Risk and Freedom

For Linda, Laura and Thomas

Risk and Freedom
The record of
road safety regulation

John G.U. Adams
University College London

LONDON   TRANSPORT PUBLISHING PROJECTS   CARDIFF

First published in 1985
by Transport Publishing Projects
59 Park Place
Cardiff CF1 3AT

Printed in Great Britain
by The Bottesford Press
1 Queen Street
Bottesford
Nottingham

ISBN 0 948537 05 1

Contents

Preface

Road safety is a subject on which everyone who survives childhood in a motorised society is an expert - a true expert in the sense that his or her survival skills have been developed and proved by experience. These skills are neither simple nor trivial; comparison with the behaviour in traffic of people in societies where motor vehicles are few suggests that an ability to read and respond to traffic danger signals is a highly complex skill which can only be learned over a period of time, and often painfully.

If one chooses a vantage point above a complex of busy urban roads one can observe a society's acquired expertise in action. One can see a mixture of vehicles - from juggernaut lorries to bicycles - and a mixture of people - from the old and anxious to the young and heedless - all managing, somehow, to find a way through the complex to get where they want, usually without a policeman in sight. The danger is manifest. Braking a split second late, moving a steering wheel an inch or two to the left or right, misreading the intentions of other road users, or misjudging their speed, miscalculating the friction between tyre and road, a simple lapse of concentration, any one of these or numerous other possibilities could spell instant death. Yet an observer would have to watch for a very long time before seeing someone killed.

There is a second, more select, class of road safety expert. Members of this class belong to what has been called "the safety community"; they are few in number and possess a quite different kind of knowledge about road safety. Some of them know a great deal about the minute particulars of accidents, which part of the body makes contact with which hard surface, the nature of the injuries sustained, the age and sex and blood alcohol levels of those involved, and numerous other details such as time of day and year, weather, road layout, types of vehicle and speeds. But usually, because individual accidents are such rare and unpredictable events, they analyse and communicate their findings with the aid of a variety of statistical methods. They deal in statistical abstractions: averages, probabilities, trends, levels of significance.

The purpose of their labours is to identify opportunities for intervening in the operation of the transport system to make it safer. Over the years many of their recommendations have been implemented.

Transport is now arguably the world's most regulated activity. The evidence surveyed in this book suggests that most of the work of the safety community has been nullified by the reactions of the common or garden experts. Most road users, it is argued, are deliberate risk takers. The risks they take are generally very small, but nonetheless real. If they cannot be persuaded to take fewer risks, they will respond to imposed safety measures in ways that reestablish the level of risk with which they were originally content. If, for example people are obliged to buy vehicles with improved brakes, they will not continue to drive as before and enjoy an additional margin of safety. They will drive faster or start braking later. In a way that often appears finely and expertly judged, they consume potential safety benefits as performance benefits.

There is a long established school of political thought which is hostile to all regulation. An exemplar of this school is Lieutenant-Colonel Moore-Brabazon, quoted here defending the rights of motorists threatened by the 1934 Road Traffic Act.

"It is true that 7000 people are killed in motor accidents, but it is not always going on like that. People are getting used to the new conditions. The fact that the road is practically the great railway of the country instead of the playground of the young has to be realised. No doubt many of the old Members of the House will recollect the numbers of chickens we killed in the old days. We used to come back with the radiator stuffed with feathers. It was the same with dogs. Dogs get out of the way of motor cars nowadays and you never kill one. There is education even in the lower animals. These things will right themselves." (quoted in **The Penguin Book of the Bicycle**.)

This book does not belong to the Moore-Brabazon school; transport in a highly mobile society must be regulated in a great many ways. Since 1934 there have been large increases in the numbers of motor vehicles, and many additions to the body of motoring legislation; the numbers of road accident fatalities have moved up and down with little apparent connection to the regulatory efforts of governments. It is not clear that "things have righted themselves". The possibilities for compelling people to be safer than they choose to be appear to be extremely limited. But attempts at safety regulation can nevertheless have real effects. The "playground of the young" has become smaller and more dangerous, and chickens and dogs, and pedestrians and cyclists, have learned to get out of the way. It is argued here that the principal achievement of road safety regulation has been a redistribution of the burden of risk from vehicle occupants to pedestrians and cyclists. There is a case for redressing the balance. Striking a desired balance is primarily a job for politicians, not experts from the safety community.

Many of the arguments in this book are highly contentious. They call into question the validity of an enormous amount of road safety regulation. The bulk of the literature on the subject is rather daunting to readers unfamiliar with statistical methods. It has been my ambition to make a part of it more accessible. Previewers of the book tell me that I have not succeeded totally. But it is my hope that the area which the non-statistical reader must accept on trust has been substantially reduced, and that some statisticians from outside the consensus of the safety community might be enticed into taking an interest in the problems discussed.

Acknowledgements

I would like to thank Eljay Crompton for designing the cover, and Anne Mason, Alick Newman and Chris Cromarty for their help in preparing the illustrations. Bill Campbell, Tony Nicholson, Colin Titcombe and Paul Schooling have given generous help with computing problems, and James Smith and Rex Galbraith have provided useful statistical advice.

Some of the evidence and arguments presented here have been rehearsed earlier in the form of discussion papers, articles and conference papers. They have on occasion provoked hostility and personal abuse (see Chapter 9). I am grateful to all of the following for encouragement, stimulation and/or criticism offered in a friendly and constructive spirit: Gerald Wilde, Chris Wright, Bob Davis, John Wardroper, Mark McCarthy, Harry Shannon, Leonard Evans, Lloyd Orr, Phil Goodwin, George Stern and Edmund Grattan.

Finally I wish to thank my "domestic" critics, Hawys Pritchard and my wife Linda. They have been unrelentingly helpful.

1　Road Safety:
perspectives on problems

Some numbers

People born before the Second World War sometimes look back nostalgically to the time of their youth when it was safe for children to play in the streets. The memory is flawed.

In 1927, the earliest year for which the figures are available, there were 2774 pedestrians killed in road accidents in Britain. In 1983, despite the fact that the country's population had increased by 25 per cent and the number of motor vehicles had increased ten fold, there were 1914 pedestrian fatalities. Figures for England and Wales reveal that in 1982 there were 413 children under the age of 15 killed in road accidents; in 1927 there were 1067.

In the United States between 1928 and 1932 the number of pedestrians killed annually averaged 12,300. By 1982, despite large increases in numbers of people and vehicles the number was 7274.

Table 1 provides some further statistics for the two countries. In both countries, since the 1920s vehicle numbers have increased enormously, pedestrian casualties have decreased, vehicle occupant

Table 1.1　Road Accident Fatalities

	pedestrian	cyclist	twmv*	other+	total	total per 100,000 population	total per 10,000 vehicles
Britain							
1927	2774	644	1175	736	5329	12.1	28.0
1983	1914	323	963	2245	5445	9.9	2.7
USA							
1928-32							
average	12300				31050	25.2	12.1
1982	7274				43721	19.0	3.1

*two wheeled motor vehicles   +"other", mostly car occupants
Sources: **Accident Facts 1978**, National Safety Council, Chicago; **Statistics of Road Traffic Accidents in Europe** UN Economic Commission for Europe, Geneva, 1983; **RAGB 1983**, Tables 1 and 2.

casualties have increased, total casualties relative to population have fluctuated but display no clear trend, and death rates per vehicle have declined very considerably.

What do the numbers signify?

There is little agreement about the significance of numbers such as these. There is no single agreed index for measuring the magnitude of the road accident problem, or even for determining whether things are getting better or worse.

Some people, principally safety experts and campaigners, consider road accidents to be "the greatest epidemic of our time" (this was the title of a BBC television documentary on the subject on August 20, 1984). They arouse a crusading zeal and provoke calls for drastic measures. Driving has become the motorised world's most regulated activity - in Britain motoring offences account for about 90 per cent of all court proceedings (TSGB 1983, Table 2.52) - and the demand for further regulation shows little sign of abating.

Others view the numbers with considerable satisfaction. The large, and continuing, decreases in deaths per vehicle are seen as impressive safety achievements - substantial progress is being made. The adherents to this view are found principally among the manufacturers of motor vehicles and the builders of roads; they consider the established trends, especially the downward trend in fatalities per vehicle, as evidence of a job well done. In recent years their satisfaction has been widely displayed in their advertisements extolling the safety benefits of their products.

Perhaps most commonly, the numbers arouse complacency. Herman Kahn exemplifies this reaction:

"... let us assume that the U.S. authorities had made a [technological assessment] of the automobile in 1890. Assume also that this study came up with an accurate estimate that its use would result eventually in more than 50,000 people a year being killed and maybe a million injured. It seems clear that if this study had been persuasive, the automobile would never have been approved. Of course some now say that it never should have been. But we would argue that society is clearly willing to live with this cost, large and horrible as it is. In Bermuda, which restricts drivers to 20 miles an hour, there are almost no fatal accidents except with cyclists.... Similar speed limits could be introduced in the United States if they were wanted, but the majority of Americans apparently prefer 50,000 deaths a year to such drastic restrictions on their driving speeds." (Kahn, 1976, p.168).

In Britain as well there is some evidence to support the view that society considers that it is getting good transport value for the price it is currently paying in life and limb. British Members of Parliament, who might be presumed to have an interest in assessing the collective will correctly, have judged that society is willing to pay even more for the benefit of driving faster. In the discussion in Parliament that preceded the rescinding of the speed limits that had been imposed in the aftermath of the 1973 oil shortage, there was no serious opposition to paying a higher price for greater speed, merely a bit of ritual lamenting:

Mr. John Ellis (asking the Secretary of State for Transport): "Does my right honourable friend agree that speed is a contributory factor to road accidents and that as a direct result of his announcement today more people will be killed and injured on our roads? Are we not guilty of having a schizophrenic approach to this matter? It is no use the House or the public throwing up their hands in favour of safety when such an approach is adopted. Is it not only fair to say that?"

The reply
Mr. Rodgers (Secretary of State for Transport): "Yes, it is only fair to say that. All of us, including me, suffer from schizophrenia. We want to save life but we like driving fast. Although we should all travel slowly, with a red flag in front of us, people do not choose to do that. We must strike a balance. It is dangerous in some respects, but that is life."
(Hansard, April 6, 1977)

The distribution of risk

How can different people contemplating the same "facts" differ so greatly on their significance? A part of the explanation is likely to lie in the uneven distribution of the burden of risk created by road traffic.

Variation by mode of travel. There are large differences between different modes of travel in the likelihood of having an accident. Per mile travelled a motorcycle is the most dangerous mode of transport. The death rate per mile for motorcyclists is about about twice that for pedal cyclists, 23 times that of car occupants, 40 times that for drivers of heavy goods vehicles, and 160 times that for bus travellers (Sabey and Taylor, 1980, p. 46) There is also a marked difference in the rates at which different vehicles kill people other than their own drivers. The differences are closely related to differences in the size and weight of the vehicles involved. Pedal cyclists and motorcyclists kill mainly themselves. For every car driver killed in a car accident in Britain in 1983 there were more than three other non-drivers killed. And for every lorry driver killed in a fatal accident involving a heavy goods vehicle there were

eighteen other people killed (**RAGB** 1983, Tables 4 and 23).
    There are also considerable variations within particular modes of
transport.   It has been shown that big cars are more likely to be
involved in accidents than small cars (Evans and Wasielewski, 1983)
but that, if they are involved in accidents, occupants of small cars
are more likely to be killed (Evans 1984).

Socio-economic   variation. The differences in the likelihood of
being killed in a traffic accident between those at the top of the
socio-economic ladder and those at   the   bottom   are   large. Table 1.2
shows that an unskilled manual worker is four and   a   half   times more
likely   to   be killed in a motor vehicle accident than a self employed
professional,   and sixteen   times   more   likely   to   be   killed while
walking.

TABLE 1.2   Mortality by Socio-Economic Group and Cause of Death
              Standardised Mortality Ratios for men aged 15-64+
                      England and Wales   1970-1972

	\multicolumn{5}{c}{Socio-economic groups}				
	1.1,2.1	1.2,2.2	3	4	11
All motor vehicle acccidents	62	98	40	83	180
Driver, not motorcycle	99	150	64	121	70
Motor cyclist	5	39	--	51	200
Pedestrian	40	38	22	44	353

+ 100 is the norm for the whole population
1.1,2.1 Employers in industry etc.
2.1,2.2 Managers in industry etc.
3   Professional workers - self employed
11   Unskilled manual workers
Source: Occupational **Mortality** 1970-72, OPCS, Series DS
no.1, Table 4B.

Geographic variation.   There   is   also   considerable geographical
variation in the burden of risk   of   road   accidents.   As Chapter   2
illustrates there   are   enormous   differences   in road accident death
rates   between   countries.   Within   countries there   are   persistent
differences between regions, and between rural and urban areas.
    An appreciation of the   geographical   variation   in road accident
casualty statistics is crucially dependent on the   type   of casualties
'eing   considered.   For   example, **Road Accidents Great Britain**
presents   a   breakdown by county of the number of injury accidents per
1000 vehicles. By   this   measure Greater   London   is by far the most
dangerous   area   in Britain with 18 casualties per   1000   vehicles   in
1983. Rural Dyfed   in   Wales,   by   contrast had only 10 per 1000.   If

fatal and serious injuries only are considered the positions are reversed. Dyfed had 4.5 fatal and serious accidents per 1000 vehicles while Greater London had only 2.8 (**RAGB** 1983 Table 46, **TSGB** 1973-83 Table 2.23). In the United States the geographical variation in road death rates appears even greater. The road accident death rate per 100,000 population in Washington D.C., which is almost entirely urban is about a quarter of that in New Mexico, which has vast wide-open spaces (**Accident Facts**, 1977).

Variation with speed and condition of road. Although there are numerous factors contributing to such differences the most important is likely to be speed. In Britain the percentage of all injury accidents which are fatal accidents is more than twice as high for accidents on roads with speed limits over 40 mph as it is for accidents on roads with speed limits less than 40 mph; in 1983 these percentages were 4.1 for roads with limits above 40 mph and 1.5 for roads with limits less than 40 mph (**RAGB** 1983 Table 3). (The statistics may exaggerate the difference between urban and rural areas. For reasons discussed more fully below, all statistics relating to non-fatal injuries should be treated with caution. It is likely that a higher proportion of slight injuries are officially recorded in urban areas than in rural areas because police and medical services are more accessible. However there is no firm evidence to support this suspicion.)

Accident and fatality rates also vary with the condition of the road. Rain, fog, snow and ice can all cause changes in driving behaviour and the pattern of accidents. When conditions become very bad the number of fatal accidents usually declines, and the percentage of injury accidents which are fatal also declines (see, for example, Chapter 4, Figures 4.1 to 4.3).

The fact that accident rates can increase while fatality rates decrease, and vice versa, can cause serious difficulties in the interpretation of accident data. Because of the infrequency of fatal and serious accidents, most local scale accident studies deal simply with total injury-accident frequencies. Accident prevention measures, such as straightening a bend in the road, which also encourage higher speeds, could have the effect of decreasing numbers of minor accidents while increasing the number of fatal and serious casualties.

Variation by mental and physical state. There are large variations in accident rates associated with variations in blood alcohol concentrations. Figure 1.1 illustrates the results of a study which attempted to estimate the way in which the probability of an accident increases with blood alcohol levels. It can be seen that both the average probability, and the range about the average increase dramatically above concentrations of 80mg/100ml.

Blood alcohol levels do not vary simply and directly with

consumption of alcohol. They depend not only on the amount consumed, but also on factors such as rate of consumption, other contents of the stomach, length of time after consumption, body weight, metabolism and experience. Alcohol is probably the most intensively studied aspect of mental and physical variation in driving ability, but numerous other factors – assorted drugs and "naturally" induced variability in mood caused by anxiety, aggression, tiredness, high spirits etc. – can also affect vigilance and driving ability.

<u>Age and sex differences.</u>   There are large differences in road accident death rates according to age and sex. At all ages males have a far higher risk of being killed in a traffic accident than females. In Britain in 1927 the ratio was 3 to 1; in 1982 it was 2.4 to 1. The difference in rates is greatest for the 15 to 24 age group; in 1927 the ratio was 6.5 to 1 and in 1982 4.1 to 1. The rates appear to be converging, but very slowly. Also over time there has been a shift in the age groups at greatest risk. It has already been noted above that since 1927 there has been a large decrease (61 per cent) in the

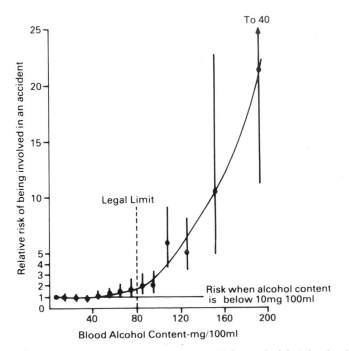

Figure 1.1   Variation in accident risk with blood alcohol content. Source: Department of the Environment 1976.

numbers of children killed under age 15, but over the same period there has been an 80 per cent increase in the number killed between the ages of 15 and 24. There has also been a very large increase in the number of elderly female pedestrians killed. In 1983 female pedestrians over the age of 70 accounted for 23 per cent of all female road accident fatalities; in contrast, male pedestrians over 70 accounted for only 7 per cent of all male casualties. (RAGB 1983 Table 30)

What distinguishes death in traffic accidents from death by most other causes (with the exception of the causes of death for infants and elderly female pedestrians) is its prematurity. In a survey of causes of death in twenty-seven countries in Europe, North America and Oceania (WHS 1974) accidents were reported to be overwhelmingly the leading cause of death for all ages from one to forty-four; traffic deaths accounted for between 30 per cent of all accidental deaths in Bulgaria, with 11.3 cars per 100 inhabitants, and 56 per cent in Australia with 36.9 cars per 100. Traffic is predominantly a killer of people in the prime of life. The traffic accident mortality rate typically reaches a peak in the late teens and declines thereafter until it experiences a rise again after the age of 65.

Over time there have been changes in the things from which people die, and the ages at which they die from them. Figure 1.2 shows that the relative importance of accidents as a cause of death has increased very considerably since 1931, especially below age 40, as other causes, especially infective diseases, have declined in significance. Figure 1.3 shows the way in which the significance of road accidents relative to all accidents varies according to age and sex in Britain.

Because there are no agreed units for measuring pain and grief, it is difficult to provide a firm statistical foundation upon which to base a judgement about the significance of the age distribution of accidental death. Of the more than 600,000 deaths in Britain every year should some be considered more tragic or lamentable than others? In Britain traffic deaths account for less than one per cent of all deaths. Compared to the major killers such as cancers and heart diseases they might be thought unimportant.

One way of highlighting the premature character of road accident deaths is by comparing the mean age at death of road accident victims with that for other causes of death. In Britain in 1983 the average age at death for all causes was 69.6 for men and 75.2 for women. The average age of death in motor vehicle accidents was 36.6 for men and 48.4 for women. For ischaemic heart disease the figures are 70.2 and 77.1 respectively; for pneumonia they are 77.7 and 81.7 (OPCS 1983 Table 24).

Another method is to calculate the number of years of life lost. This involves measuring age at death against some standard. Since there is no universally agreed age at which people should die, the choice of standard must be arbitrary. This calculation has been done for England and Wales using age 65 (a common age of retirement) as the standard. By this method motor vehicle accidents, which claimed 5059 lives in 1983, accounted for 136 thousand years of life lost. This compares with ischaemic heart disease, which claimed 157,000 lives and 263 thousand years of life lost, and pneumonia which claimed 55,000 lives, but only 44,000 years of life lost (OPCS 1983 Table 24). In the United States, where the motor vehicle accident death rate and homicide rate are much higher than in Britain, similar calculations show that accidents and violence account for more years of life lost "pre-retirement" than all cancers and cardiovascular diseases put together (Robertson, 1983, p.9).

Some Controversies

Variations in the distribution of road accident risks have been much studied in the hope that they might reveal the treatable causes of accidents. So far such studies have yielded a voluminous literature, but little agreement about what should be done.

What should be done?

Accidents are unintended and unforseen events. With the benefit of hindsight their immediate causes usually seem obvious. In the case of road accidents the list of causes identified after the event is very large, but the causes, and proposed remedies, are commonly assigned to one of three categories - vehicle, road, or road user.

Studies which have attempted to allocate responsibility for accidents amongst these categories usually conclude that road users deserve most of the blame. Sabey and Taylor (1980), for example, attempted to identify the "main contributory factors" responsible for 2130 accidents which they investigated in great detail. They concluded that 8.5 per cent of the blame could be assigned to vehicles, 28 per cent to the road environment, and 95 per cent to road users; these add up to more than 100 per cent because many accidents were considered to be the result of more than one contributory factor.

Such categorisations however are almost wholly arbitrary. Joksch (1980, p. 67) has observed that the attribution of responsibility follows "established folklore". It is possible, depending upon the assumptions one makes, to allocate all the blame to the user, or all blame to the road and vehicle. If one accepts human nature and human fallibility as given, then accidents are seen as the result of the failure of vehicle manufacturers and road builders to make proper allowance for well known human limitations. At the other extreme road users can be considered totally responsible for their actions, and

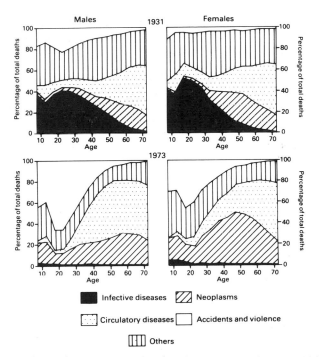

Figure 1.2 Mortality by cause of death, age and sex: 1931 and 1973. Source: **Trends in Mortality: England and Wales 1951–75**, OPCS 1978, DH1 No. 3.

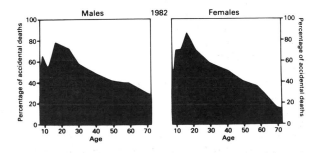

Figure 1.3   Road   accident   deaths as a percentage of all accidental deaths. Source: **RAGB 1982** Table 11.

held accountable for their failures to make proper allowance for the hazards in their environment, and the limitations of their vehicles, or themselves.

Judgements about whether safety can be promoted by means of vehicle and road engineering, or by altering road user behaviour, depend on the views taken about the possibilities for making roads and vehicles more "foolproof" on the one hand, and for making human beings less "foolish" on the other.

Who should decide?

Perceptions of problems are influenced by experience, and, as we have seen above, personal experience of road accident risks is highly variable. However, the influence of experience is not direct and straightforward. One might expect that those groups upon whom risks bear most heavily would manifest the greatest concern about safety. In some cases the opposite appears to be happen. Young male motorcyclists, with very high accident rates appear to be much less concerned about road safety than their mothers, who have very low accident rates. One hypothesis, which will be discussed more fully in Chapter 8, suggests that accident rates are a consequence of levels of concern, rather than causes of them; young men might have higher accident rates than their mothers because they are less concerned about safety.

The level of concern about a particular risk is also likely to be influenced by whether or not it is borne voluntarily. (The definition of "acceptable risk" has been pursued at length, but inconclusively, by Fischhoff et al (1981)). Some leisure pursuits, such as hang gliding or mountain climbing, and occupations, such as deep sea diving or putting out oil well fires, are highly dangerous, but are pursued voluntarily either for the thrills provided, or the lucrative rewards, or both. Other risks are imposed, and are borne reluctantly and resentfully; dangerous working and living conditions endured for reasons of poverty and necessity, risks posed by drunken and reckless motorists, insidious threats posed by radiation, drugs and chemicals are examples.

The risk of death or injury creates intractable political problems. Who should decide what risks are acceptable? Some would draw a sharp line between voluntary and involuntary risks, and say that individuals should be free to impose whatever risks they choose upon themselves, but should be prevented, by the state, from imposing any risks upon others. Others argue that life, and death, are not that simple. Should children be free to take whatever risks they choose? If not, at what age should they become free? Should adults be permitted to risk becoming "a burden on society" if they become seriously injured? Should they be allowed to let their dependents become a burden on society if they are killed or become incapacitated

as a result of risks voluntarily borne? Should manufacturers be free
to produce, and people free to buy, products with concealed and
potentially lethal defects? Can risks which are borne in ignorance be
said to be risks borne voluntarily?

How does one define a risk "voluntarily borne"? Except for
prisoners in police custody, and children in parental custody, people
are not compelled to travel by car, but they are often under
extremely strong pressure to do so. In the real world most actions are
neither totally free nor totally constrained, but somewhere in
between. Even the very poor have choices, albeit far fewer than the
wealthy. "SAFETY AT WORK OR A SAFE JOB?" was the headline of a
newspaper story (Sunday Times, 23.12.1984) describing the dilemma of
workers in an asbestos factory faced with closure if compelled to
meet more stringent safety standards. The union, on behalf of its
members agreed to a fibre concentration standard which had been
estimated to cause asbestos related cancers in 4 out of every 100
workers with 25 years exposure. Although usually not so carefully and
explicitly calculated, such trade-offs are extremely common. They are
made routinely in driving as motorists continuously balance time
saving gains against risk taking costs. For some this will be a free
choice, but for many it will be a choice made under external pressure
to save time.

Legislators around the world routinely intervene in such balancing
acts. Driving is one of the most closely regulated activities on
earth; in highly motorised countries road traffic offences far
outnumber all other offences brought before the courts. Every feature
of motor vehicles and road construction has been closely scrutinised
in order to minimise the threat it poses. Driver behaviour has been
minutely examined in an attempt to eradicate risk. And legislators
everywhere seem always to be arguing over how the balance between
freedom and regulation should be struck.

How to decide?

The ultimate goal of students of decision-making is a
comprehensive, systematic and consistent method embodying, in
quantified form, the principles of optimization and distributive
justice, into which can be fed accurately measured valuations of all
the relevant variables. This goal remains distant. In the vanguard
of researchers pursuing this goal in the realm of transport planning
are the cost-benefit analysts. Cost benefit analysis proceeds by
attempting to identify all potential winners and losers associated
with a proposal. It attempts to estimate the magnitude of the impacts
of the proposal and then to place a cash value on the potential
winnings and losses. If the winnings exceed the losses the proposal
is considered justified, if not, it is rejected. In principle the
method is commendably straightforward. In practice it has foundered

on problems of measurement and valuation.

A notorious example of the failure of cost benefit analysis to resolve safety issues is provided by the case of the Ford Pinto fuel tank. The Ford Pinto had a fuel tank which tended to rupture when the car was struck from behind. Ford was aware of the problem and contemplated reducing (not eliminating) the problem by adding protection which would have cost eleven dollars per car. Although an apparently trivial sum relative to the selling price of the car, when multiplied by the 12.5 million vehicles to which it was proposed that the modification might be made, it produced an impressively large number. Ford rejected the proposed modification on the basis of a cost-benefit calculation which assumed that the added protection would save 180 lives and 180 injuries; each life saved was valued in the Ford analysis at $200,000, and each injury at $67,000. Subsequently, in a court case, a person injured in a fire resulting from a ruptured Pinto fuel tank was awarded $128 million. On appeal this award was reduced to $6 million (Robertson, 1983, p.179). The fact that there can be a 2000 fold difference of opinion about the appropriate value to assign to one of the central numbers (the price to attach to an injury) in a cost benefit analysis suggests that the method is lacking in precision.

Will it work?

Leaving aside for the moment the problems concerning the value of life and limb, there remains considerable doubt attaching to estimates made of the number of lives and injuries that would be saved (or lost) as a result of regulating vehicles or traffic. Estimates, such as the 180 lives that might be saved by improving a fuel tank, are commonly presented as firm facts in discussions about safety. It is frequently assumed that the experts know quite precisely what the effect would be of implementing a particular proposal. An example which will be discussed in Chapter 5 is the much repeated claim made in the British Parliament over a number of years that a seat belt law would save 1000 lives a year in Britain. It is further commonly assumed in debates about road safety that the means exist virtually to eradicate the accident problem – if only the economic resources and political will could be mustered.

Robertson, for example, in his book **Injuries** argues
"Using the principles of science, we know how to build vehicles that would seldom kill occupants in a crash and would reduce pedestrian injury. ... Persuading the producers and users to adopt the technology or forcing the recalcitrant to do so in the political arena has been a far more difficult task than developing the technology" (Robertson, 1983, p.191).

Others are much less certain. Frank Haight has been editor of

Accident Analysis and Prevention for many years; there can be few safety researchers who have reviewed more published and unpublished work in this field. He observes

"One sees time and again large sums of money spent [on road safety] in industrialized countries, the effect of which is so difficult to detect that further sums must be spent in highly sophisticated evaluation techniques if one is to obtain even a clue as to the effectiveness of the intervention" (Haight 1985).

Order from chaos?

The above brief survey suggests that we are adrift on a sea of statistics, with no clear idea of our speed or direction, and with no agreement about the port we ought to be trying to reach. Beneath the statistical surface are strong emotional currents; the statistics relate to death and injury, matters which arouse strong feelings. The following chapters attempt to extract some order from the apparent chaos of road accident research, and speculate about the way in which the emotional currents have influenced the treatment of the statistical evidence.

Chapter 2 introduces a remarkable regularity that has been found in accident statistics from a wide variety of countries over many years. "Smeed's Law" describes the relationship that exists between a country's level of motorisation and its road accident fatality rate per vehicle. There are very large differences in death rates per vehicle between the least motorised countries and the most motorised. These differences are similar to the differences within highly motorised countries between death rates per vehicle in the early stages of motorisation and current levels. It is suggested that the relationship described by the Smeed Law is sufficiently consistent to justify using the Law as a standard against which to rank the road accident records of different countries at different levels of motorisation.

The direction of change in the death rates deserves comment. As the number of vehicles in a country increases, the opportunities for any individual vehicle to collide with another also increase; but the death rate per vehicle decreases. There are many claimants of the credit for this decrease. Some attribute it primarily to improvements in vehicles and roads. Others attribute it mainly to the regulation of road users. A few, including the writer, believe it may be mostly attributed to a spontaneous phenomenon called "risk compensation" or "risk homeostasis". This last explanation suggests that motorists alter their behaviour in response to perceived "safety improvements", and that potential safety benefits are commonly consumed as performance benefits - for example, if improved brakes reduce stopping distances, drivers will respond by driving faster or braking later.

Chapters 3 and 4 review the claims of the advocates of engineering solutions to road safety problems, and find them wanting. The claims for vehicle safety regulation are doubted for two main reasons. The first reason is based on the Smeed Law; the fact that countries in the Third World, with relatively modern cars, are achieving death rates similar to those achieved in Britain and the United States in the Model-T era, suggests that the safety technology built into modern cars can account for little of the reduction in death rates achieved in the highly motorised countries. The second reason relates to the plausibility of the statistical analysis upon which the claims are based. The United States has the largest, and one of the most regulated, vehicle fleets in the world. The life-saving benefits of the US regulations have been much disputed. Chapter 3 considers the most recent evidence advanced in support of regulation and finds it unconvincing.

Chapter 4 examines the argument that improved roads have been responsible for much of the reduction of death rates per vehicle, or per vehicle mile. Because the proportion of a country's road network that can be improved in any one year is small, even in countries pursuing major road building programmes, national time series data cannot settle the argument. The case for the safety benefits of improved roads rests mainly on the differences in accidents between types of roads, and on reductions in accidents associated with "black spot treatment". Again the evidence is found to be unsatisfactory. The principal objection to the evidence which is adduced to support the claims for road improvements is that it is myopic. The claims for black spot treatment are shown to be based on statistical evidence which does not allow for the possibility of behavioural responses beyond the treated site. Many of the claims are also shown to be seriously flawed statistically. Evidence is reviewed which suggests that the response of motorists to improvements in road conditions, like the response to vehicle improvements, leads to potential safety benefits being consumed as performance benefits.

Chapters 5, 6 and 7 examine the claims for the safety benefits of measures which seek to regulate road user behaviour. Chapter 5 looks in considerable detail at the statistical aftermath of seat belt legislation, the measure which has been the principal focus of road safety legislative efforts around the world in the past fifteen years. It finds a dearth of evidence that seat belt laws have achieved the savings in life and limb commonly attributed to them. Chapter 6 scrutinises the claims for motorcycle helmet legislation and finds a similar lack of convincing evidence. In both cases it is argued that the evidence is consistent with the hypothesis that protecting motorists from the consequences of bad driving encourages bad driving.

Chapter 7 looks at the record in Britain and the United States of the major safety initiatives since the Second World War: speed limits, drink-drive laws, insurance, training and, in Britain, seat belt legislation. Once again a similar picture emerges; there is no

clear evidence that attempts to regulate behaviour have had any
lasting benefit. The remarkable success of the Partyka model in
explaining most of the variation in road accident death rates in the
United Sates by means of employment variables appears to leave little
room for regulatory measures to account for anything. In Britain
modified versions of both the Smeed and Partyka models can also
account for most of the variation in the numbers of road accident
fatalities in a way which suggests that road safety initiatives have
had little effect.

Chapter 8 considers possible explanations for the apparent lack of
effect road safety endeavours. The explanation which appears to
account best for the evidence reviewed in the preceding chapters is
Wilde's Risk Homeostasis Theory. It suggests that risk-taking
behaviour involves an attempt to balance perceived risk and desired
risk, and that people adjust their behavior in response to changes in
perceived risk. It leads to the conclusion that the principal, and
perhaps only, determinant of aggregate accident rates is what Wilde
calls the "target level of risk"; and this leads to the conclusion
that the only measures which are likely to have more than a transient
effect on accident rates are measures which alter attitudes to risk
taking.

Both the interpretation of the evidence reviewed in Chapters 2 to
7, and the explanation offered in Chapter 8 are highly
contentious. If they were to be subjected to any test of opinion,
either expert or lay, they would almost certainly be rejected by a
wide margin. Chapter 9, "The Emperor's New Clothes", proffers reasons
for supposing that in this case the majority may be wrong.

In the absence of any risk compensation effect, safety measures
which eliminate the immediate and specific causes of accidents
should work. An impressive volume of safety regulation all around
the world has been based upon research which either ignores or denies
the possibility that road users will adjust their behaviour in
response to measures intended to make them safer. An impressive
amount of political and intellectual face has been invested in safety
measures which should work. Impressive amounts of money and effort
have also been invested. In the name of safety, billions of pounds
have been spent on roads, countless hours of police and court time
have been devoted to the enforcement of regulations, innumerable
campaigning groups and legislators have devoted their energies to
securing the implementation of safety measures. To suggest that most
of this activity has been ineffectual will offend a great many people.

Chapter 10, "Risk and Freedom" addresses the question at the
centre of the controversy - do people desire risk? The implicit
assumption of most safety campaigners, safety researchers, and
legislators who vote for safety legislation is that people do not.

If enough people take enough risks of a given magnitude the result
will be a predictable number of accidents. If the desired end is the
reduction of accidents, the obvious means is the reduction of risk.

But it appears that people positively desire a certain measure of excitement in their lives. The "accident problem" is rooted in human ambivalence. People do not desire accidents, but they do desire risk. And you cannot have the latter without the former. To the extent that accident rates reflect risk taking rates, and risk taking rates reflect a willingness to take risks, then accidents can only be reduced by compelling people to be safer than they voluntarily choose to be. In a free society the scope for such measures would appear to be severely limited.

The tendency for potential safety benefits to be consumed as performance benefits has consequences for the distribution of the burden of risk. If safety measures alter driver behaviour, this will have consequences for other road users. For example, measures aimed at promoting pedestrian safety frequently restrict the freedom of pedestrians and increase the freedom of motorists; measures which make vehicle occupants less vulnerable in accidents are likely to make pedestrians and cyclists more vulnerable. While safety regulation appears to have had little impact on the total numbers killed and injured on the roads, it has had a considerable impact on the distribution of the burden of risk, and on the order of precedence and deference which governs the behaviour of road users.

2 Engineering Theology and Smeed's Law

A Regularity

Chapter 1 described some of the considerable variability which characterises road safety issues. This chapter focuses on a remarkable regularity.

During this century, as the world's motor vehicle population has increased, most countries have experienced dramatic reductions in their death rates per vehicle. In the United States, for example, the number of road accident deaths has dropped from over 50 per 10 000 registered vehicles in 1905 to 3.1 in 1982. In Britain this number has dropped from over 90 per 10 000 registered vehicles in 1909 to under 3 in 1983. Evidence is presented below to show that such decreases are extremely common.

There is no shortage of claimants of the credit for these decreases, but there is at the present time sharp disagreement among them. Broadly, the claims, and claimants, can be allocated to the same categories used in Chapter 1 for allocating the responsibility for accidents: **safer vehicles**, **safer roads** and **safer road users**. The claimants assignable to the first two categories favour engineering solutions to road safety problems. Those assignable to the third category favour solutions involving behaviour modification. At the present time the engineers appear to be in the ascendant. Their claims will be examined first.

Engineering Theology

Murray Mackay, head of the Birmingham Accident Research Unit, and probably the most prominent accident researcher in Britain, is emphatic about the efficacy of engineering solutions, and dismissive of the possibilities for improving road user behaviour.

"All people are as God made them, and often worse than that, and programmes for changing road user behaviour very quickly founder on the subtleties of human response and the political limitations of the social manipulation of drivers and other users of the highway." (Mackay, 1982a)

Having dismissed the possibility of making progress by changing behaviour Mackay concludes

"The major gains which have been made in transport safety have come about predominantly from **engineering** solutions; that is, engineering of either the road environment or the vehicles involved."

Safety measures which depend on the modification of human behaviour Mackay suggests should be relegated to the realms of folklore; safety measures which focus on the prevention of accidents he thinks are likely to prove futile.

"The traditional approach to road accidents has been based on the premise that it is 'obvious' that they should be prevented from taking place, and because the predominant causes of road accidents rest on road user errors of one sort or another, it is again 'obvious' that road user behaviour needs to be changed."

Mackay describes safety measures aimed at modifying road user behaviour as the "traditional approach". For a number of years this approach has been under attack by those favouring engineering solutions to safety problems. Mackay's view that "human response" renders behavioural measures futile is echoed widely in the safety literature. Robertson, a prominent American proponent of this view, complains (1983, p.65), of the "chorous of 'experts'" who insist that the injury problem is essentially a problem of errant human behaviour. Like Mackay he recommends concentrating safety efforts on measures which acknowledge human fallibility, and protect people from its consequences.

"A comprehensive approach to regulating for motor vehicle injury reduction could be stated in a simple standard. A new vehicle sold in the United States should not be capable of exceeding a speed on a level road at any point in a five-mile test run that would injure with life-threatening severity in a frontal or front-angle crash, according to crash forces measured on a test dummy in crash tests into a solid barrier at the vehicle's maximum speed." (p.204)

Senior safety researchers at Britain's Transport and Road Research Laboratory also favour engineering solutions. Sabey and Taylor (1980) for example argue that, notwithstanding the fact that accidents are caused mainly by "human factors", engineering measures are usually more cost effective.

"Although human factors play the largest part in contributing to accidents they are difficult to identify and costly to remedy. In the accident situation described here, remedial measures of an engineering nature, which are easier to identify and often readily and cheaply effected, can be applied to counter human failings" (Sabey and Taylor, 1980, p.52).

Senior safety experts at the Greater London Council take a similar view.
"Despite [the] high involvement of the road-user factor in accidents, it has proved to be extremely difficult to devise a cost-effective method of reducing significantly such accidents by training and publicity. ... Attention to the road environment, however, has been shown to be very cost effective ... Simply by concentrating the effort on identifying patterns of accidents, solutions can be devised which reduce the number of opportunities for road users to make mistakes" (Huddart and Dean, 1981, p.51).

The engineering approach to road safety has considerable intuitive appeal. As Mackay notes, people are killed or injured in car accidents "because some part of the structure of the car has struck some part of the human frame with a force greater than can be tolerated without some major injury". He argues
"... biomechanics and vehicle crash protective design go directly to the immediate, specific problem of transport accidents, namely the relationship between design and injury."

and
"What the science of biomechanics has done is to show that the majority of deaths and injuries now occurring can be prevented by correct, crash protective design. This power for good, through the introduction of crash-protective concepts has been, and still is enormous." (Mackay 1982a)

Smeed's Law

In 1949 the late R.J. Smeed proposed a "law" which related the rate of road accident fatalities to the level of motorisation. It is a law which has stood the test of time remarkably well. It has some interesting implications for the current debate between the "behaviouralists" and the "biomechanics".

The law, in its most general form is described by an equation

$$D/N = a(N/P)^{-b}$$

D represents the number of road accident deaths in a country, N the number of registered motor vehicles, and P the population.

In his 1949 paper Smeed fitted this function to 1938 data for 20 countries, deriving a value for a of .0003 and a value b of .667. a, it can be seen is effectively a lower bound for the death rate,

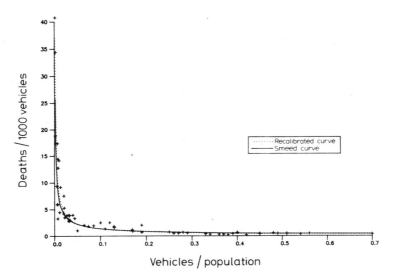

Figure 2.1 The relationship between levels of motorisation and road accident death rates per vehicle. Source: Table 2.1.

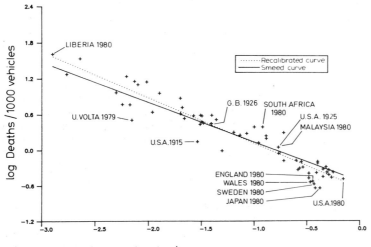

Figure 2.2 The relationship between levels of motorisation and road accident death rates per vehicle - transformed data. Source: Table 2.1.

being the level reached when there is one motor vehicle for every inhabitant. He found that this law also provided a reasonable approximation of the relationship between death rates and vehicle ownership in Britain for the period 1909 and 1947. In 1968 he tested the law against data from 16 countries for the years 1957-1966 and found that it performed well with the coefficients derived using the 1938 data. In 1970 he tested it once more against data from 68 countries for the period 1960-67 and found that it still performed well with the same coefficents. His last paper on the subject (1972) contained further tests, this time using time series data. Again the law performed well.

Figure 2.1 suggests that the law is still holding up remarkably well. The solid line in Figure 2.1 represents the curve that Smeed fitted to his original 1938 data. The dotted line shows the effect, or lack of it, of fitting the same function to 1980 data for 62 countries. Figure 2.2 displays the data represented by Figure 2.1 transformed into logarithms to permit easier identification of the residuals from the line of best fit. The highest level of car ownership in 1938 was in the United States with about .23 cars per head. Smeed's work thus represents an impressive forecasting achievement.

Table 2.1 lists the data displayed in Figures 2.1 and 2.2. The table suggests three alternative ways of ranking countries in terms of their road safety records - deaths per capita, deaths per vehicle, and the size and direction of the deviation of death rates per vehicle from the rates estimated by Smeed's Law.

By the first criterion, deaths per capita, the poorest countries fare quite well, by the second they fare very badly. Using the third index one can make comparisons among countries at equivalent levels of motorisation. Amongst the most highly motorised countries (countries with more than .3 vehicles per capita) the countries with the poorest performance are Austria, Belgium, France and Australia. The countries with the best records are Norway, Japan, Sweden and Wales.

The data for the poorest countries are the most variable from year to year, and the least reliable. The countries with the fewest cars also have the least resources to devote to collecting and analysing state data. The deficiencies in their data probably lead to an understating of the death rates per vehicle. In these countries many people live beyond the purview of the collectors of official statistics and an unknown number of deaths are likely to go unreported. (Sayer and Hitchcock (1984) found that only 41 per cent of road accident fatalities recorded by Colombo Hospital were also reported on police records, the official source of such data. By developing country standards they considered Colombo to have very good road accident statistics.) Mackay (1984) has reported evidence from Nigeria to the effect that only 30 per cent deaths are reported in that country.

2. Engineering theology and Smeed's Law

All the motor vehicles in the poorest countries are imported, and most likely to be counted at that time. They are less likely to have their scrapping officially noted, and an unknown number could stay on the books after they have left the road; death rates per vehicle therefore are likely to have inflated denominators. Thus from what is known of road accident statistics in developing countries it appears that they tend to be inaccurate and to underestimate deaths per vehicle, possibly substantially. It is possible that a similar bias might have been at work in the statistics of many of the currently highly motorised countries when they were in the early stages of motorisation. This caveat should be borne in mind when considering Figures 2.1 and 2.2 and all the graphs which follow in this chapter.

For many years R.J. Smeed remained intrigued by the relationship between road accident fatality rates and levels of motorisation, first formalised in his 1949 paper. He periodically retested his original

Table 2.1   Road Accident Death Rates for 62 Countries: 1980*

	Death	Rates					
	per 100 000 population		per 1000 vehicles		Standardised residuals		Vehicles/ population
	rank	rate	rank	rate	rank	residual	
Upper Volta	1	2.27	41	3.25	1	-2.8	.007
Ethiopia	2	3.22	60	18.84	11	-1.1	.002
India	3	3.38	52	5.59	4	-1.7	.006
Niger	4	3.95	51	5.91	8	-1.4	.007
Pakistan	5	4.65	55	9.35	13	-0.8	.005
Sierra Leone	6	4.79	49	4.42	10	-1.2	.011
Dominican Rep	7	4.84	27	0.98	2	-2.0	.050
Liberia	8	5.13	62	40.75	36	0.2	.001
Sri Lanka	9	7.50	43	3.45	17	-0.5	.022
Cameroon	10	7.87	61	34.42	54	1.0	.002
Senegal	11	8.27	48	4.16	23	-0.2	.020
Colombia	12	8.42	38	2.75	19	-0.4	.031
Norway	13	9.00	1.5	0.23	3	-1.8	.380
Yemen Arab Rep	14	9.55	40	3.01	25	-0.1	.032
Thailand	15	9.56	39	2.90	24	-0.2	.033
Sweden	17	10.00	3	0.27	6	-1.5	.370
Japan	17	10.00	1.5	0.23	5	-1.6	.420
Wales	17	10.00	4	0.29	7	-1.4	.340
Lesotho	19	10.15	56	12.75	49	0.8	.008
Turkey	20	10.25	45	3.85	30	0.1	.027
Nigeria	21	10.68	58	14.45	55	1.0	.007
Malawi	22	10.77	59	17.35	56	1.1	.006
Togo	23	10.92	50	5.28	39	0.4	.021
England	24	11.00	5	0.30	9	-1.2	.360

Table 2.1 Continued

	Death Rates per 100 000 population		per 1000 vehicles		Standardised residuals		Vehicles/ poulation
	rank	rate	rank	rate	rank	residual	
Egypt	25	11.55	54	9.17	51	0.9	.013
Finland	26.5	12.00	7	0.34	12	-1.1	.330
East Germany	26.5	12.00	15.5	0.47	14	-0.8	.260
Botswana	28	12.16	47	3.93	42	0.5	.031
Morocco	29	12.21	44	3.82	40	0.5	.032
Chile	30	12.91	35	2.02	33	0.2	.064
Denmark	31.5	13.00	11	0.41	15	-0.6	.330
Czechoslovakia	31.5	13.00	24	0.67	18	-0.5	.190
Mauritius	33	13.30	32	1.81	32	0.2	.073
Kenya	34	13.58	57	14.13	59	1.4	.010
Netherlands	35.5	14.00	12	0.42	22	-0.3	.390
Scotland	35.5	14.00	18	0.50	16	-0.5	.270
Jordan	37	14.41	42	3.30	46	0.7	.044
South Korea	38	14.97	53	7.54	58	1.2	.020
N. Ireland	40	15.00	19	0.52	21	-0.3	.290
Greece	40	15.00	29	1.35	35	0.2	.110
Hungary	40	15.00	26	0.89	27	0.0	.170
Tunisia	42	15.51	46	3.92	52	0.9	.040
Italy	43	16.00	9	0.36	20	-0.4	.450
Panama	44	16.41	33	1.93	45	0.6	.085
Ireland	45.5	17.00	25	0.68	29	0.1	.250
Poland	45.5	17.00	30	1.60	53	0.9	.130
Spain	47	18.00	22	0.64	31	0.1	.280
New Zealand	48	19.00	8	0.35	26	-0.1	.540
Malaysia (W)	49	19.06	28	1.13	44	0.6	.170
Switzerland	50	20.00	10	0.39	28	0.0	.510
West Germany	51	21.00	17	0.48	38	0.3	.450
Australia	52	22.00	15.5	0.47	43	0.5	.510
Taiwan	53	22.91	31	1.77	57	1.2	.130
United States	54	23.00	6	0.33	37	0.2	.700
Yugoslavia	56.5	24.00	36.5	2.50	60	1.5	.100
Belgium	56.5	24.00	21	0.61	48	0.7	.400
Canada	56.5	24.00	13.5	0.43	41	0.5	.560
Luxembourg	56.5	24.00	13.5	0.43	34	0.2	.490
Austria	59.5	26.00	23	0.65	50	0.8	.400
France	59.5	26.00	20	0.53	47	0.7	.480
Portugal	61	29.00	36.5	2.50	61	1.9	.120
South Africa	62	31.85	34	2.00	62	2.2	.190

*For some Third World Countries data are for 1978 or 1979. Sources: RAGB 1981, Table 45, and Transport and Road Research Laboratory, unpublished data for 32 countries 1978-1980, provided by I.A Sayer 1984.

formulation with new data. He was working on this problem at the time of his death. The graphs reproduced below in Figure 2.3 had been prepared by him for publication but were never published. They were found in his files some time after his death and are reproduced here with the permission of the Department of Transport Studies at University College London, his old department.

Where possible they have been checked against available data sources. His original data sources have not been found and in many cases it has not been possible to verify the graphs. But they are presented as he left them because he had a reputation as a meticulous and scrupulous researcher, the graphs form a unique collection of data, and they represent, collectively, impressive support for his "law".

The solid lines on the graphs in Figure 2.3 do not represent lines of best fit but Smeed's superimposition of the curve that he calculated originally using 1938 data. For a number of countries there appears to be no correspondence with the Smeed Law; Pakistan (Figure 2.3.34) provides the worst fit of the countries examined. Generally the countries which fit worst are those with very short time series and/or those most likely to suffer from the data deficiencies discussed above. All the developed countries with reasonably long times series exhibit the tendency described by Smeed's Law, although some lie persistently above or below Smeed's curve.

Joubert (1985) has objected that the relationship plotted by Smeed "gives rise to large spurious correlations" because the number of vehicles is incorporated in the variables on both axes. Having vehicle numbers represented on both axes undoubtedly improves the correlation (see Figure 2.3.48 in which they appear only on the horizontal axis), but whether the correlation is spurious is another matter. The graphs show that as the number of vehicles increases, the death rates per vehicle decrease in a remarkably consistent way.

It is frequently thought appropriate in accident studies to use a measure of exposure to risk. If attention is confined only to the number killed in road accidents, or the number killed relative to population (columns one and two in Table 2.1) then it is very difficult to make meaningful comparisons between countries at different levels of motorisation. Using a control for exposure, such as numbers of vehicles, permits inferences to be drawn about the dangerousness of the activity. Other things being equal one would expect more car accidents in countries with many cars than in countries with few, because where vehicle ownership is high there are more opportunities for collisions to occur. Thus the relationship plotted by Smeed calls attention to the interesting and significant fact that other things do not remain equal. As the volume of motor traffic increases, motoring per unit of exposure becomes dramatically safer.

2. Engineering theology and Smeed's Law

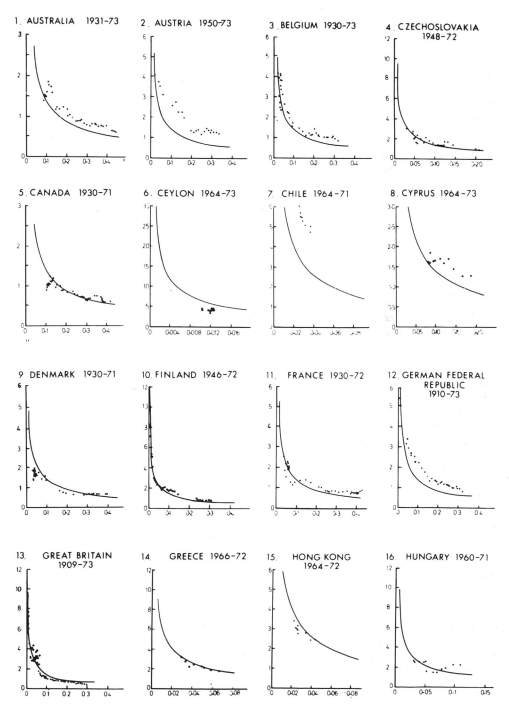

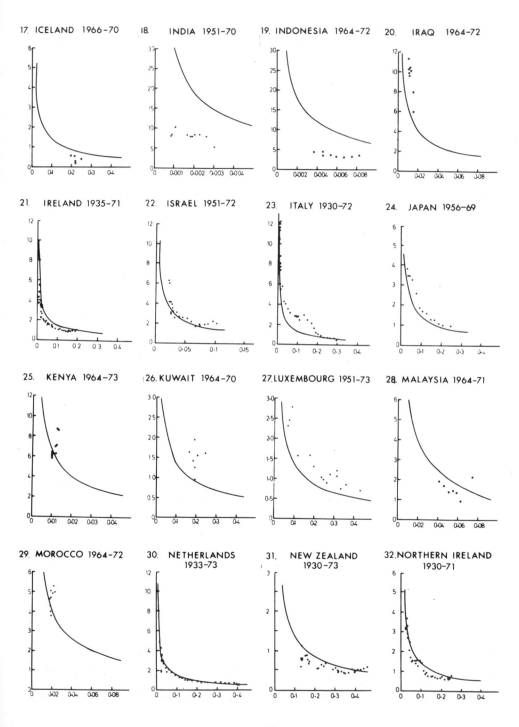

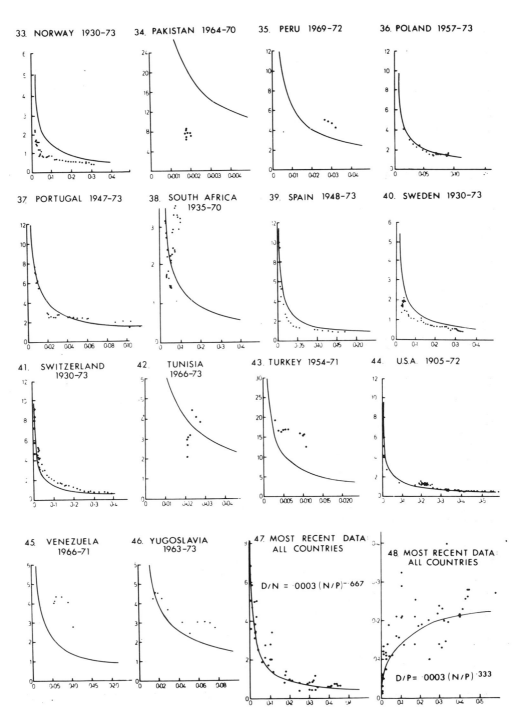

33. NORWAY 1930-73
34. PAKISTAN 1964-70
35. PERU 1969-72
36. POLAND 1957-73
37. PORTUGAL 1947-73
38. SOUTH AFRICA 1935-70
39. SPAIN 1948-73
40. SWEDEN 1930-73
41. SWITZERLAND 1930-73
42. TUNISIA 1966-73
43. TURKEY 1954-71
44. U.S.A. 1905-72
45. VENEZUELA 1966-71
46. YUGOSLAVIA 1963-73
47. MOST RECENT DATA ALL COUNTRIES

$$D/N = \cdot 0003 \, (N/P)^{-\cdot 667}$$

48. MOST RECENT DATA ALL COUNTRIES

$$D/P = \cdot 0003 \, (N/P)^{\cdot 333}$$

Figure 2.3 Smeed curves for 46 countries. Horizontal axes represent motor vehicles/population; vertical axes of Figures 2.3.1 to 2.3.47 represent road accident deaths per 1000 motor vehicles; vertical axis of Figure 2.3.48 represents road accident deaths per 1000 population. Figures 2.3.47 and 2.3.48 display data for the most recent year shown for each of the individual countries in Figures 2.3.1 to 2.3.46. Source: personal files of the late R.J. Smeed.

Failure to appreciate the almost universal occurrence of this phenomenon can lead to misunderstandings. For example, Joubert, who is critical of Smeed, also uses per vehicle death rates in an analysis which purports to demonstrate the efficacy of seat belt legislation in Australia. He plots (Joubert 1985) deaths per vehicle in the state of Victoria over a period from 1960 to 1980, and notes that after the seat belt law was passed this index decreased. This appears rather unimpressive evidence when it is appreciated that this index has been falling in almost every country in the world ever since the first cars appeared on the road. Joubert plotted deaths per vehicle on time, rather than on levels of vehicle ownership per head of population, but wherever vehicle ownership is increasing steadily over time, as was the case in Austrlia, and where these increases are large relative to population, then the plots on time will be very similar to the plots on vehicle ownership. Joubert has, in effect, done what he criticises Smeed for doing, and then miscontrued the result.

If one does not use some means of relating road accident deaths to exposure to risk it is virtually impossible to make any sense of international road accident statistics. What, for example should one make of the fact that in 1980 Malaysia had a death rate per 10,000 vehicles more than three times higher than that of the United States? Figure 2.2 shows that Malaysia's death rate in 1980 is virtually the same as that of the United States in 1925, and that its vehicle ownership rate in 1980 is also very similar to that of the United States in 1925. Judged by a simple comparison with the United States using current data, Malaysia would be considered to have a very bad accident record. Judged by its position relative to the Smeed curve Malaysia might be judged much less harshly.

Smeed's Law also provides a helpful back-cloth against which the claims for different "solutions" to road safety problems can be viewed. In the following chapters the claims are considered under two principal headings: engineering solutions, and behavioural solutions. Engineering solutions are examined first.

3   Engineering Solutions:
safer vehicles

The fact that Smeed's Law performs so well when applied both to time series data for individual countries going back almost to the beginning of this century, and to to data for a number of different countries at given points in time, calls into question the claims discussed in the last chapter for the primacy of engineering solutions to road safety problems.

Few developing countries have their own car industries. Most of the vehicles in the least motorised countries in the world today are relatively modern imported vehicles. They incorporate most of the engineering impovements found in modern vehicles in the most highly motorised countries. The variation in vehicle age is almost certainly greater in developing countries; those vehicles which avoid major accidents tend to be kept on the road longer. However, because both the vehicle population growth rates and the accident attrition rates in the less motorised countries are often very high, the average age of the vehicles in many of these countries is possibly less than that in highly motorised countries where growth rates have slowed as ownership saturation levels are approached. Yet the death rates per vehicle being achieved today with modern "safe" vehicles in the less motorised countries are on average higher than those recorded in the early stages of motorisation in the currently highly motorised countries.

The differences in death rates per vehicle between the highly motorised countries and those with few vehicles are enormous. Liberia lies at one end of the recalibrated curve in Figure 2.1 and the United States at the other. Both are small residuals from the line of best fit. If the United States with over 150 million registered vehicles in 1980 had had Liberia's death rate per vehicle, more than 6 million people would have been killed on the roads; the actual number was 51088. The Liberian death rate applied to Britain in the same year would have yielded about 800,000 deaths, instead of the actual total of 6010.

The composition of vehicle fleets has varied over time, and varies from country to country, but does not seem to be related to death rates in a way that assists the argument of the advocates of engineering solutions. Japan currently has one of the lowest death rates per vehicle and one of the highest proportions of two wheeled vehicles in its vehicle population (25 per cent in 1981 (IRF 1983)). In Britain in 1930, two wheeled motor vehicles comprised 31 per cent of the total motor vehicle population; the over-all motor vehicle death rate was 3.2 per 1000 vehicles (RAGB) - a level which is exceeded by most developing countries, with more modern vehicles and lower proportions of two wheeled vehicles, over 50 years later. There are also marked differences between countries in the average sizes of vehicles. In the United States in 1982 the market share of "large" and "very large" cars (cars with engine sizes greater than 1800 cc, and weighing more than 2400 pounds) was more than 55 per cent; in the United Kingdom it was about 11 per cent (MIT 1984, p.130). There is considerable evidence to the effect that, if they are involved in a crash, occupants of large cars are less likely to be killed than occupants of small cars (see for example Evans and Wasielewski 1983). In 1982 there were 1.48 car user deaths per 100 million car kilometres in the United States, but only 1.10 in Britain.

Superior casualty services at the scene of an accident, and subsequently in hospital, must save some lives in the more highly motorised countries which would be lost in similar accident circumstances in developing countries. But the availability of effective medical services in less motorised countries today probably does not differ greatly from that found in Britain and the United States in the early days of motoring. Since both vehicle ownership and modern medical facilities tend to be concentrated in major urban areas in Third World countries it is possible that casualty treatment for the average accident victim in developing countries today may be superior to that available in the early decades of this century in the currently developed countries. However, there appears to be no firm evidence on the subject.

It is sometimes objected that comparisons of accident statistics for industrialized countries with those for developing countries are misleading because they ignore numerous variables which could render such comparisons invalid. This may be the case; given the uncertainty attaching to Third World data it is an objection which is incapable of conclusive refutation. However, evidence discussed in Chapter 2 suggests that death rates per vehicle in Third World countries are likely to be understated, and no variables have been named whose known effects in developed countries could begin to account for the enormous differences which exist between the death rates of countries at the top of Smeed curve and those at the bottom.

Vehicle Safety Regulation

The United States has led the world in most matters connected with the car; as recently as 1965 it accounted for more than half the world's car population (Adams, 1981, p.12). In the mid-1960s it began to implement a series of unprecedented vehicle safety regulations.

3. Engineering solutions: safer vehicles

The National Highway and Traffic Administration was formed and empowered to set vehicle safety standards.

The NHTSA required a number of design changes such as padded instrument panels, tougher windscreens, energy absorbing steering columns and seat belts, with the aim of improving the chances of a car's occupants surviving a crash. Although it also required design changes aimed at preventing crashes, such as dual brake systems, the emphasis in its regulations was on protecting car occupants during a crash. It was a development of global significance. Mackay notes (1982a, p.6)

"The effects of those standards have reverberated through the automotive world ever since. They have been copied, modified and adopted by almost every country with a significant car population and they have changed car design from a free market, styling-dominated activity, to one in which certification, or passing the standards, with all the attendant engineering problems, is of prime importance in the priorities of car manufacturers."

Despite the fact that these standards were adopted so widely and enthusiastically, there has been, since the mid-1970s, heated controversy about whether or not they have worked. Peltzman (1975a, 1975b), in a study which provoked a controversy which still continues concluded that they had not; "the one result of this study that can be put forward most confidently is that auto safety regulation has not affected the highway death rate" (1975a, p.717). In brief, Peltzman fitted a multi-variable regression model to road death rates per vehicle for a period before the regulations came into effect (1947-1964) and used the coefficients estimated for the model to calculate the "expected" rates for a period after the regulations came into effect (1965-1972). He found that the actual and "expected" rates did not differ significantly. He advanced a hypothesis to explain why they had not worked: "design regulation encourages a trade of more accident risk for a lower cost per accident" (1975b, p.28).

It is a peculiarly economic explanation. Peltzman suggests that the death rate of a society at any particular time represents the "equilibrium price", paid in lives and limbs, as well as property damage, of a given level of "driving intensity"; if a government attempts to impose, by regulation, vehicles which are safer than society wants, then society will restore the equilibrium by driving more dangerously.

Since the publication of Peltzman's work both his conclusion, that regulation had had no effect, and his explanation have been hotly disputed. Discussion of the explanation will be reserved for Chapters 8 and 10. In this chapter the debate about his conclusion will be considered. Peltzman's findings were the subject of considerable comment in the safety literature. Robertson (1977) was the most prominent, and scathing of the Peltzman critics. The controversy was settled, to the satisfaction of the **American Journal of Public Health,** in a further article by Robertson (1981); in an editorial which accompanied the article the **Journal** said

"... it is good to know that, in 1975-1978, the automobile safety standards laid down by the federal government some years earlier resulted in the saving of 37 000 lives. This is the figure Robertson comes up with in an article published in this month's issue of the **Journal**.... The estimate appears to be quite sturdy: a number of possible confounders were examined and discarded. Thus the study provides assurance that the specifics of the public health actions taken by the federal government were based on scientific knowledge and achieved their goal." (Yankauer, 1981)

Robertson estimated these savings using a regression model having the following form

$$D = a - .72F - .36S + 1.35T + .027A + .012A^2 - .0008A^3$$

where D = deaths per 100 million vehicle miles,
  a = a constant estimated by model
  F = federal regulation (1 = 1968-1977 cars; otherwise 0)
  S = state and GSA regulation (1 = 1964-1977 cars; otherwise 0)
  T = type vehicles (0 = truck; 1 = car)
  A = age of vehicle in years
  R-squared = .91

The coefficent of F is interpreted by Robertson as indicating that the regulations, which came into effect in 1968, reduced the car occupant death rate by .72 per 100 million miles, and the coefficient of S as indicating that the state and GSA regulations caused a reduction of .36, a combined effect of 1.08.

The most compelling graphical summary of Robertson's findings is reproduced here as Figure 3.1. It shows that over the period 1975 to 1978 those cars which were the subject of the regulations made under the National Traffic and Motor Vehicle Safety Act (1968 model cars and later) had death rates per vehicle mile about half those of unregulated cars. Robertson translates these differences into an estimated saving of 37,000 lives over the four year period.

Unfortunately the controversy still will not die. Both the

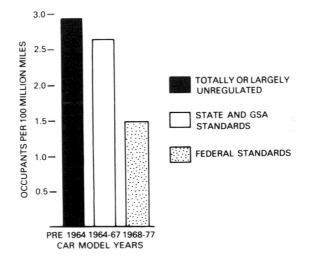

Figure 3.1   Average annual fatal crashes per 100 million miles: United States 1975-1978.   Source: Robertson 1981, p.819.

Robertson model and Peltzman's model appear to   contain within them a number of "confounders"; certainly both are statistically complex and leave scope for dispute about the interpretation of the results.   As a result, for most observers the debate has been confusing and inconclusive.

A full account of the operation of the   confounders   in Robertson's analysis can be found in Orr (1984).   Orr re-analyses Robertson's data and   demonstrates   that Robertson's claims for the efficacy of regulation are greatly exaggerated.   Orr concludes

"Statistical analysis with these data reveals a multicollinearity   problem that makes the prediction of the effects of regulation uncertain.   There is also bias in regression results due to the inappropriate inclusion of truck data in the regressions.   Regressions on the car data reveal a life saving effect of regulation that, at best, is one-fourth the value reported by Robertson."

Orr's study uses a modification of Robertson's methods.   The result is a range of possible life saving effects attributable to legislation; the range embraces a zero effect.

The data when examined with the help of a much simpler statistical method, suggest very strongly that Robertson's claim is completely untenable.   Discarding half of Robertson's observations (those relating to trucks, which were not affected by the

33

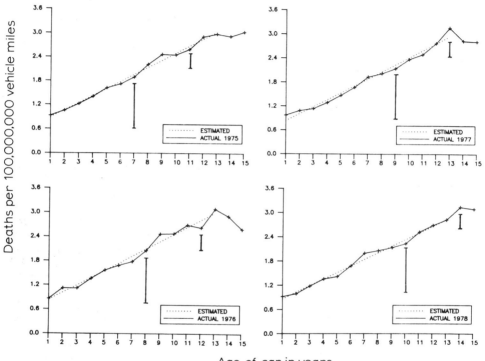

Figure 3.2 The non-effect of vehicle safety regulation. The long vertical bars represent the decrease (.72 deaths per 100 million vehicle miles) attributed by Robertson to the US federal safety regulations. The short bars represent the decrease (.36) that he attributes to the GSA regulations. The bars are positioned on each graph to show the size and location of the steps which Robertson's analysis indicates should appear in the trends. They correspond to the coefficients of the S and F variables in Robertson's regression model.

regulations), and applying a much simpler linear regression model to the data for each year in turn, and using only one independent variable (vehicle age), gives a much better fit to the data (average R squared = .98), and reveals no trace of the dramatic effects which Robertson's model suggests are associated with the regulations which came into effect in 1964 and 1968 (see Figure 3.2).

The pronounced steps in Figure 3.1, which Robertson attributes to vehicle safety regulations, appear to be artefacts of an inappropriate method. Figure 3.2 reveals a very steady, linear increase in death rates with vehicle age. There are no sharp breaks associated with the imposition of the regulations. If one takes the average of the death rates for all the cars manufactured in 1968 or after, and compares it with the average for all the cars manufactured prior to 1964 there is a very substantial difference. But this difference is connected to the steps in the graph in Figure 3.1 only by the prior assumptions of Robertson's method, or, as Orr observes, "The results are a matter of number-crunching on a foregone conclusion of effective regulation" (Orr 1985).

In a rejoinder to Orr, Robertson (1984) argues that one should not expect the steps to be visible because "the regulations and compliance with them were implemented gradually rather than in the abrupt fashion estimated in dummy-variable regression models [i.e Robertson's own models]." This represents a significant retreat from his argument that the **American Journal of Public Health** found so convincing. Having in effect conceded that his first analysis discovered steps in the death rates which do not exist, he now argues that he has discovered a much more gradual effect.

He proposes a brand new regression model which assumes that death rates per car mile are a function of car model year, calendar year, and the index of industrial production. Since the age of a car is related to both model year and calendar year, this has the effect of sharing the clear age effect, illustrated in Figure 3.2, between the two variables in an arbitrary way. The result is a statistical model which explains less of the variation in the death rate (89 per cent) than his previous model (91 per cent), or the simple age model (98 per cent). In interpreting his results he simply **assumes** that differences in death rates between model years are caused by regulation. His new model produces an estimate of 45,000 lives saved by vehicle safety regulation from 1975 to 1978.

It has already been noted in Chapter 2 that the overall death rate per vehicle (or per vehicle mile, see Chapter 7) in the United States has followed the long term downward trend characteristic of the Smeed Law. Over the four year period covered by Robertson's study, deaths per 100 million vehicle miles were relatively stable: 1975, 3.45; 1976, 3.33; 1977, 3.35; 1978, 3.40. If Robertson's conclusions are valid, but for the imposition of vehicle safety regulations, the death rate over this period should have risen sharply, against the long term trend.

It appears that Robertson has simply discovered that there is a strong relationship between vehicle age and death-rates, and claimed it for regulation. The strength of the correlation between vehicle age and death rate is striking and merits further study. Studies by Evans (1983) and Evans and Wasielewski (1983) revealing the way in which driver age had confounded conclusions about the relationship between vehicle size and accident involvment, suggest that the positive correlation between vehicle age and death rate found in Robertson's data might be substantially accounted for by a negative correlation between vehicle age and driver age, i.e. younger drivers might tend to drive older as well as smaller cars.

In the United States there appears to be no clear evidence that vehicle safety regulations have reduced road death rates per vehicle mile, and the argument continues. But there is no dispute about what happened to the total number of road accident deaths in the seven years after the regulations were introduced. They increased by fourteen per cent, from 49,163 in 1965 to 56,278 in 1972. (Adjusted for population growth this represents a 6 per cent increase.)

In the less motorised countries modern vehicles with vastly superior handling qualities and crash-protection characteristics are being driven in such a manner that they are killing people at a higher rate than their primitive predecessors did in Britain and the United States in the early decades of this century. Since the mid-1960s the safety record of less motorised countries has become worse. Jacobs and Sayer (1983, 1984) have recalibrated the Smeed function for a collection of developing countries using data for 1965, 1968, 1971, 1978 and 1980. Over this period the slope of the line has become progressively steeper and the intercept higher, i.e. since 1965 the average death rate per vehicle, relative to level of motorisation, has been increasing in the least motorised countries. Figure 2.2 reveals a similar change between 1938 and 1980; the upper left end of the recalibrated line is higher than the line originally fitted by Smeed to 1938 data.

It would appear that engineering solutions cannot escape the subtleties of human response which, their advocates insist, render behavioural safety measures ineffectual.

Bicycle Safety Regulation

The idea that people might adjust their behaviour in such a way as to off-set the safety benefit of vehicle safety regulation strikes many people as implausible.

For the past fifteen years I have cycled to work, a mode of travel that accident statistics inform me is dangerous. I cycle in both wet weather and dry. Until recently my bicycle was fitted with conventional rim brakes which are very inefficient in wet weather.

The result was that in wet weather I would pedal slowly, and often assist my brakes by putting a foot on the ground. I then discovered a new development in bicycle brake blocks which dramatically improved wet weather braking performance. Although they were more expensive I purchased them. I now travel much faster in wet weather. To the extent that I am capable of judging, I am taking neither more risks nor fewer. If I have overestimated my new brakes' efficiency I am at greater risk. If I have underestimated, I am safer. If I have judged their efficiency accurately I have consumed a potential safety benefit as a performance benefit.

Shortly after I discovered these new brake blocks Britain's Department of Transport also discovered them. It has now introduceed a regulation (BS6102) which makes it illegal for any manufacturer, or retailer, or importer to supply a new bicycle which is not fitted with them. The Department of Transport offers no evidence that this regulation will save any lives. It appears to be a regulation which compels an improvement in performance in the name of safety.

Personal anecdotes prove nothing. But behavioural theories must pass many tests before gaining general acceptance. One test is that of plausibility in the light of personal experience.

4 Engineering Solutions: safer roads

Blackspot   treatment

The highway engineering equivalent to the manufacture of more "crashworthy" vehicles is the construction of safer roads. As in the case of vehicle engineering solutions, large claims are made for the safety benefits of road improvements.

The most direct and specific of the highway engineering solutions advocated is the set of measures commonly referred to as "blackspot treatment". A report from Britain's Transport and Road Research Laboratory contends

"There has been increasing evidence from the UK and the US that relatively detailed local accident investigation, combined with low cost engineering remedial measures can be highly effective." (Jacobs and Sayer 1983)

However, much of such evidence has recently been called into question.

Regression to the mean. Hauer (1980) and Abbess, Jarrett and Wright (1981) have shown that the conventional before-and-after studies upon which most of the claims rest, contain a systematic bias. The cause of this bias is known by statisticians as the "regression-to-mean effect". Hauer explains the effect for the layman as follows

"Consider a group of 100 persons each throwing a fair die once. Select from the group those who have thrown a six. There might be some 16 such persons. (This is roughly analagous to the arranging of all road sections in the order of increasing number of accidents and selecting the top 16 per cent). In an effort to cure the 'proneness to throw sixes', each of the selected persons is administered a glass of water and asked to throw the die again. One can expect that all but two or three persons have been cured. This 'success' of the water cure is attributable entirely to the process of selection for treatment."

Because there is a substantial random element in the distribution of accidents in any given time period, there is a high probability that a section of road experiencing an exceptionally large number of accidents in a given time period - the definition of an accident black spot - will have a lower number in the succeeding time period without any treatment at all. Hauer demonstrates that in certain circumstances it is possible for the bias in before-and-after studies to account for all of the effect claimed for a particular treatment.

Hauer notes that the cumulative effect of studies which exaggerate the efficacy of blackspot treatment is the development of an erroneous consensus about the effectiveness of certain treatments, and that this consensus finds its way into highway engineering manuals and handbooks, and can lead to the implementation of projects of doubtful validity.

An illustration of the way in which a consensus can develop by the accretion of citations is provided by the TRRL study referred to above. One of the pieces of evidence it cites for the effectiveness of blackspot treatment is a study 13 years earlier by Duff (1971) which reported a number of cases where blackspot treatment appeared to have been successful. But reference to Duff's paper reveals that the results he was reporting were collected in a survey in which respondents were asked to report only schemes which they considered had been successful in reducing accidents. (The tendency of believers in particular safety measures to report only those results which confirm their beliefs is discussed in Chapter 9.)

The potential for the successes claimed for blackspot treatment to mislead extends beyond the realm of road safety. For example, in "Road Accident Prevention: the Lessons for Crime Control", Mayhew (1979) accepts at face value the claims for road accident blackspot treatment, and advocates, on the basis of these claims, engineering solutions to the problem of crime prevention.

Accident migration. Ebbecke and Shuster (1977) conducted a study of a safety programme in Philadelphia which converted a large number intersections from two-way to four-way stop sign control. The result appeared to be a substantial reduction in the numbers of accidents at the converted intersections. But something else also appeared to be happening at the same time.

"... the 4-way stop ... generally reduces accidents by about 50% where installed. ... [Therefore] with traffic volumes remaining constant ... one should reasonably expect the total accidents per year for the study location to be constantly decreasing, that is unless 4-way stops were having some deleterious effects on the 'other' intersections. ... total study location accidents have remained substantially constant over the past four years. **The total area accidents are not being reduced, they are just being rearranged.**" (my emphasis)

Wright and Boyle (1984) have observed a similar phenomenon in London. They call it the "accident migration effect". In a study of black spot treatment in London they detected a tendency for accident frequencies at treated blackspots to decrease, but to increase in the immediate vicinity of the treated site. They venture this hypothesis to account for their findings

"... an untreated blackspot, which by definition has more accidents than the average location on the road network, also has a higher than average incidence of near misses or conflicts. This will mean that a proportion of drivers leaving an untreated blackspot will have been involved in some form of conflict and will be driving more cautiously. Among commuters the effects of a near miss on one day may persist over a long period. This higher level of caution among a proportion of drivers will, it is argued, artificially deflate the numbers of accidents in the surrounding area. Successful treatment of the black spot will reduce the proportion of drivers leaving the blackspot who are behaving cautiously so that the number of accidents in the surrounding areas will tend to increase towards their 'natural' levels."

Wright and Boyle estimated that accident frequencies at treated blackspots decreased by 22.3 percent and increased by 10 percent in immediately adjacent links and nodes. They note that their method could well produce a substantial underestimate of the migration effect:

"there are no a priori grounds for supposing that this is the limit of the effect ... using a larger surrounding area might well result in additional numbers of accidents being involved in the migration process."

Migration effects have been noted in other areas where attempts have been made to suppress undesired behaviour. Physical measures to suppress crime are frequently believed to have the effect of simply displacing it to less secure targets (Mayhew 1979, p.26). And a related phenomenon has been noted by Smith (1981), investigating the problem of fault detection in industries such as atomic power, where faults are potentially catastrophic. He notes that "events which have had extraordinarily small 'probabilities' associated with them actually seem to occur with monotonous regularity." The reason, he suggests, is that vigilance is related to the fault inspector's perception of the probability of finding a fault; "the 'safer' a system is made the less effort is put into a search for any faults in that system." He concludes that "we cannot guarantee to increase the safety of a system by, for example, increasing the number of fault detectors or the number of inspectors." In certain circumstances, he demonstrates, increasing the number of inspectors can actually decrease the probability of detecting a fault; if sufficient inspectors are appointed such that the probability of any one inspector finding a fault is reduced to a level which falls below the inspectors' threshold of concern, then the over-all level of vigilance will fall.

Road surface and vehicle handling

One can also consider improvements to vehicle handling characteristics under the heading of safer roads. Considered as safety measures, better tyres, brakes, suspensions and steering – changes which increase a driver's control over his vehicle – operate like road improvements to reduce the chances of unwanted contact with other road users or other unfriendly parts of the adjacent environment. Such measures are also the subject of numerous safety claims.

Everyday observation suggests that improvements in vehicle handling characteristics and in roads are, at least partly, consumed not as safety benefits but as performance benefits. The study by Rumar et al (1976) provides compelling statistical support for this impression. The study recorded the speeds of several thousand vehicles travelling around two consecutive bends in a road near Uppsala in Sweden. The vehicles were divided into two groups depending on whether or not they were fitted with studded tyres for winter driving. Speeds were recorded for dry (high friction) conditions and icy (low friction) conditions.

The first of the two bends had a radius of 105 m and the second 45 m. The study found that speeds were markedly lower on the tighter bend (by 26% on average). No clear difference was found in the speeds for the two groups in dry conditions – this would appear to refute the argument of Robertson (1983, p. 144) that "the possibility that those who drive faster more often buy studded tyres is at least as reasonable an interpretation of the finding as an attempted adjustment of driving speed to the equipment once purchased. And both groups travelled more slowly in icy conditions (on average speeds were 17% lower). But in icy conditions the cars fitted with studded tyres were driven faster than cars fitted with unstudded tyres (6% on average). Figure 4.1 redrawn from Rumar et al summarizes their findings for the first bend in the road. It shows that the greatest differences in speed occur at the highest speeds, i.e. at speeds most likely to be associated with loss of control. The fastest two and a half per cent of unstudded cars were travelling at 57 kph or more; the fastest two and a half per cent of studded cars were travelling at 63 kph or faster.

The Rumar study suggests very strongly that drivers are sensitive to variations in the security of their grip on the road, whether caused by variations attributable to the road surface (dry/icy), or

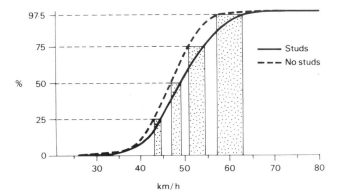

Figure 4.1 Cumulative speed distributions of cars rounding a curve in Sweden in low friction conditions. Source: Rumar et al 1976.

road   curvature   (long   radius/short   radius),   or   car   tyres (studded/unstudded).

On the question of whether cars fitted with studded tyres enjoyed a net safety benefit despite being driven faster the evidence was inconclusive. Rumar et al attempted to translate their speed curves into estimates of "the proportion of side friction used" and the "proportion of maximum speed used" in order to estimate which group of cars was driven with the largest safety margin. The authors concluded that cars with studded tyres probably did enjoy a safety advantage over   cars without, but acknowledged that this conclusion was supported by only one of their indices for one of their two bends in the road, and was dependent on the calculation of a coefficient of side friction for studded tyres whose estimation was "difficult".

The study showed that in dry conditions both studded and unstudded cars were driven with a much greater margin of safety, by their criteria, than in icy conditions.   But the study did not pursue the implications of the evidence that the speed at which an accident happened was likely to be lowest for unstudded cars in icy conditions, and highest for both sets of cars in dry conditions. To the extent that the severity of an accident is dependent on speed the Rumar study suggests that there are likely to be more, but less serious accidents involving unstudded cars on ice, and fewer, but more serious accidents with both types of car in dry conditions.

Evidence from Ontario suggests that the severity of winter accidents is much less than that of summer accidents.   Figure 4.2 shows that over a ten year period the number of injuries was lowest in February and highest in August. The pattern for fatalities is similar

42

but the difference between February and August is much more pronounced. Traffic levels decrease when road conditions are bad, but this is probably, at least in part, a response to perceived danger, a perception amplified by news bulletins urging people to stay at home unless their journeys are essential.

Figure 4.3 shows the annual variation in the ratio of deaths to injuries. By this crude index of accident severity it would appear that the average August accident is 33 per cent more severe than the

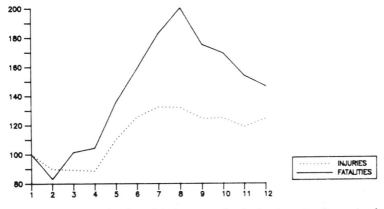

Figure 4.2 Indices of fatalities and injuries in Ontario by month, 1970–1979. The average for all Januaries (month 1) is set equal to 100. Source: **Motor Vehicle Accident Facts 1979**, Ont. Min. of Transportation and Communications.

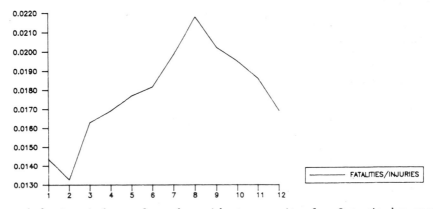

Figure 4.3 An index of road accident severity for Ontario by month, 1970–1979. Source: Figure 4.2.

average February accident.   Accidents in Ontario are recorded by
severity of injury and road surface condition.   The figures for the
period 1974-1980 are shown in Table 4.1.   They indicate that accidents
occurring in dry conditions are, on average, much more severe than
those occurring in slippery conditions. (The caveats concerning the
use of injury statistics must be repeated here. It is possible that
some of the differences displayed in Table 4.1 could be attributed to
reporting bias - in good weather people may be more inclined to wait
about to report an accident.   Nevertheless the differences in Table
4.1 are consistent with the Rumar evidence to the effect that average
speeds are lower when road conditions are bad.)

In Sweden for the period 1961-1964, (a period for which damage
only accidents were published), damage only accidents were more
numerous in January and February, the months when driving conditions
are worst, than in July and August.   But fatalities in January and
February were considerably less numerous (Statistics Sweden). This
suggests that Swedish drivers view risk, like Lowrance (1980), as "a
compound measure of the probability **and** magnitude of adverse
effect"; in their driving they appear to respond to difficult
conditions in a way which increases the probability of an adverse
effect, but which at the same time decreases the probability of the
adverse effects of the greatest magnitude.

Table 4.1   Road accidents in Ontario:
road condition and severity of accident

Road Surface Condition	Fatal	Personal Injury	Fatal/ P.I.
Dry	6494	274873	.024
Wet	1878	113051	.017
Loose snow	214	16448	.013
Slush	179	11000	.016
Packed snow	226	12413	.018
Ice	289	19446	.015

Source: **Motor Vehicle Accident Facts**, Ontario Ministry
Transportation and Communications, annual.

A similar response appears to be made to the differences between
urban and rural driving conditions. In Britain the death rate per 100
million vehicle kilometres is lower in built-up areas where traffic
densities are highest than in non-built-up areas (2.8 compared to
3.5, (RAGB 1982 Table 43)). Conversely the "all severities" rate is
very much lower in non-built-up areas (non-built-up 79, built-up 234).
The lowest rates for both categories are found on motorways (death
rate 1.4, all severities rate 29). But this does not necessarily

mean that building more motorways saves lives. In Britain 83 per cent
of car journeys are less than 10 miles in length (NTS 1983 Table
3.3). The scope for consolidating a significant part of these journeys
on to motorways is therefore very limited. Outside urban areas the
development of the motorway network has diverted longer distance
inter-city traffic from rail to road, and fostered the growth of
traffic in the tributary parts of the road network which remain
unimproved.   The death rate per 100 million passenger kilometres by
train in Britain is about 0.07 (TSGB 1983 Table 3.26); for car
occupants the death rate is about 1 per 100 million kilometres.
(RAGB 1982 Table Z). Wilde (1982) cites Canadian evidence to the
effect that, per passenger kilometre, travelling by train is 30 times
safer.

A speculation.   If all roads were to be paved with a substance
having the same coefficient of friction as ice, the number of people
killed on the roads would be substantially reduced. (The **performance**
of the road network as a transportation system might also be reduced
- but that is a separate matter.)
    In Sweden in September 1967 when all drivers were obliged to
change from driving on the left to driving on the right - a "safety
measure" as bizarre as paving the roads with ice - the number of
people killed on the roads plummeted. Figure 4.4 suggests that the
country, having demonstrated that it was capable of halving its road
death toll, decided that it had over-compensated for a perceived
danger and fairly quickly reverted to its "acceptable" rate of
killing.   Wilde (1982a) reports evidence from Iceland of a
considerable drop in fatal and personal injury accidents in that
country when it changed from left to right, followed by a return to

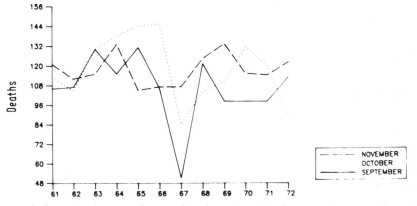

Figure 4.4 Road accident deaths in Sweden.   Source: Statistics
Sweden.

pre-existing trends after two and a half months.

This suggests a gradation of accident severity according to the perceived difficulty of road conditions relative to the handling characteristics of the vehicle. The worse the road conditions the less likely an accident is to be fatal. This evidence appears to weaken the Rumar study's tentative conclusion that studded tyres convey a net safety benefit.

Radical alteration of traffic environments

In newer built environments (less frequently in old) attempts are sometimes made to segregate vehicles and people to provide traffic-free neighbourhood environments, especially for the benefit of children. Pedestrian precincts in shopping centres have been established for both amenity and safety reasons. More recently, planners have been experimenting with mixing vehicles and pedestrians in circumstances which require the vehicles to travel at very low speeds and defer to the pedestrians.

Measures such as the establishment of pedestrian precincts are bound to have an effect on the pattern of motor vehicle accidents. If traffic is removed from an area then traffic accidents in that area are no longer possible. But, as yet, I am aware of no study which specifically addresses the possibility that accidents will be transfered elsewhere in such circumstances.

A study by by Levin and Bruce (1968) on the location of primary schools suggests that this is a possibility deserving further research. Their study compared accessibility to primary schools in St. Albans and Stevenage in England. The towns are comparable in size, but St. Albans is an "old" town and Stevenage a new town. St. Albans was largely built before the age of mass car ownership and accommodates motor vehicle traffic as best it can on roads not designed for it. Stevenage was built with the problems posed by traffic very much in mind; it has a hierarchical road network for motor vehicles, and segregated footpaths and cycleways with their own bridges and underpasses; and residential areas have been designed to provide traffic free play areas.

The study reported traffic accidents to primary school children (aged 5 to 11) recorded by the police during 1962-66. Over the five years there were 120 injuries to primary school children in Stevenage and 80 in St. Albans. The accident rates per 1000 per year were very similar: 2.97 in Stevenage and 3.16 in St. Albans. But there were interesting differences in the patterns of accidents. The serious and fatal accident rates were twice as high in Stevenage as St. Albans. The numbers of casualties in each category were: 78 slight, 39 serious and 3 fatal in Stevenage; 68 slight, 11 serious and 1 fatal in St. Albans. In Stevenage 9 per cent of road accidents happened on the way to or from school; in St. Albans school journeys accounted for

30.5 per cent. In St. Albans a very much lower percentage of school journeys was "unescorted"; almost 50 per cent of afternoon journeys of 1 mile were unescorted in Stevenage, while less than 15 per cent were unescorted in St. Albans. In both towns close to 90 per cent of the accidents were attributed to children running into the road or stepping off the kerb without looking.

The study did not explicitly address hypotheses such as "risk compensation" or "accident migration", but it presents photographic evidence of behaviour which fits comfortably with such ideas. It pictures pedestrians in Stevenage crossing roads at "dangerous" unofficial crossing points within close reach of a purpose-built pedestrian underpass. It also pictures a child crossing a road on a pedestrian bridge on the **outside** of the safety railings. Such behaviour is very poorly documented in the safety literature, but is a phenomenon commonly discussed at public inquiries into road schemes in which I have participated.

Although the evidence reported by Levin and Bruce suggests that children and parents in Stevenage may be "compensating" for their safer environment, it is far from conclusive. Only traffic accident data are reported, so whether there are significant differences in the patterns of other accidents is not known. Differences between the two towns in socio-economic indicators known to be associated with differences in accident rates have not been explored. At present it can only be noted that the "safer" traffic environment of Stevenage was not reflected in its road accident statistics for primary school children.

The contribution of "safer" roads

Road conditions usually improve as vehicle ownership increases and death rates per vehicle decrease. The evidence with respect to the contribution, if any, of safer roads to these decreasing death rates is less clear cut than the evidence with respect to improved vehicles discussed in Chapter 3.

At best it appears that road improvements can be credited with a very small share of the reductions in road accident death rates illustrated by the graphs in Chapters 2 and 3. The claims that are often made for the safety benefit of improved roads, while large, are sufficient to account for only a small part of the **very** large reductions in death rates exemplified by the Smeed Law. And there is reason to suppose that many of these claims have been inflated by a failure to consider regression-to-mean effects and the possibility of accident migration.

There is clear evidence that drivers tend to consume improvements both in vehicle handling characteristics and road quality, at least in part, as performance benefits rather than safety benefits. With respect to vehicles, the evidence reviewed in Chapter 3 suggests that all of the potential safety benefit is consumed. There is no obvious reason why the behavioural response to road improvements should be different.

Some of the most conspicuous road improvements in less developed countries - such as the dual carriageway roads linking Lagos to Ibadan, and Cairo to Alexandria - are internationally notorious for their accident records. Recent work by Jacobs at Britain's Transport and Road Research Laboratory, applying the Smeed Law to less developed countries, reveals that some of the largest positive residuals from the line of best fit are oil rich middle eastern countries which have made extravagant investments in road improvement. In Kuwait between 1961 and 1979 there was almost a four fold increase in the length of paved roads (Jadan and Salter, 1982). Yet Kuwait, when tested against the Smeed Law (see Figure 2.3.26), consistently has more fatalities than predicted.

The United States has enjoyed a very large lead over the rest of the world in vehicle ownership. A large proportion of its built environment was designed for the car. By contrast Britain has smaller cars and higher speed limits, and a much larger proportion of its road system predates mass car ownership. Yet Britain's road safety record is superior to that of the United States, judged either by deaths per 100,000 population, deaths per vehicle or by their respective positions relative to the Smeed Curve (see Figure 2.2 and Table 2.1).

5   Behavioural Solutions:
   seat belts

As a safety measure the seat belt can be classified as an engineering solution. However the controversy which surrounds seat belts is largely concerned with behavioural responses to measures intended to promote their use. Should motorists be compelled to use them? Will lives be saved if motorists are compelled to use them? For many years there has been a strong consensus amongst road safety experts and campaigners that the answer to both questions should be an emphatic "yes".

Expectations

In the British parliamentary debate in 1979 William Rodgers, then Secretary of State for Transport, claimed
"On the best available evidence of accidents in this country – evidence which has not been seriously contested – compulsion could save up to 1000 lives and 10,000 injuries a year." (**Hansard**, March 22, 1979)

Although the magnitude of the savings attributed to seat belts has varied, the claims made in the scientific literature have been consistently large. A report by the Transport and Road Research Laboratory in the same year concluded "seat belts reduce deaths of car occupants by at least 40 per cent" (Grime 1979). Hurst (1979), in a paper in the journal **Accident Analysis and Prevention** cited Swedish evidence that "belt use reduces chances of fatal injury by about 83 per cent for drivers and about 80 per cent for front seat passengers."
The Royal Society for the Prevention of Accidents produced a campaign pamphlet which cited American evidence that "... for belted occupants the deaths were reduced by 77 per cent in full frontal crashes and 91 per cent in roll overs." The pamphlet concluded "no other single practical piece of legislation could achieve such dramatic savings in lives and serious injuries" (RoSPA, 1981).
In the 1981 parliamentary debates which preceded the passage of Britain's seat belt law the claim that 1000 lives and 10,000 injuries a year would be saved was repeated frequently. David Ennals, former Secretary of State for Health, asserted that not wearing a belt increased six-fold a motorist's chances of being killed in an

accident (Hansard, Janaury 13, 1981). Although a new note of caution and uncertainty about the magnitude of the probable accident savings was introduced by Norman Fowler, then Secretary of State for Transport, he was quite clear that there would be savings.
   "I stress that there should still be savings. No one would deny that." (Hansard, July 28 1981)

How well the British expectations have stood the test of events since the law came into effect will be considered below. But first the basis of the expectations will be examined. The following are some optimistic claims culled from evidence presented to a United States Congressional Inquiry into seat belts in 1978. They are but a small sample from a large number of similar claims made in many different countries during the 1970s when seat belt legislation was the principal objective of road safety campaigners around the world.

   "Mandatory safety belt usage ... [holds] the potential to save 89,000 lives on the highways over the next ten years." (DoT 1978, p.130)

   "The potential for saving lives right now is tremendous with estimates ranging from 10,000 to 20,000 lives per year if everybody always wore lap and shoulder belts." (DoT 1978, p.152)

   "French police have estimated that seat belts have reduced fatalities in France by 63 per cent." (ASBC 1978, p.229)

   "Two separate studies [in Sweden] ... found that seat belts reduced fatalities and serious injuries by 50 to 70 per cent, minor injuries by 20 per cent." (ASBC 1978, p.235)

   "The [German] government estimates that 1,700 deaths and 30,000 injuries are prevented annually by the use of seat belts." (ASBC 1978, p.238)

   "... occupant restraints is the largest highway safety issue that we have ever had since the automobile came on the scene. It is more important than the safety aspects of the interstate, more important than getting drunk drivers off the road. In my opinion, it is the number-one issue, and I base that on the profound benefits that can be obtained from occupant restraint." (B.J. Campbell (Director of Highway Safety Research Centre, University of North Carolina) DOT 1978, p.361)

The evidence that the use of a seat belt greatly improves a car occupant's chances of surviving a crash appears to be overwhelming. That a person travelling at speed inside a hard metal shell will stand a better chance of surviving a crash if he is restrained from rattling about inside the shell is both intuitively obvious and supported by an impressive body of empirical evidence.

Results

The claims cited above promise very substantial reductions in numbers killed on the highways if most car occupants could be persuaded, or compelled, to use seat belts. Generally, the higher a country's level of car ownership, the larger its ratio of car occupant fatalities to total road accident fatalities, and, therefore, the greater the potential benefit of measures that reduce occupant fatalities.

In Sweden, for example, the seat belt law is estimated to have increased wearing rates from between 8 and 33 per cent before the law to between 85 and 90 per cent after the law (American Seat Belt Council 1980). Car occupant fatalities accounted for 50 per cent of all road deaths in Sweden before the law came into effect (NRTRI 1978, p.6). Therefore, applying the Swedish fatality reduction estimates of 80-83 per cent cited by Hurst, the law should have resulted, all other influences remaining constant, in a reduction in occupant fatalities of at least 57 per cent, and in total road deaths of at least 28 per cent. As Figures 5.14 and 5.15 below show, in Sweden this did not happen.

As the other graphs in this chapter show, in no country in which a seat belt law has been passed have reductions in fatalities occurred which remotely approach the dramatic reductions promised in the claims cited above. There have been reductions in fatalities in some countries in which seat belt laws have been passed, but they have not been as great as the reductions that have occurred in the same period in countries in which seat belt laws have not been passed.

Caveats

Road death statistics can fluctuate substantially from year to year in a way that frequently mystifies the experts. For example, in explaining Ontario's road fatality statistics to the 1978 United States Congressional Inquiry, an Ontario Government safety expert said: "If you go back to 1970, there was a big drop for no apparent reason and a very substantial increase from that year to the next. That kind of increase in the order of 20 per cent in fatalities in one year causes a great deal of panic among certain legislators, but I don't think there is any particular systematic reason for it, at least not one we know" (Lonero, 1978, p.189).

One must be careful not to be overly impressed by the statistics for one particular year. Nevertheless, the abundant evidence about the effectiveness of seat belts in reducing the severity of injuries __in crashes__ suggests that, in general, one should expect a large reduction in fatalities immediately following a law that produces large increases in wearing rates. Because the safety benefit of a seat belt is conferred as soon as it is securely in place there should be no delay in its effect. The fatality statistics should record an instant drop that is directly related to the increase in wearing rates.

In a particular country, in a particular year, other influences might obscure, or exaggerate, the effect of a seat belt law. Almost all countries have a variety of road safety campaigns underway at any given time which could, if allowance were not made for their effect, exaggerate the influence of seat belt legislation. Also, during the 1970s, the energy crisis affected some countries more severely than others. But probably all motorists everywhere have been exposed to information about the economic benefits of light-footed driving. In some countries the economic incentive to drive more slowly was reinforced by a lowering of speed limits and a physical shortage of fuel. In global terms 1973, the year of the "energy crisis", was a watershed year for road deaths. Before 1973 the death toll in the major motorized countries of the world had been rising for many years. Since 1973 it has declined substantially.

Evidence

Prior to the passage of Britain's seat belt law a study (Adams 1981b) compared the road accident fatality records of 13 countries having "effective" seat belt laws with the records of four countries without. The thirteen countries with effective laws were Belgium, Denmark, Finland, France, West Germany, Netherlands, Norway, Spain, Switzerland, Sweden, Israel, Australia and New Zealand. The four countries without effective laws were Britain, Italy, Japan, and the United States.

"Effective" legislation is defined as a law that was followed by substantial increases in wearing rates. Japan was included amongst the countries without seat belt laws because, although it had a law, it was not enforced and wearing rates were reported to be less than a third of those in Britain during the 1970s (Japanese Government 1980).

The choice of countries included in the study was constrained by the availability of relevant information. Bulgaria, Czechoslovakia, Greece, Hungary, Ireland, Luxembourg, Malaysia, South Africa, and the U.S.S.R. were all reported to have passed seat belt laws, but insufficient was known at the time about enforcement, wearing rates and changes in road death rates to include them in the study. Austria was also excluded because, although like Japan it had a law, it was apparently not enforced, but reported wearing rates were about three times higher than those in Japan.

Together all the countries included in the study contained over 80

per cent of the world's car population. The road death tolls of all
seventeen countries were converted to indices with 1973, the year of
the "energy crisis" set equal to 100. These indices included
all road accident deaths, i.e. cars occupants plus all other road
users. Two composite indices consisting of the average of the indices
of the thirteen countries with seat belt laws, and the average of the
four countries without laws were calculated. These are displayed in
Figure 5.1. It shows that the index for countries with seat belt laws
fell 17 points between 1972 and 1978, while the index for countries
without laws fell by 25 points over the same period.

Figure 5.1 has been criticized by Mackay (1982b) who argues
"This comparison purported to show that the greater reduction
in the four "non-law" countries in comparison to the 13 "law",
was because the introduction of seat belt laws increased road
deaths. The methodology however is flawed because in the "law"
group not all those countries introduced that law in 1971. The
laws were introduced at different times between 1970 and 1977.
If the analysis is conducted by shifting the countries from the
"non-law" to the "law" group at the time that each country
actually introduced a seat belt law, then the conclusion drawn
by Adams is reversed."

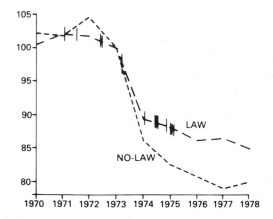

Figure 5.1 Indices of road accident deaths for countries with
seat belt laws, and without. Bars indicate the dates at which
laws came into effect in countries in the "law" group. Source:
IRF Table VII.

This criticism was repeated in another paper (Mackay 1982a) but
has never been explained. Firstly, I have not argued that seat belt
laws have increased road accident deaths, only that there is no
evidence that they have reduced them. Secondly, he wrongly assumes

that my data were "standardised" to a 1971 base; the indices for both groups were set to equal 100 in 1973. If the indices of all countries are set to 100 in 1973, and if all transfers from the "no-law" to the "law" group had been completed by 1976, then whether one uses my method of summarizing the data, or Mackay's transferable-group-membership method, both "law" and "no-law" indices must have the same values in 1973, 1977 and 1978. The paths of the two graphs between 1973 and 1977 are not identical, but they do not differ in a way which will alter the conclusions drawn about the efficacy of seat belt legislation.

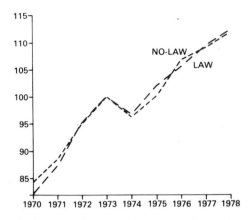

Figure 5.2 Indices of petrol consumption in law and no-law countries. Source: IRF, Table VI.

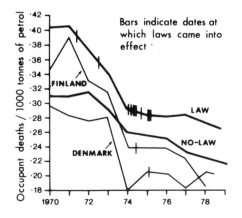

Figure 5.3 Road accident deaths per thousand tonnes of petrol consumed. Source: Adams 1982.

Figure 5.2 shows the changes that occurred in petrol consumption in the "law" and "no-law" countries. It suggests that the experience of the energy crisis was similar in the two sets of countries. Figure 5.3 is comparable to Figure 5.1, but represents car occupant deaths only, divided by petrol consumption measured in thousands of tonnes. Thus it attempts to control for the effects of the energy crisis, and to separate car occupants from other road users. The "effect" of seat belt legislation is no more apparent in this graph than in Figure 5.1.

Figure 5.4 shows the changes that occurred in the indices of road traffic injuries for the same period for the two sets of countries. Injury statistics for individual countries behaved in a more erratic way than the fatality statistics. Injury statistics are inherently less reliable than fatality statistics; in industrialized countries almost all deaths get recorded, while only an unknown and variable percentage of injuries gets recorded. The composite indices for the "law" and "no-law" countries indicate that in both sets of countries the decrease in injuries following the energy crisis was less than the decrease in fatalities. As with the fatality indices, the decrease was greater in those countries that did not pass effective laws than in those that did. A comparison of injury graphs for individual countries supports the same conclusions as a comparison of fatality graphs, but because of their greater reliabilty the following discussion is confined to fatality statistics. (The inadequacies of non-fatal injury data will be discussed more fully in the section dealing with seat belt legislation in Britain.)

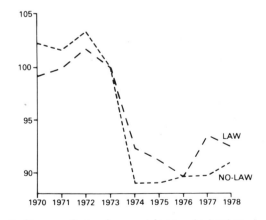

Figure 5.4 Indices of road accident injuries. Source: IRF, Table VII.

Road death indices for individual countries

Highly aggregated statistics such as those summarized in Figure 5.1 can be misleading (Chapter 6 provides an illustration of the pitfalls of careless aggregation). This section presents the road death indices for all the individual countries so that the reader can confirm that in none of the countries which passed seat belt laws can any clear beneficial effect be seen.

Belgium. Figure 5.5 compares the Belgian road death index with the average index for the no-law countries. The seat belt law was passed in Belgium on June 1, 1975. (Unless otherwise indicated all the dates and wearing rates quoted in this section are from ASBC, 1980.) The decrease in fatalities which began in 1972 continued through 1975, but from 1976, the first full year of the law's operation, the Belgian death toll increased steadily, while in the no-law countries it continued to drop until 1978 when a small rise occurred. The Belgian Transportation Administation attributed the decline in 1975 not only to the seat belt law, but also to harsher drunk-driving laws and stiffer penalties for violations of the traffic code (ASBC 1978. p. 223). Belt usage was estimated to have increased from 17 per cent before the law to between 63 and 86 per cent after the law. The graph of occupant fatalities divided by petrol consumption also reveals no

Figure 5.5   Figure 5.6

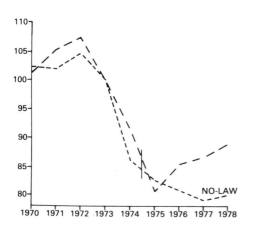
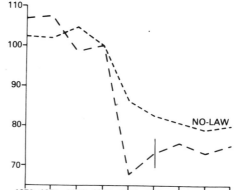

Figures 5.5 and 5.6   Indices of road accident deaths for Belgium and Denmark compared with index for the no-law group of countries. Source for remaining graphs in this chapter – unless otherwise indicated – IRF Table VII.

apparent effect attributable to seat belt legislation. (Graphs showing fatalities divided by petrol consumption have been drawn for all the countries discussed below (Adams 1982). For none of them do the graphs alter the impression formed by the graphs of total road death indices.)

Denmark. Figure 5.6 compares the Danish road death index with the no-law index. Denmark experienced a dramatic drop of 32.5 points in 1974. But its belt law did not come into effect until January 1 1976; the death toll in this year increased by 2.5 points. Belt usage was estimated to have increased from 25 per cent before the law to 70 per cent after the law. The Danish Council of Road Safety Research published a critique of my 1981 study and concluded
    "It is not surprising that Adams does not find that the fatality indices for the law group decrease. The same thing was found in the Danish Council of Road Safety Research analysis of the effect of the [Danish] seat belt law..." and "... it is difficult to see the big death-reducing effect of seat belts which some researchers think they can see." (Lund 1981).

Finland. Figure 5.7 compares the Finnish road death index with the no-law index. The Finnish law came into effect in July 1975. This is the only year between 1972 and 1978 in which Finland experienced an increase in road deaths. Tolonen (1984) reports an increase in belt wearing rates in rural areas from 20-30 per cent before legislation to 60 per cent after legislation; the reported increase in built-up areas was from 5 per cent to 35 per cent. There were no effective sanctions for non-compliance with the law and by 1980 wearing rates were reported to be about 50 per cent in rural areas and 20 per cent in built-up areas.
    The downward trend in fatalities shown in Figure 5.7 continued, with a slight interruption in 1979, until 1981. On April 1 1982 the non-use of seat belts was made an offence punishable by a fine, and wearing rates increased to 93 per cent in rural areas and 70 per cent in built up areas. Tolonen reports that in 1982 road accident fatalities increased, and that this increase continued strongly into 1983. In the first quarter of 1983 traffic deaths increased by 46.7 per cent compared to the same period the previous year (i.e. compared to the last quarter before fines began to be imposed, and wearing rates increased sharply). He reports "The reasons for this are not known but experts believe that increased speeds on the the highways as well as misbehaviour in road traffic contribute to this negative development" (p.9).

France. Figure 5.8 compares the French road death index to the no-law index. The French law came into effect on July 1, 1973; initially, the law did not compel wearing in urban areas. On January 15, 1975 the law was extended to urban motorways, and to all urban

Figure 5.7   Figure 5.8

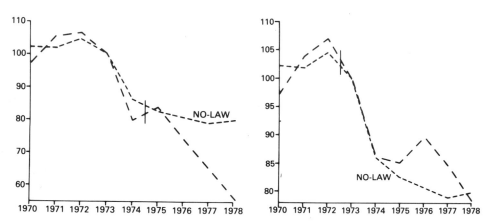

Indices of road accident deaths for Finland (Figure 5.7) and France (Figure 5.8) compared with index for no-law countries.

roads during the period 2200 – 0600 hours. On October 1, 1979 the law was extended to all areas and all hours (RoSPA 1981b). France experienced a slightly greater decline in its death rate in 1973 than the no-law countries, 7 points and 5 points respectively, But from 1974 until 1978 the no-law index was below the French index. Belt usage is estimated to have increased from 20 per cent before the law to between 50 and 90 per cent after the law. The decline in fatalities in France in 1973 appears to be associated not with the seat belt law which came into effect in July, but with the energy crisis later in the year. Chodkiewicz and Dubarry (1977) concluded:
"... the seat belt seems to be an indispensable tool in reducing the number of car accidents however, it is insufficient alone. On the highways in France, the death rate, **which was not affected by the compulsory use of the belt**, decreased in a few months by 57 per cent when a complementary measure limiting speed was introduced." (Chodkiewicz and Dubarry 1977)

West Germany. Figure 5.9 compares the German road death index with the no-law index. The German law came into effect on January 1, 1976. In 1976 the German index remained at its 1975 level, 91 points, while the no-law index dropped by 2 points. Belt usage estimates range from 22 to 64 per cent before the law, to 45 to 85 per cent after the law.

Figure 5.9   Figure 5.10

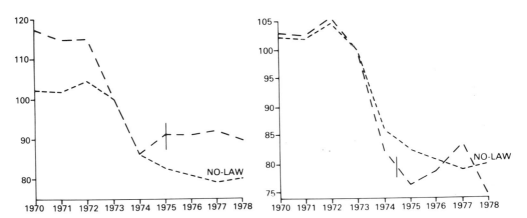

Indices of road accident deaths for West Germany (Figure 5.9) and the
Netherlands (Figure 5.10) compared with index for no-law countries.

Netherlands. Figure 5.10 compares the Dutch road death index with
the no-law index. The Dutch law came into effect on June 1, 1975. In
1975 the Dutch index dropped 4 points while the no-law index dropped
3.5 points. In 1976, the first full year of the Dutch law's
operation, the Dutch index increased by 2 points while the no-law
index continued to decrease by a further 2 points. Because of lower
speed limits and drink-drive legislation implemented around the same
time Dutch officials say that it is difficult to separate the effect
of the belt law from the effects of the other measures (ASBC 1978, p.
231). Belt usage estimates range from 13 to 28 per cent before the
law, to 40 to 75 per cent after the law.

Norway. Figure 5.11 compares the Norwegian road death index with
the no-law index. The Norwegian law came into effect on September 1,
1975. In 1975 the Norwegian index increased by 6 points while the
no-law index dropped 3.5 points. In 1976, the first full year of the
law's operation, the Norwegian index dropped 13 points, to 92,
compared to a drop of 2 points, to 81, in the no-law countries. Belt
usage estimates range from 13 to 35 per cent before the law, to 30 to
64 per cent after the law. When car occupant fatalities are
divided by petrol consumption - as in Figure 5.3 - the large decrease
in 1976 disappears (Adams 1982).

Spain. Figure 5.12 compares the Spanish road death index to the
no-law index. The Spanish law came into effect in April 1975; as in
France the law did not apply in urban areas. In 1975 the Spanish

5. Behavioural solutions: seat belts

Figure 5.11   Figure 5.12

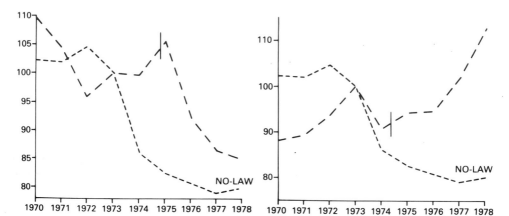

Indices of road accident deaths for Norway (Figure 5.11) and Spain (Figure 5.12) compared with index for no-law countries.

index rose 3.5 points and continued to rise thereafter. Pre-law usage statistics are not available; after the law wearing rates were estimated at 67 per cent.

Switzerland. Figure 5.13 compares the Swiss road death index to the no-law index. The Swiss law came into effect on January 1, 1976 and was repealed in September 1977. In 1976 the Swiss index dropped 4 points compared to 2 points in the no-law countries. In the following year, during nine months of which the law was in operation, the Swiss index increased by 8 points, compared to a decrease of a further 2 points in the no-law index. In the first full year after the law was repealed the Swiss index dropped by more than 2 points while the index for the no-law countries increased by one point. Belt usage estimates range from 19 to 42 per cent before the law, to 78 to 92 per cent during the period in which the law was in force. After the repeal of the law usage was estimated to have dropped by one-third.

Sweden. Figure 5.14 compares the Swedish road death index to the no-law index. The Swedish law came into effect on January 1, 1975. In 1975 the Swedish index dropped 2 points compared to a drop of 3.5 points in the no-law index. Also in 1975 there was a campaign against drinking and driving which was reported to have had "some positive effect" (ASBC 1978, p.19). The ASBC belt usage estimates range from 8 to 33 per cent before the law, to 85 to 90 per cent after the law. Figure 5.15 presents wearing rate figures superimposed on graphs of fatalities and serious injuries to car occupants. The fatality and

5. Behavioural solutions: seat belts

Figure 5.13   Figure 5.14

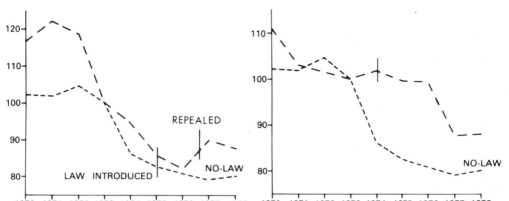

Indices of road accident deaths for Switzerland (Figure 5.13) and Sweden (Figure 5.14) compared with index for no-law countries.

injury graphs appear remarkably unperturbed by the sharp increase in wearing rates.

A Swedish study (Bohlin 1967) of 28,000 car crashes is still widely regarded as one of the best guides to the benefits of seat belts in crashes. In a 1976 paper Bohlin (with Aasberg) describes the apparent failure of the law in Sweden as a "paradox". In a conference paper a year later the paradox remained unresolved.

"Since January 1, 1975 we have in Sweden compulsory use of the safety belt in cars in front seats. Now after two years we are motivated to ask for the effect of that law. So far, however, no comprehensive report in this regard has been issued.

If we hope to find a simple direct answer in the number of annual car occupant fatalities, we may not at once be too enthusiastic over the result... Some people may say: rather poor results, which contradict those reported from other countries (Australia and France). Has the belt in Swedish cars failed to come up to the predicted positive value? Certainly not. I think that the explanation - when officially analyzed - will be partly related to the fact that the belt-use-law in Sweden had a worse 'starting point' compared to most other countries when proving its value, particularly in terms of occupant fatalities." (Bohlin 1977)

Ten years after the Swedish belt law came into effect an "official" explanation is still not available for the apparent

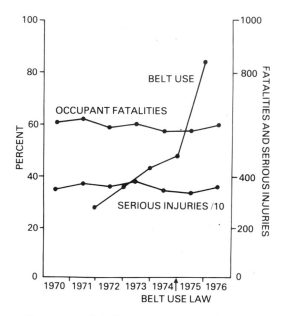

Figure 5.15 Motor vehicle occupant fatalities and serious injuries; seat belt wearing rates: Sweden. Source: IIHS, Figure 9, p.261.

non-effect illustrated by Figures 5.14 and 5.15. Tingvall (1982), in the **Journal of Traffic Medicine** has attempted an explanation in an article entitled "Is Adams Right? Some aspects on a theory concerning effects of seat-belt legislation." The argument is rather tortuous.
   "By a multi-factor discussion, we can come to the conclusion that the space for reducing especially the number of fatally injured car occupants is limited and that the outcome of the seat belt legislation well fits into what can be expected. As far as can be seen, there is no space for explanations such as the theory of John Adams [risk compensation], which implies that the B-group [those who belted up in response to legislation] has increased its injury risk (when the belt use effect is omitted) when starting to use belts." (sic. Square brackets are mine, round brackets are his.)

"The followings of John Adams' hypothesis are also examined, showing that there is no indication found that there is an increased accident or injury risk (when the belt use effect is omitted) due to seat belt use."

The argument is based on the mistaken assumption that the risk compensation hypothesis predicts an increase in the risk of injury following belt use. But perhaps most noteworthy is the conclusion that the behaviour of the graphs in Figures 5.14 and 5.15 is what one should have expected following a belt law in Sweden. "In the Swedish case 74/75 the space for reducing the injury figures, even if the marginal increase of seat belt use seems big, is limited."

Tingvall notes that the hypothesis predicts an increase in damage-only accidents following a large increase in seat belt wearing rates. He produces police accident data to show that this did not happen. This introduces a complication which Tingvall does not resolve. If there has been a large increase in belt wearing rates in Sweden - which there has - and if belts are effective in reducing death and injury in accidents - which they appear to be - and if one does not find a decrease in deaths and injuries following legislation - which Tingvall does not - then one should find an increase in damage only accidents - which he also did not find. The explanation may lie in the quality of Tingvall's accident data, which he acknowledges is suspect. Damage-only accident data collected by the police are notoriously unreliable. An unknown, and almost certainly large and variable, fraction of accidents are not reported. The number recorded

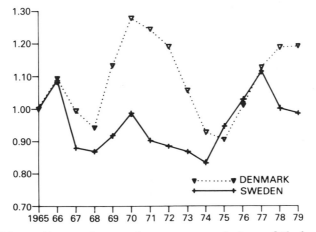

Figure 5.16 Indices of car insurance claims filed in Denamrk and Sweden. Sources: **Road Accident Statisics 1980**, Danmarks Statistik, Table 1.1; **Trafiksakerhetsverkets anslags framstallning for budgetaret 1981/1982**, Diagram 2.1.

often is simply a reflection of the police man-power available for this purpose at the time. Insurance data probably provide a better indication of change over time in total accident levels (see Figure 5.16).

From 1965 to 1975 the indices for car insurance claims filed in Sweden and Denmark moved up and down together. From 1970 to 1974 both countries experienced a downward trend. At the beginning of 1975 Sweden passed a law and Denmark did not, and for the first year in ten the two countries were out of phase. The graph for Sweden turned up sharply while the graph for Denmark continued to decline. One year later Denmark passed a law and its graph turned up sharply. This could be coincidence. Clearly other factors have caused the indices to move up and down in other years. It has been reported that a change in insurance policy, permitting smaller claims, was associated with the large rise in Denmark in 1970, and that this policy was gradually reversed in subsequent years (Lund 1982).

However, Sweden and Denmark experienced small **increases** in the numbers killed in the years in which the laws were introduced (Figures 5.6 and 5.15). If one accepts that seat belts afford protection in crashes, and there is no decrease in the numbers of deaths, then it is plausible that the numbers of crashes should have increased.

Israel. Figure 5.17 compares the Israeli road death index to the no-law index. The Israeli law, for inter-urban travel only, came into effect on July 1, 1975. In 1975 Israel experienced a drop in its index of 10 points. But Israel has the distinction of being one of only two countries among those surveyed in the study to have experienced an increase in road deaths in 1974 (the other was Sweden). In 1974 its index increased by 5 points while that of the no-law countries decreased by 14 points. Throughout the whole of the period after 1973 the Israeli index was above the no-law index. The Israeli Ministry of Transportation reports that after the law came into effect there was "an actual, as well as proportional decrease in the number of driver and passenger fatalities in the face of a relatively stable, even increasing (in 1977), accident and injury incidence" (ASBC 1980, p.10). Belt usage was estimated to have increased from 8 per cent before the law to 80 per cent after the law.

Hakkert et al (1981) claim "On the basis of the trend of fatalities and casualties to car drivers and passengers on urban roads during a 2.5 year period after the introduction of the seat belt law it is estimated that a reduction of 42% in car driver fatalities and 44% in car passenger fatalities occurred on interurban roads during the the 2.5 years after the law."

The claim is suspect. It rests upon very small numbers, and despite the reference to the "trend of fatalities" the study did not examine trends at all. The estimate was derived by comparing the number of fatalities on interurban roads in the year and half before the law with those occuring in a two and a half year period after the

law. This difference was compared to the difference in the numbers of
fatalities on urban roads in the same two periods. In other words
the urban areas, where the law did not apply, were used as a "control
group". However, the numbers in both groups were so small as to
make talk of "percentage" changes misleading. In the one and a
half years before the law there were only 19 fatalities on roads in
the urban control group, and 90 on interurban roads. In the first
year and a half after the law the number in the control group
increased by 8, while the number on interurban roads decreased by 7.
The study made no attempt to place these numbers in the context of
long term trends in order to assist judgements about their statistical
significance.

Figure 5.17   Figure 5.18

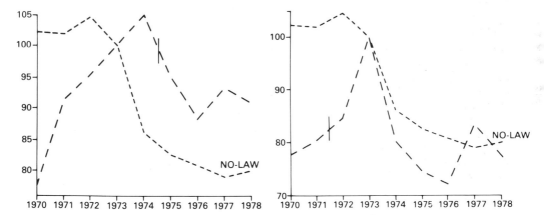

Indices of road accident deaths for Israel (Figure 5.17) and New
Zealand (Figure 5.18) compared with index for no-law countries.

New Zealand. Figure 5.18 compares the New Zealand road death index
to the no-law index. The New Zealand law came into effect on June 1,
1972. In 1972 the New Zealand index rose 4 points while that of the
no-law countries rose by 2.5. In 1973, the first full year of the
law's operation, the New Zealand index jumped 15.5 points, to an
all-time high, while that of the no-law countries dropped by 4.5
points. Belt usage estimates ranged from 33 to 55 per cent before the
law, to 85 per cent after the law. In New Zealand, as in Israel, a
decrease was observed in the ratio of car-occupant fatalities to
non-occupant fatalties. As in Israel, this shift has been construed as
evidence to support the view that the seat belt law has had a
beneficial effect: "this slight increase [in occupant fatalities] was

accompanied by a considerably sharper rise in fatalities of other road
users, suggesting certain savings from increased belt use subsequent
to passage of the law" (Hurst 1979, p.27).

Australia.

In Britain the evidence that was most frequently cited by the
advocates of legislation prior to the passage of the British belt law
was a Transport and Road Research Laboratory Report published in 1979
entitled "The Protection Afforded by Seat Belts" (Grime). The report
reviewed sixteen studies of the effects of seat belts, but stated
"for direct evidence on deaths, however, it is necessary to rely on
recent Australian data."

The State of Victoria implemented a seat belt law on December 22,
1970. This was the first seat belt law to be implemented in a
country with reliable road accident statistics; the Ivory Coast is
reported to have passed a law earlier but no analyses are available of
the result. The other states followed in 1971, and by January 1, 1972
they had all implemented laws. The Australian experience has been
extremely influential. Although there existed a considerable volume
of evidence concerning the effect of seat belts in crashes, for
countries contemplating seat belt legislation in the mid-1970s,
Australia provided the only source of evidence concerning the efficacy
of legislation.

Figure 5.19 compares the Australian road death index to the no-law
index. Between 1970 and 1972 the Australian index dropped 10 points
while that of the no-law countries increased by 2 points. But in 1973
the Australian index increased by 7 points while that of the no-law

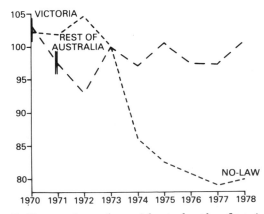

Figure 5.19 Indices of road accident deaths for Australia and
no-law countries.

countries dropped 4.5. Between 1973 and 1978 the Australian index increased very slightly while the index for the no-law countries dropped 20 points. Of the seventeen countries covered by the survey only Australia and Spain had more deaths in 1978 than 1973.

Belt usage estimates range widely. When the first law was passed not all cars were required to be fitted with belts, and the requirement to wear a belt applied only to those cars which were fitted with belts. The American Seat Belt Council (1980) cites wearing rates before the law ranging from 19 to 37 per cent before the law, and wearing rates after the law from 69 to 94 per cent. However, Vulcan (1977) cites rates for Victoria which suggest that wearing rates after the law increased from an average of only 40 per cent in the first year after the law to an average of 81 per cent in 1976.

There have been a number of studies of the effect of seat belt legislation in Australia. The four most commonly cited by the advocates of legislation are considered briefly here.

1. The Foldvary and Lane Study. One of the earliest studies of the effect of seat belt legislation, and still one of the most commonly cited, is that by Foldvary and Lane (1974) of the effect of Victoria's belt law. Despite the fact that the study is so often cited by the advocates of legislation it provides very little support for their cause. Foldvary and Lane found a statistically significant reduction in fatalities in urban areas, but not in the rural areas of Victoria which accounted for 58 per cent of all fatalities. They say "the reasons for the absence of a significant reduction in the non-metropolitan area of Victoria are not obvious."

They note that during the "after" period of their study "a road safety campaign was mounted by a widely circulated Victorian daily newspaper and was continued almost daily..." They rule out the possibility that this could have had a depressing effect on occupant fatalities because they found no significant reduction in non-occupant fatalities. They assert "while the belt wearing law could affect only vehicle occupants, the newspaper campaign and any other general factor should affect all road users in some degree." Thus they treat non-occupant fatalities as an independent control against which occupant fatalities can be compared. They assume that which needs proving: that the sense of security provided by belts has no effect on driving behaviour which could affect other road users.

Foldvary and Lane also make a very crude attempt to control for the effect of the national economy. They say "periods of buoyant economy appear to increase the number of road accidents while periods of recession have the opposite effect." Their method of controlling for this effect is to compare graphs over a period of years of road fatalities and the number of houses and flats starting construction. They provide no measure of the strength of the correlation between these variables, and a visual inspection of their graphs suggests that the year by year changes in the two variables are not highly correlated. They conclude from examining the peaks and troughs of the two graphs that a down turn in fatalities in Victoria should not have occurred until 1972 and, therefore, that the economic recession in 1971 did not contribute to the down turn in fatalities in that year. They describe fairly well what would be necessary for their housing-starts variable to make a convincing control variable.

"A more detailed study would be needed to define more exactly the lead-lag relationships between the curves, and to express the strength of the regularity of these relationships by correlation coefficients. For such an analysis monthly data – not available at present – would be required."

Another serious deficiency for a study which purports to be a study of the efficacy of seat belt legislation, is that it considers no measures of the presumed increase in wearing rates that followed legislation. Neither does it contain information about wearing rates in other Australian states. whose fatalities are compared with those of Victoria. Thus differences in fatality rates between states, and between the before and after periods, are attributed to presumed differences in wearing rates of an unspecified magnitude. As noted above Vulcan cites evidence that wearing rates in Victoria in 1971 were only around 40 per cent. Other studies discussed below argue that such a wearing rate is not high enough to achieve a measurable reduction in death rates.

Like the study of Hakkert et al in Israel it was a before-and after study using a "control". Also like the Hakkert study, no account was taken of established trends or variability in the time-series data. The before and after periods were shorter than Hakkert's, only nine months, this being the period during which Victoria was the only Australian state with a belt law. It referred to no before or after seat belt wearing rates for either Victoria or the control (rest of Australia). It did not control for differences in exposure, i.e. possible differences in growth rates of vehicle ownership or petrol consumption.

2. The Crinion, Foldvary and Lane Study (1975).

This is also a before-and after study using what is essentially the same method as that employed in the previous Foldvary and Lane study. It differs from the earlier study in that it makes some attempt to "control" for the effect of changes in exposure to accidents between the before and after periods. But the variable used to control for accident exposure is not volume of traffic or petrol consumption, but the number of cars involved in accidents. The study finds a significant reduction in the ratio of car occupant fatalities to damaged cars.

Three observations might be made about the significance of this finding. Firstly, the numbers involved are very small - the decrease in fatalities is from 87 to 65. Secondly, damage only accident data is notoriously unreliable. And thirdly, the decrease in the ratio of fatalities to accidents is consistent with the expectations of the risk compensation hypothesis.

3. **The Vaughan Study** (1977). Vaughan fitted a straight line to the trend of occupant fatalities in New South Wales for the period 1961 to 1971 and projected it to 1975. The method used was similar to that illustrated by Figure 5.21 below for the whole of Australia. He compared the actual fatality statistics with the number "expected" according to his projection. This is what he found.

"The four year period following the introduction of the law saw a reduction in the numbers of vehicle occupant fatalities in both rural and urban areas. The reductions were statistically significant in urban areas in two of the four years, and in rural areas, in one of the years only."

In other words, in five out of eight cases there was no statistically significant reduction in fatalities following the law. Thus the Vaughan study does not appear to be an impressive demonstration of the efficacy of seat belt legislation, especially when viewed in the context of trends in other countries during the same period. The rising trend in fatalities experienced by New South Wales during the 1960s was experienced by almost all highly motorized countries, and departures below this trend in the 1970s were much greater in the countries that did not pass belt laws than the departure found by Vaughan in New South Wales.

4. **The Vulcan Study**. Vulcan's study (1977) of Victoria is similar to Vaughan's in that it involves fitting a straight line to the trend of the 1960s and projecting it into the 1970s, although unlike Vaughan he does not attempt to assess the statistical significance of departures from the trend.

Vulcan'study contains a list of other factors which he suggests might have had a depressing effect on the fatality statistics. It includes: the introduction of a new 70mph speed limit in 1972, the reduction of this limit to 60mph a year later, and various measures aimed at drinking drivers. In addition he notes, "there has been a progressive implementation of improved traffic management and sustained road safety publicity, with considerable media and community involvement." A further factor not mentioned by Vulcan, nor by Vaughan, nor by Crinion et al is the effect of the economic recession which Foldvary and Lane in their 1974 study suggested should have had a depressing effect on fatalities beginning in 1972.

The Australian "Trend". Figure 5.20 illustrates the nature of the evidence upon which most of the seat belt laws in the world have been justified. It shows a rising trend in road accident fatalities in Australia which levelled-off around the time that belt laws were passed. The gap between the projected trend and the actual level of fatalities was the basis of most expectations about what would be achieved by legislation in other countries.

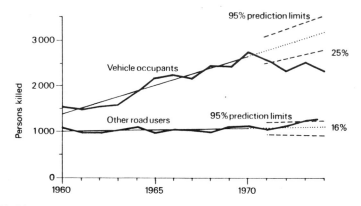

Figure 5.20 Road accident deaths in Australia. Source: Australian House of Representatives, Standing Committee, 1976.

This expectation depends on the assumption that the trend of the 1960s was linear and the graph of the number of road deaths would have continued to follow a strictly linear path indefinitely, but for the effect of seat belt legislation. I am aware of no country in the world whose road fatality statistics have behaved in such a manner as to make this assumption credible. What is most noteworthy about the Australian graph (Figure 5.20) is not the distance by which the actual number of road deaths fell below the projected trend of the 1960s, but the distance by which the Australian index exceeded the index of the no-law countries in the 1970s. Of the countries covered by Figures 5.6 to 5.20, only Spain had a worse record of achievement during the 1970s, and Spain also passed a belt law.

The No-Law Countries

Figures 5.21-5.24 compare the road death indices of Great Britain, Italy, the United States and Japan to the average indices of the law countries. In every case the "energy-crisis drop" (1972-1975) in the indices of the no-law countries is greater than that of the average index for the law countries. During this period eight of the thirteen countries in the law group implemented their laws. In Italy and Japan the decrease continued until 1978. In Britain and the United States the indices began to rise again after 1975. During this period belt

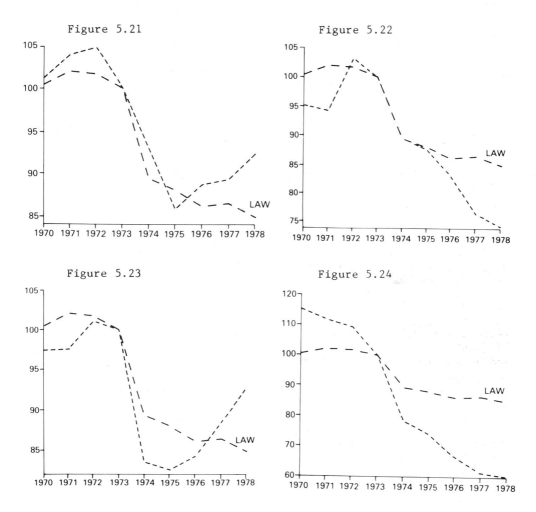

Indices of road accident deaths for Britain (Figure 5.21), Italy (Figure 5.22), United States (Figure 5.23) and Japan (Figure 5.24) compared with the index for the no-law countries.

5. Behavioural solutions: seat belts

usage in Britain was estimated to range from 20 per cent in urban areas to over 40 per cent on motorways (Grime 1979, Fig.4) In Japan usage estimates range from a high of 14.5 per cent for drivers on motorways down to 5.8 per cent for passengers on other roads (Japanese Government 1980, Table Table 23). Estimates are not available for Italy and the United States for this period, but Hedlund (1984) reports United States wearing rates in the early 1980s between 11 and 14 per cent.

The most dramatic decrease in the road death toll in the 17 countries surveyed in the study was in Japan, 55 points between 1970 and 1978. Japan was also the country which experienced the most rapid rate of growth in car ownership over this period. With the possible exception of Italy and the United States, for which figures are not available, Japan had the lowest seat belt wearing rate of the countries surveyed.

Other Countries

Since the results of the study discussed above (Adams 1981b, 1982) more evidence about the efficacy of seat belt legislation has become available from Ireland, Canada and Britain.

Ireland. The wearing of seat belts by front seat occupants of cars and light vans was made compulsory in Ireland from February 1 1979. In May of the same year the 60 mph speed limit on rural roads was reduced to 55 mph. Figure 5.25 shows that in 1979 there was a small increase in the numbers of car occupants and pedestrians killed.

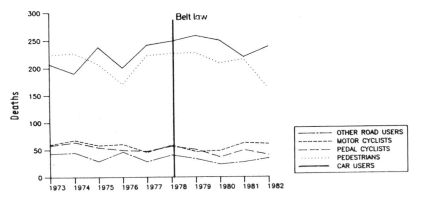

Figure 5.25 Road accident deaths in Ireland. Seat belt legislation was effective from February 1, 1979. Source: **Road Accident Facts 1982: Ireland.**

In a study of the impact of the Irish seat belt legislation Hearne (1981) found no significant decrease in deaths or serious injuries attributable to the legislation. But he was anxious that his findings should not be construed as evidence that seat belts are not effective injury reducing devices.

"In attempting to interpret these results, it is important to be clear that they cannot be taken to mean that the safety-belt, when properly worn, is not an effective device for reducing the severity of injury."

He concluded that while seat belt use doubled in Ireland, from 25 per cent before the law to 50 per cent after, much higher wearing rates still would be required before substantial effects would become manifest. He suggested that it was probably the most safety conscious motorists who belted up while the most reckless continued unbelted.

Canada. In Canada different provinces implemented belt laws at different times. This permits a comparison of the road safety records of the "law" and "no-law" provinces. Figure 5.26, illustrating road accident death rates for all road users, suggests that over the relevant period, when some provinces were passing laws while others were not, the road safety record of the no-law provinces showed a greater improvement than that of the law provinces.

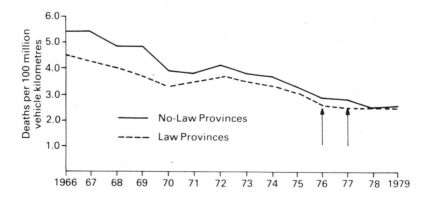

Figure 5.26 Road accident death rates in Canada. Seat belt laws came into effect in Ontario and Quebec in 1976, and in British Columbia and Saskatchewan in 1977. Source: Wilde and Kunkel 1984.

5. Behavioural solutions: seat belts

In a paper entitled "The Effectiveness of the Canadian Mandatory Seat Belt Use Laws" for the Road Safety Directorate of Transport Canada, Jonah and Lawson (1983) fitted linear trend lines to the road accident data of the provinces that had passed laws and to the "control group" that had not in order to calculate the "expected" number of fatalities in each province in the period after legislation.

Both the law and no-law provinces fell below the established linear trends after 1976. Table 5.1 (derived from Jonah and Lawson's Table 2) shows in more detail how the law and no-law provinces fared with respect to occupant fatalities after the laws were passed.

Table 5.1 Ratio of actual to predicted occupant fatality rates for post law years by province

	1977	1978	1979	1980	1981
Ontario	.68	.71	.77	.75	.74
Quebec	.75	.94	.92	.81	.81
Saskatchewan	.84	.87	.75	.69	.64
British Columbia	.84	.68	.69	.70	.71
Average all law	.78	.79	.78	.74	.73
Unlegislated provinces	.74	.71	.80	.76	.69

Dates at which seat belt laws came into effect: Ontario – January 1976, Quebec – August 1976, Saskatchewan – July 1977, British Columbia – October 1977. Predicted occupant fatality rates were based on linear regressions applied to data for a period running from 1960 to the date of legislation.

In their conclusion Jonah and Lawson speculate that "the impact of the seat belt use laws fell short of expectations because it was mainly the safe drivers who buckled up in response to the law." Jonah, Lawson and Hearne clearly find the results of legislation in their respective countries disappointing. But it is important to note how far short of expectations these results fell. In Ireland deaths to motorists and pedestrians increased and in Canada the provinces which passed legislation fared worse than the provinces that did not. A corollary to their suggestion that a perceptible beneficial effect should only be expected following considerably larger increases in wearing rates would seem to be that it is not necessary for the prudent majority to wear belts because they are protected by their careful driving.

Britain.   In Britain the use of seat belts by the front seat occupants of cars and light vans became compulsory on the 31st of January 1983.   The result is discussed in Chapter 7 as part of a review of the record of major British efforts at road safety regulation since World War II.

6 Behavioural Solutions: motorcycle helmets

Legislation compelling motorcyclists to wear helmets rivals seat belt legislation in the magnitude of the claims made on its behalf. Although the absolute number of lives saved attributed to motorcycle helmets is not as great as that attributed to seat belts this is primarily because in most parts of the world there are fewer motorcyclists than car occupants. The proportional reduction in fatalities usually attributed to helmet legislation is even greater than that attributed to seat belt legislation.

The problem of evidence is similar to that encountered in the last chapter. There is abundant evidence to the effect that if one falls on one's head the chances of escaping death or injury are greatly increased if one is wearing a helmet. On the basis of such evidence many countries have passed laws compelling the wearing of helmets for motorcycling. There is also, as in the case of seat belts, a dearth of evidence that the legislation has met the claims made for it. In this chapter five recent pieces of evidence will be considered: three from the United States, one from Nigeria, and one from Malaysia.

The United States

An "experiment" was conducted in the United States in the 1970s which is widely believed to have proved conclusively that helmet legislation is a highly effective public health measure. It appeared to be an ideal "controlled" experiment; over a period of a few years a set of geographically diverse states, containing about 47 per cent of the country's motorcycles, repealed laws compelling motorcyclists to wear helmets. It was widely predicted that these repeals would cause a substantial increase in the numbers of motorcyclists killed. How have the predictions fared?

Readers of the **American Journal of Public Health** and the **British Medical Journal** who have not had a chance to examine the data for themselves are probably of the opinion that they have fared extremely well. The **British Medical Journal** in an editorial entitled "A Grim Experiment" told its readers on August 9, 1980
"The immediate effect was a drop in the proportion of motorcyclists using helmets from 100% to 50%. Deaths from

motorcycle accidents rose by an average of 38% in the states which had repealed their laws, while remaining constant in the other states. ... Deaths and injuries on the road are one of the few subjects where preventive medicine can be based on reliable statistics on the effects of intervention. ... The refusal by successive governments to take action on these data is a continuing disgrace."

The immediate cause of the **British Medical Journal's** indignation was an article in the **American Journal** of **Public Health** of June 1980 by G.S. Watson, P.L. Zador and A. Wilks entitled "The Repeal of Helmet Use Laws and Increased Motorcyclist Mortality Rates in the United States, 1975-1978". An editorial in the same issue of the AJPH (Baker 1980) described the evidence of Watson et al as "new and impressive" and called the widespread repeal of helmet laws "tragic". The editorial noted that the conclusions of Watson et al were consistent with those of a previous study by the National Highway Traffic Safety Administration (NHTSA 1979) on the same subject.
The studies by the NHTSA and Watson et al bear the stamp of authority and the editorial seal of approval of prestigious journals. Together they appear to have settled the debate about the efficacy of helmet legislation once and for all. This appearance is deceptive. Both studies commit elementary statistical mistakes that completely invalidate their results.

The NHTSA's Mistake

The NHTSA's mistake will be considered first because it is simplest and easiest to explain. Figure 6.1 is a reproduction of the front cover of the NHTSA's report to Congress (1980). The graph was taken from the body of the report and put on the front cover because, presumably, it was considered such compelling evidence in support of legislation. The **Report** concludes (p. VIII-4) that the decline in helmet use associated with helmet law repeal is "the single most significant factor" responsible for the dramatic increase in the motorcyclist death rate after 1975. And Watson et al considered the figure such compelling evidence for the efficacy of legislation that they reproduced it in a second article on the subject a year later in the AJPH entitled "Helmet Use, Helmet Use Laws, and Motorcyclist Fatalities" (Watson, Zador, Wilks, 1981).
The elementary mistake of the NHTSA was to base its conclusion on data that were too highly aggregated to support any defensible inferences about the effect of helmet legislation. Figure 6.2 shows that when dissaggregated the data do not support the NHTSA's conclusion. Plotting the death rate for repeal and non-repeal states separately for the period after 1975 we can see that the blame for the increase in the death rate cannot be placed on helmet law repeal

A REPORT TO THE CONGRESS

ON

THE EFFECT OF MOTORCYCLE HELMET USE LAW REPEAL -- A CASE FOR HELMET USE.

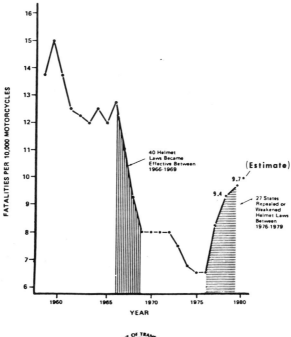

APRIL 1980

U.S. Department of Transportation
National Highway Traffic Safety Administration

Figure 6.1   Front cover of NHTSA Report to the Congress

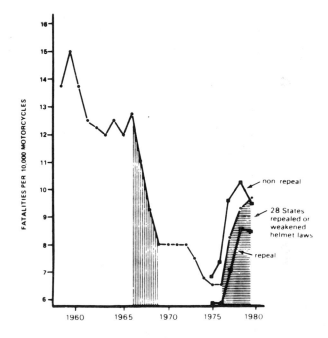

Figure 6.2   Disaggregated data for fatalities per 10,000 motorcycles registered 1975-1979.   Figure 6.1 gives the number of repeal states as 27.   Watson et al (1980) list Nebraska as a repeal state in 1977, but NHTSA does not. Actual fatalities in 1979 were substantially below the estimate recorded in Figure 6.1.   Sources: Motorcycle Fatalities by State and Month for 1975-1979, Submission 95 (9-2-80) FARS 9-5-80; and Comparison of State Total Motor Vehicle Registrations 1975-1979, supplied by National Center for Statistics and Analysis, US Department of Transportation, 400 Seventh Street SW, Washington DC.

because, for most of this period, the increase was greatest in the states that did not repeal their laws.   In 1976 9 states repealed their helmet laws, in 1977 a further 14, and in 1978 a further 4. Between 1975 and 1978 the death rate in repeal states increased by 46.7 per cent while in non-repeal states it increased by 48.2 per cent.   In 1979 the death rate decreased by 2.6 per cent in the 28 repeal states and by 7.8 per cent in the non-repeal states. Throughout this period the death rate in the repeal states was on average 19 per cent lower than that of the non-repeal states.

The Mistakes of Watson, Zador and Wilks

Watson et al conclude their 1980 paper on the same note of indignation as that found in the editorials quoted above.
"The repeals of motorcycle helmet laws have been one of the most tragic decisions made recently in the USA from the standpoint of public health. ... The retention of existing laws and the reinstatement of repealed laws should be an urgent issue for public health workers and everyone else concerned with lowering unnecessary mortality and morbidity, and the huge medical and other economic losses that result."

The statistical analysis upon which their indignation rests is more sophisticated than that illustrated by Figures 6.1 and 6.2. This is how they describe their method.
"The states that repealed or weakened their helmet laws were matched with one or more states from the same geographic region that either did not have helmet use laws or did not change such existing laws in this four-year period. The effect of weakening the law in each state was then estimated in three steps: 1) the mortality data from each state prior to repeal were regressed on smoothed data from the matched states; 2) these equations were used to predict the numbers of motorcyclist deaths that would have been expected in each state in the period following repeal or weakening of the law if the laws had not been changed; 3) these numbers of expected deaths were then compared with the actual numbers of deaths that occurred." (Watson et al, p.579)
They concluded that
"It is estimated that the repeals or weakening of motorcyclist helmet use laws were typically followed by almost 40 per cent increases in the numbers of fatally injured motorcyclists." (Watson et al, P.579)

Table 6.1 summarises their results. At first sight their evidence, like the NHTSA's, appears to be compelling support for legislation - so compelling that it was reproduced in the NHTSA's own report. Also like the NHTSA's evidence it is completely misleading. The method adopted by Watson et al involves prediction based on regression equations, and is crucially dependent for its plausibility on the "matching" states being a good match. To quote one prominent authority, "unless the correlation is reasonably high (say .7 or above), it may be rather misleading to make use of prediction equations", and "correlations of a very high order are necessary for even moderately accurate prediction." (Blalock, 1960, pages 285, 299) A worrying symptom in a report which is dependent on the use of

6. Behavioural solutions: motorcycle helmets

Table 6.1 Estimates of the Effect of Helmet Legislation

	Actual deaths post repeal	Expected deaths if no repeal	Per cent increase Watson et al	Per cent increase Chenier, Evans
Utah	43	22	95.5	35.7
Montana	28	15	86.7	20.4
Colorado	113	62	82.3	46.9
Ohio	139	83	67.5	12.4
Indiana	157	95	65.3	-9.3
New Hampshire	39	24	62.5	20.7
Idaho	24	15	60.0	11.6
South Dakota	24	15	60.0	9.1
Iowa	53	34	55.9	*
New Mexico	43	28	53.6	70.4
Minnesota	195	127	53.5	19.8
Kansas	128	84	52.4	17.9
Arizona	194	129	50.4	16.5
Wisconson	106	76	39.5	29.1
Texas	419	310	35.2	39.3
Rhode Island	47	35	32.3	22.7
Louisiana	189	143	32.2	52.0
Iowa **	156	123	26.8	*
North Dakota	17	14	21.4	53.6
Connecticut	168	140	20.0	59.3
Washington	130	113	15.0	52.6
Oregon	77	71	8.5	17.8
Oklahoma	22	24	8.3	*
Nebraska	34	36	5.6	*
Oklahoma **	22	24	-8.3	*
Maine	9	23	-60.9	15.6

* omitted from Chenier-Evans study.

** there were two law changes in Iowa and Oklahoma.

prediction equations is that none of the correlations between repeal
and control states is given. This omission is of particular
significance for this study because, as explained below, the weaker
the correlation between repeal and control states, the greater will be
the bias of the method in favour of the authors' conclusions about the
efficacy of helmet legislation.

Figures 6.3a and 6.3b are graphs of the raw data to which Watson
et al applied the method that led to their conclusion that Utah had
95.5 per cent more fatalities after the repeal of its helmet law than
expected on the basis of its relationship with the control states,
Nevada and Wyoming. Utah is used in the following critique of the
method because, according to Watson et al it is the state which

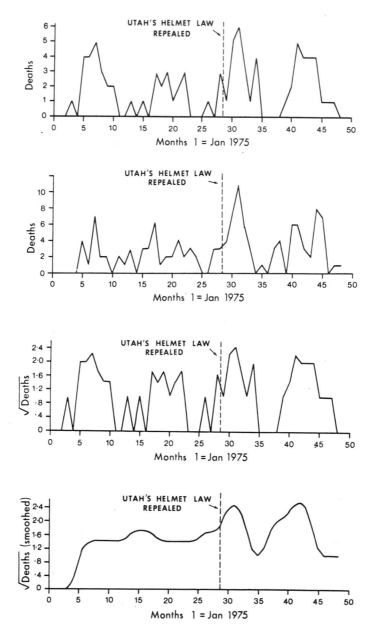

Figure 6.3 Motorcycle fatalities per month (a) in Utah, (b) in control states – Nevada and Wyoming, (c) in Utah – transformed data, and (d) in control states – transformed data. Source: Motorcycle Fatalities by State and Month (see Figure 2).

experienced the largest post-repeal increase in fatalities. It is, in other words, the case that contributes most to their estimate that helmet law repeal has increased fatalites by an average of 40 per cent.

Figures 6.3c and 6.3d display the results of the data transformations that Watson et al employed before proceeding to the regression stage of their analysis. First they took the square roots of the data for both Utah and the control states. Then, in addition, they subjected the control state data – but not the Utah data – to a procedure known as a "3RSSH twice smooth". This has the effect of removing the peaks and troughs from the time-series data. It seems a curious thing to do to the data. The point of smoothing, according to Tukey (1977, p.205), the author of the method, is to give a "clearer view of the general once it is unencumbered by detail." But a comparison of Figures 6.3b and 6.3d suggests that the smoothing operation performed by Watson et al gets rid of the general along with the detail. For the period before repeal, no trace of the seasonal fluctuations apparent in the raw data displayed in Figure 6.3b remains in Figure 6.3d. The main justification of the matching method is that the repeal and control states share a common pattern of seasonal fluctuation: "Since motorcyclist fatalities display strong seasonal variation, the similarity of such variation was an important part of the matching criteria." (Watson et al 1980, p.581) There was a weak correlation between the raw data for Utah and the control states in the period before repeal (r-squared, adjusted for degrees of freedom, 25.5 per cent). But the data transformations employed by Watson et al reduce this correlation almost to zero (r-squared, adjusted, 1 per cent).

Figure 6.4 illustrates the relationship between the transformed data for Utah and that for its control states for the period before repeal. The most important thing to note about this correlation is that it means that any prediction based upon the "matching" of Utah with its control states will not only be very unreliable, but also strongly biased. This is because the weaker the correlation between the variables, the flatter will be the regression line which describes their relationship. If, as is the case here, there is a pronounced increase in the average values of both variables in the period after repeal – the period for which the prediction is being made – most of the residuals from regression for the prediction period will lie above the flattened regression line; that is, the regression line will produce an underestimate of the number of deaths in the repeal state.

Figure 6.5 illustrates the nature of the bias injected by a weak correlation when a regression model is used for purposes of prediction in the way in which Watson et al have used it. It shows, for period 1, variable Y plotted on variable X. The slope of the line on the graph will be determined by the standard deviations of the two variables, the graphing scale, and the strength of the correlation. If the correlation is zero, as in this illustration, the regression

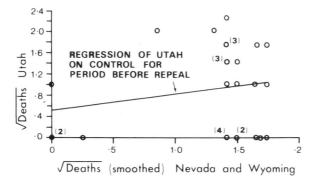

Figure 6.4 Regression of transformed data for Utah on control states for the period prior to repeal. Numbers in brackets indicate multiple observations. Source: see Figure 6.2.

line will be flat, regardless of standard deviations and graphing scales.

In Figure 6.5 it is assumed that both X and Y have means of one in period 1, and means of three and two respectively in period 2. It can be seen that if the regression line fitted to the data for period 1 were used to calculate the "expected" values of Y in period 2 (using actual values of X in period 2), all the residuals would be positive, even though the increase in X was, on average, twice the increase in Y. Thus the method will be very powerfully biased in cases where there is a weak correlation and a significant increase in the average

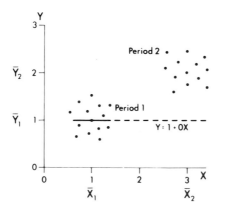

Figure 6.5 The effect of a weak correlation.

value of both variables between the period for which the regression line is calculated and the subsequent period for which "expected" values are estimated. If the values of both variables were to decrease the bias would be in the opposite direction.

Figure 6.6 illustrates this biasing effect with the example of Utah. It should be noted that most of the post-repeal observations lie beyond the range of the data to which the regression line was fitted. The line in Figure 6.6 illustrating the regression of the control state data on Utah shows that the method, allied to a weak correlation, can be made to prove anything. If the "expected" fatalities for the control states after repeal are predicted from this regression line, the location of the residuals for the post-repeal period indicates that Nevada and Wyoming had many more fatalities than expected.

In Figure 6.7 the monthly fatalities in the control states have been subtracted from the monthly fatalities in Utah - the two time series have been reduced to one which represents the difference between them. If helmet law repeal had had the effect of increasing the number of fatalities in Utah by 95.5 per cent relative to the control states, this effect would be noticable as a sudden large upward jump of the graph after month 28, the time of repeal. In fact, after month 28 the average level of the graph decreases, from -.54 to -1.5.

Registration data are not available on a monthly basis. Figure 6.8 compares annual fatalities per 10,000 registered motorcycles in Utah, Montana and Colorado with those in Nevada and Wyoming. Nevada and Wyoming were also used by Watson et al as control states for Montana and Colorado. Montana and Colorado are the repeal states

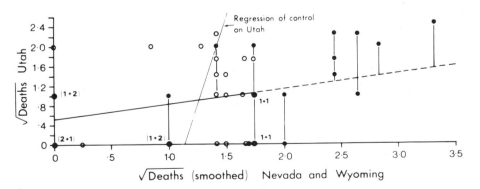

Figure 6.6   Regression of Utah on control states for period 1975-1978. Numbers in brackets indicate multiple observations; where there are two numbers, the second number indicates post repeal observations.

which, according to their analysis, experienced the second and third largest increases in fatalities following repeal (see Table 6.1). Thus Figure 6.8 shows that the three states that are purported to support the conclusions of Watson et al most strongly, all have substantially lower death rates than the control states, and did not experience significant increases in their death rates relative to the control states at the time of repeal.

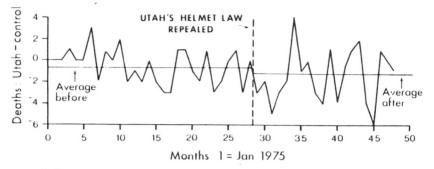

Figure 6.7   Motorcycle fatalities per month, Utah minus control, 1975-1978.

The large percentage increases attributed to helmet law repeal by Watson et al would appear to be artefacts of an inappropriate statistical method. The data transformation process employed altered the strength of the correlations between repeal states and their controls in a way which appears random; in 15 of the 26 cases listed in Table 6.1 it strengthened the correlation and in 11 it weakened it. While it sharply reduced the r-squared value in the case of Utah, in the case of Oklahoma it transformed a negative correlation with an r-squared of 16.6 to a positive correlation with an r-squared of 68.1 (Thrumble 1983). But whether the transformation process increased or decreased the strength of the correlation, it throws the results into doubt. Where it weakens the correlation, as in the case of Utah, it increases the bias of the method. Where it strengthens the correlation, as in the case of Oklahoma it suggests that the result is an arbitrary product of the method and not a "real" effect.

The Chenier - Evans Study

A third survey of the effect of helmet legislation in the United States attributes smaller, though still substantial fatality increases to helmet law repeal. The study by Chenier and Evans (1984) estimated that states which repealed their helmet laws experienced a 28 per cent increase in fatalities. This study, while much more plausible

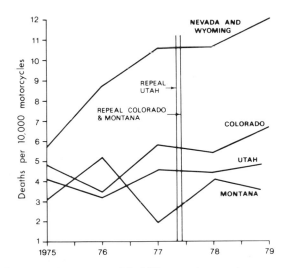

Figure 6.8   Deaths per 10,000 registered motorcycles in Utah, Colorado, Montana and the control states. Source: see Figure 2.

statistically than the work of NHTSA and Watson et al, must also be considered inconclusive.

Table 6.1 presents their estimates of post-repeal fatality increases alongside those from the study of Watson et al. Although both studies attribute increases in fatalities to the repeal of helmet laws, they cannot be said to provide support for each other because their estimates of post-repeal fatality increases are weakly and negatively correlated.

The method used by Chenier and Evans might be described as a before-and-after comparison with national controls. For each state which repealed (or weakened) a mandatory helmet wearing law the ratio of post-repeal fatalities to pre-repeal fatalities was calculated and compared to the same ratio for all states which did not change their helmet wearing laws. It employed a longer time series than Watson et al - 1975-1982 compared to 1975-1978. Like the Watson study it was based on simple numbers of deaths and did not attempt to control for variations in exposure. Unlike the Watson study it made no attempt to ensure a match between repeal states and the control - it simply used all non-repeal states as a control.

When the claims made by Chenier and Evans for the effect of repeal are viewed alongside the original data they appear no more convincing than those of the Watson study. The magnitude of the seasonal variation in motorcycle fatalities, and its monthly pattern, differs from state to state, mainly with differences in temperature and rainfall. Thus the method will be biased depending on the time of year in which laws were repealed and whether the seasonal variation in the repeal state is greater or lesser than the average variation in the national control. Although the attempt of Watson et al to match repeal and control states was not very successful, it did at least attempt to deal with a serious source of bias.

It can be seen from Table 6.1 that the Chenier and Evans method attributes a 35.7 per cent increase in fatalities to the repeal in Utah. Viewed alongside Figures 6.3a, 6.3b, 6.7 and 6.8 this appears rather implausible. The increase estimated by Chenier and Evans appears to be mainly attributable to an abnormally large number of deaths in Utah in 1980 and 1981. This is an implausibly delayed reaction to a law which came into effect in May 1977.

The increase in fatalities which Chenier and Evans attribute to repeals in Colorado and Montana, while smaller than those claimed by Watson et al, are still substantial. They also appear implausible in the light of Figure 6.8.

Another reason why it is important to view the results of the Chenier method in the context of the original data is that the method is capable of mistaking a trend for a before-and-after difference. This is a well-known problem with before-and-after comparisons (see, for example, the discussion of the Australian evidence in Chapter 5). The problem is illustrated by Figure 6.9. It can be seen that in Texas, in the period before repeal, the number of fatalities was increasing relative to the Watson controls. The dotted line projects this trend into the post-repeal period. The upper dashed line represents the post-repeal trend; and the lower dashed line represents the same trend after reducing the monthly fatalities in Texas by 39.3 per cent - the amount by which Chenier and Evans estimate that deaths increased after the helmet-law was repealed in Texas. Again the effect of repeal claimed by Chenier and Evans appears implausible. While the examples of Utah, Colorado and Montana might be dismissed because of their small numbers of fatalities, Texas is more difficult to dismiss; it accounts for 17 per cent of all repeal state fatalities.

Control for Exposure

Figure 6.1 suggests that the period from 1958 to 1975 was one in which considerable progress was being made in reducing motorcyclist fatalites. In fact, during this period fatalities increased by more than four fold, from 720 to 3189. In the same period the number of registered motorcycles increased from 521,290 to 4,964,070 - an almost ten-fold increase. The reader is invited to conclude from Figure 6.1 that the passage of motorcycle helmet laws was a significant cause of the decrease in deaths per motorcycle during this

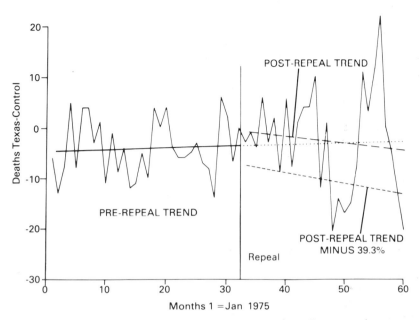

Figure 6.9 Motorcycle fatalities per month, Texas minus control (Arkansas, Georgia, Florida). Solid line represents pre-repeal trend; dotted line represents pre-repeal trend projected into post-repeal period; top dashed line represents post-repeal trend; bottom dashed line represents post-repeal trend implied by the estimate of Chenier and Evans. Source of data: see Figure 2.

period. But the Smeed Law suggests that other forces might have been at work.

As Chapter 2 illustrates the early stages of the motorisation process have been characterised almost everywhere in the world by large increases in numbers killed, and even larger decreases in numbers killed per vehicle. Despite the rapid growth of motorcycle ownership in the United States, by 1975 the number of motorcycles per head was still well under .03, well within the range over which countries in the early stages of motorisation experience the greatest decreases in fatalities per vehicle.

The most serious omission from the studies of Watson et al and Chenier and Evans is an adequate control for exposure. Chenier and Evans show that the number of fatalities increased by more in the repeal states than in the non-repeal states. But Figure 6.2 shows that when an exposure control in the form of numbers of registered motorcycles is introduced this difference disappears; Figure 6.2 also indicates that repeal states have consistently had much lower death rates per vehicle.

Apparently the registration data are of uncertain accuracy. In their 1980 paper Watson et al give this as their reason for using a method of analysis that takes no account of exposure at all: "Because credible registration data were not available, we felt that no such data could be used in this study" (p. 581). They are not, however, consistent in their rejection of evidence based on registration data. In their 1980 paper they cite as evidence supporting their conclusions a study by Robertson based on registration data (p.580), and in their 1981 paper they actually reproduce the graph (shown here as Figure 6.1) and assert without any caveats at all that it shows that "the repeal of 27 state helmet laws between 1976 and 1979 coincided with a rise in the fatality rate from 6.7 to 9.7, a 31 per cent increase." (An increase from 6.7 to 9.7 is an increase of 44.7 per cent, not 31 per cent. But as Figure 6.2 indicates, the actual death rate in 1979 was considerably below the estimate shown in Figure 6.1; it was 8.8. Thus the increase from 1976 to 1979 was, coincidentally, 31 per cent.) Their clear implication is that repeal was the cause of the post-1975 increases shown in Figure 6.1.

The validity of the basis of the NHTSA graph is also accepted by Ross and McLeary (1983). Speaking of this graph they assert "few quasi-experiments are as valid or as interpretable as this one." The following excerpt demonstrates the power of the graph to mislead, and shows that once misconceptions get established in the literature they can be very difficult to dislodge. (The work of Ross (1976) debunking the "Scandinavian Myth" about drink drive legislation suggests that he is a critical and sceptical researcher.) Ross and McLeary observe

"The impact in Figure 3 [my Figure 6.1] is so visually striking that a lay audience would not question the causal interpretation of these data. However, social scientists do not decide questions of validity on the basis of popular response, and it is necessary to rule out formally any plausible alternative explanations.

In this example two rival explanations might be suggested. First, the 1966-69 reduction might be interpreted as a simple continuation of an historical trend evident in the early 1960s. Second, the change might simply reflect the removal by Selective Service of young drivers from U.S. highways to Vietnam. The first explanation is easily ruled out by the post-1976 increase coincident with the repeal of the helmet laws. To rule out the second hypothesis we might be able to disaggregate the national series into 47 different state series. Although we cannot do so here, analyses of the disaggregated data would likely show reductions at 47 different times during the 1966-69 period and 27 increases at different times between 1976 and 1979. ... The illustration is obviously an ideal case, where data are of the highest possible quality, the intervention is precise and well-defined for the fatality series, and a great many controls are available."

So suggestive is the coincidence in Figure 6.1 between the repeal of helmet laws and the fatality increase beginning in 1976 that Ross and McCleary assume that helmet law repeals caused it. So convinced are they of what the data "would likely show" if disaggregated that they do not bother to do it before pronouncing on the excellence of the evidence and analysis.

The Insurance Institute for Highway Safety also considers Figure 6.1 visually striking. It reproduces it in **Teenage Drivers** as evidence of the "dramatic" effect that changes in helmets laws have had on motorcyclist fatalities.

The NHTSA (1980) admits to reservations about the reliability of the registration data (p.V-25), but these reservations were apparently not sufficiently strong to dissuade it from displaying Figure 6.1 on the cover of its report to Congress, a gesture which the unwary might reasonably construe as a manifestation of confidence in the evidence. Certainly none of the studies referred to above provide any reasons for supposing that the registration data are biased in any particular direction.

There is one further serious deficiency in the American data. Even if the registration data are not biased, there is reason to suspect that they provide an unsatisfactory measure of exposure. The best measure of exposure would be, not numbers of motorcycles, but motorcycle mileage. This is not available in the United States. It

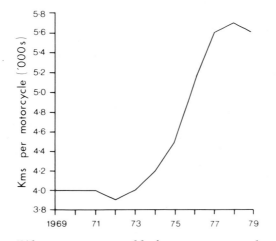

Figure 6.10 Kilometres travelled per motorcycle per year, Britain 1969-1979. Source: <u>TSGB 1969-79</u>, Table 2.9.

6. Behavioural solutions: motorcycle helmets

is available in Britain. Figure 6.10 shows that the distance travelled annually by the average motorcycle, which had been stable for a number of years, increased by 44 per cent between 1973 and 1978. The beginning of the upturn in Figure 6.10 coincides with the energy crisis in late 1973. If the distance travelled per motorcycle in the United States behaved in a similar way over this period, then the picture of fatalities per unit of exposure (measured in vehicle miles) would look very different from the one displayed in Figure 6.1.

The fact that levels of exposure probably varied substantially over the period covered by the above studies, and that it cannot be assumed that this variation occurred uniformly in all the different states, renders all the above evidence less than conclusive. However, scrutiny of the raw monthly data for individual states (as in Figures 6.3, 6.7 and 6.9) reveals none of the sudden large increases in fatalties which should be visible if the claims made in the studies discussed above are valid. It would require an exceptional amount of coincidence for all these presumed increases to be masked by sudden large decreases in levels of exposure in repeal states relative to controls. On the evidence so far published for the United States it cannot be safely concluded that helmet legislation has saved any lives.

Nigeria

There is one study which appears to run counter to the usual claims for helmet legislation. The study by Asogwa (1980) was published in **Accident Analysis and Prevention**, the preeminent journal in the field of safety research. It reports that in the Nigerian State of Anambra a law passed in 1976 was followed by an increase in the number of motorcyclists killed and injured, despite the fact that wearing rates after legislation were reported to be 96.4 per cent. Although motorcycle registrations were higher in the period after the law, the increase was much smaller than the increase in deaths and injuries.

The study however must be regarded as completely inconclusive. It was a simple before-and-after study and suffers from the serious limitions of such studies discussed above, and in the previous Chapter with respect to seat belts. It is also based on extremely small numbers: 5 deaths in the before period, 18 after. And it is based on Nigerian data which, as noted in Chapter 2 are widely considered to be unreliable.

Malaysia

A Malaysian study, also published in **Accident Analysis and Prevention**, (Supramaniam, Van Belle and Sung, 1983) concludes

"An odds ratio of .70 is the estimated risk of deaths associated with motorcycle accidents after the introduction of the helmet law compared with no helmet law. The 30 per cent estimated reduction in fatalities in Malaysia is similar in magnitude to that reported in the U.S.A. It is estimated that in 1979 the number of fatalities in Penninsular Malaysia was about 140 lower than could have been expected without the helmet law."

The study begins by noting that "the death rate on Malaysian roads [is] one of the highest in the world." The authority cited for this statement is a newspaper, **The New Straits Times** of Malaysia. The Malaysian statistics presented in Chapter 2 suggest, on the contrary, that Malaysia's road accident record is unexceptional.

The Malaysian study is oblivious to the possibility of driver compensation. The evidence upon which the 30 per cent reduction claim rests is based on an estimate of the beneficial effect of helmets **in accidents** - the 30 per cent reduction refers to a reduction in the number of deaths per 100 accidents.

The reduction estimate was derived using a linear regression model. The model contains both a time trend and a law/no-law variable and is thus prone to the same problems encountered by Robertson's model discussed in Chapter 3. Certainly the estimated reduction in fatalities per 100 accidents appears to be an artefact of the model and not a real effect. Figure 6.11, reproduced from the Malaysian study, shows that the reported results are contradicted by the data. For two of the three groups of states the number of fatalities per

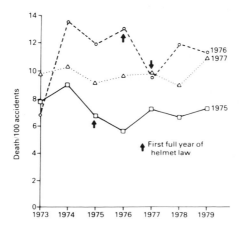

Figure 6.11 Deaths per 100 accidents for states grouped by first full year of helmet law, Malaysia. Source: Supramaniam et al 1984.

accident **increased** during the first full year of operation of the helmet law.

In any event, the authors of the study acknowledge data problems which by themselves are sufficiently serious as to suggest that little reliance should be placed on the study.

"No standard definition is used for the motorcycle rider killed. It may include only those killed on the spot and/or those who die as a result of the accident soon after hospital admission. There may be variations from State to State or from individuals to individuals as well as over time in recording this vital information resulting in misreporting. This could affect the results either way.

However unreliable the fatality data may be the accident data are almost certainly much worse. With a large measure of uncertainty attaching to the numerator of their index and even more uncertainty attaching to the denominator their measure of the benefits of a helmet law can be expected to bear a very tenuous relationship to reality.

Britain

A law requiring the wearing of helmets by motorcyclists came into effect in Britain in June 1973. In 1973 fatality rates per 100 million miles travelled on two-wheeled motor vehicles decreased by 2 per cent; fatality rates for all classes of road user decreased by 9 per cent. In 1974, the first full year of the law's operation, fatality rates for motorcycle riders increased by 2 per cent while fatality rates for all classes of road user decreased by 3 per cent (RAGB 1976). The excuse usually offered for the failure of helmet legislation in Britain to make a discernible beneficial impact is that voluntary wearing rates were already above 85 per cent before the law made helmets compulsory. This explanation conflicts with the explanation usually offered to account for the failure of seat belt legislation – that the most accident prone drivers are concentrated in the group of non-users, and that one should not expect to see an effect in the accident statistics until very high usage rates are attained.

The official Department of Transport view of the critique of the American evidence presented above is contained in a letter from Lynda Chalker, Minister in the Department of Transport, to Member of Parliament Brian Sedgemore (December 6, 1983)

"I am aware of the work carried out by Mr. Adams on the American experience of compulsory helmet wearing ... My officials have recently studied the two re-analyses presented by Mr. Adams and have found inconsistencies in his approach to the data. I do not propose to give a critique of the studies here, but I would like to say that doubt has been cast on only one element of a number of studies which show adverse effects of helmet law repeals. There have been many analyses of the American studies and elsewhere which have supported helmet use. I believe that the benefits of helmet wearing are amply proven and recent Governments have taken the view that helmet wearing should be required by law."

On being asked what the alleged inconsistencies in my analysis were the Department replied (February 27, 1985):
"I should emphasise that the Department has not had access to the full US data, so we have not been able to analyse it. Therefore we have no views on whether the National Highway Traffic Safety Administration paper, and the subsequent analyses by Watson et al, are correct. Nor have we made any judgement about the validity of your criticisms of these papers. However we did note two apparent inconsistencies in your article.
First, you did not appear to take full account of the fact that the 27 states repealed their laws at different times over a period of nearly 4 years. For example, Ohio appears to be counted as a repeal state for each year from 1975, despite not having repealed its law until July 1978.
Second, you criticise the use of fatality rate by registration, on the grounds of unreliability and because motorcycle use may have varied in a very different way from registrations. But in criticising Watson et al and re-analysing the data for one repeal state and its control group, you appear to use the same measure."

Both these criticisms betray a hasty reading of my paper (Adams 1983). What the Department sees as the significance of the first criticism is not made clear, but in any event it is a comment more appropriately directed at NHTSA and Watson et al, ·because they both deploy the data in the way criticised. The second criticism was anticipated and dealt with in my article where I note that uncertainty about exposure levels diminishes the certainty with which any view about the American experience can be held. What was originally seen as an ideal "controlled" experiment has been shown to be far from ideal. It has not been proven conclusively that helmet legislation has not saved lives in the United States, but neither has it been proven that it has.

Conclusion

The above survey of evidence on motorcycle helmet legislation is not exhaustive, but it covers the most recent evidence available, and the most "authoritative". I am aware of no other more convincing

6. Behavioural solutions: motorcycle helmets

studies. The evidence fails to support the widely accepted view that motorcycle helmet legislation has produced dramatic reductions in fatalities. In Britain, as elsewhere, legislation would appear to be based more on faith than hard evidence.

7 Behavioural Solutions:
the United States and Great Britain

Laws and incentives

In Britain in 1983 there were 2,123,000 findings of guilt for
motor vehicle offences (TSGB 1983, Table 2.52). There were
4,619,000 fixed penalty notices issued, mostly for parking offences.
In addition 308,000 written warnings were issued for motoring
offences. In total, there was one official encounter with the law
each year for every three vehicles. Table 7.1 lists these offences in
rank order.

Table 7.1 Motor Vehicle Offences: Britain 1983
Findings of Guilt or Fixed Penalty Notices

	Thousands
Waiting and parking (fixed penalty)	4,417
Licence, insurance and record keeping	709
Vehicle test and condition	304
Speeding	266
Neglect of traffic signs, directions, and pedestrian rights	147
Careless driving etc.	146
Non-display of valid vehicle excise licence (fixed penalty)	142
Driving after consuming alcohol or drugs	98
Obstruction, waiting and parking	89
Lighting and noise	70
Unauthorized taking or theft of motor vehicle	52
Accident offences	48
Lighting offences (fixed penalty)	41
Load and trailer offences	37
Disregarding precribed route (fixed penalty)	16
Offences peculiar to motorcycles	13
Reckless driving	5
Other	142
Total	6742

Source: TSGB 1973-83, Tables 2.52 and 2.53

The great majority of these offences are violations of fixed rules, such as driving without the prescribed documents, or above a certain speed, or with more than a specified amount of alcohol in the blood. Only a relatively small number require judgements by the police about whether or not the offending behaviour is actually dangerous – e.g. careless driving and reckless driving. There is however a large measure of police discretion involved in bringing charges. It is widely acknowledged that the offences listed above represent only the tip of the iceberg of motoring offences. Speed limits are widely flouted with impunity; this fact is frequently adduced in Britain as evidence of the need to increase the limits to more "realistic" levels. A British Home Office study has estimated that less than one in every 250 drink driving offences results in a conviction (Riley 1984). In North America estimates of the chances of a driver being caught while over the limit have been calculated at 1 in 2000 (Borkenstein 1972).

Throughout the world enormous amounts of time and money are devoted to devising regulations governing road user behaviour, to passing laws giving these regulations the official support of the state, and to applying sanctions to ensure compliance. Legislators, civil servants, police, judges, magistrates and lawyers are all involved in this highly labour-intensive business. In Britain, over the past 10 years, motor vehicle offences have accounted for 90 per cent of all court proceedings, excluding fixed penalty offences (TSGB 1973-83, Table 2.52). Although parking regulations often have a safety purpose, their primary function is to minimize congestion and promote the smooth flow of traffic in areas where the demand for road space exceeds supply. But most of the rest of the regulations listed above (with the exception of theft) are invoked primarily in the name of safety. Even the record keeping regulations have a safety purpose in that they facilitate the apprehension of those violating other regulations. Yet there is a dearth of conclusive evidence that any of the regulations have been responsible for a lasting reduction in the numbers killed and injured on the roads.

The United States

Consider the example of the United States. Figure 7.1 describes the history of road accident fatalities between 1960 and 1983. It also presents the results of a model which attempts to account for this history. The model which has achieved this is a simple regression model with the following form.

$$\text{Fatalities} = -96781 - 1.8569 \text{ x Unemployed Workers}/1000$$
$$+ 0.4971 \text{ x Employed Workers}/1000$$
$$+ 0.9616 \text{ x Non-labour Force}/1000$$
$$- 3995 \text{ if } 1974$$
$$- 4824 \text{ if } 1974 \text{ or later}$$

This model accounts for 97.8 per cent of the variability in the numbers of fatalities since 1960, but it does not **explain** the variability. It is accompanied by a warning that

"... the model does not imply that other factors (such as safety programs and improvements) are unrelated to fatality decreases. ... a model describes the observed coinciding of changes among variables, but does not of itself imply cause and effect." (Partyka, 1984)

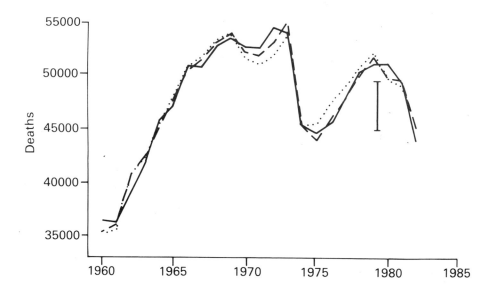

Figure 7.1 The Partyka model. Solid line represents actual road accident fatalities; dashed line represents fit of the Partyka model; vertical bar represents the effect that the model attributes to the national 55 mph speed limit; dotted line represents the fit of the model with the speed limit variable removed.

Having issued this caution Partyka proceeds immediately to disregard it. The "1974 or later" variable is described as the variable which accounts for the "effect" of the national 55mph speed limit which was imposed in 1974. It is interpreted as signifying that the law **caused** an annual reduction in fatalities of 4824. Figure 7.1 suggests that this is improbable. If the "1974 and after" variable is removed from the regression equation the model produces a fit which is almost as good (r-square = 95.7). An examination of the residuals for the years 1973 and 1975 from the fit produced with the "1974 and after" variable removed suggests that there was a downward step in fatalities in 1974 which persisted for a few years, but that the magnitude of this step has been greatly exaggerated by the Partyka model. 4824, represented in Figure 7.1 by a vertical bar, appears an excessive amount of credit to attribute to this variable

While the Partyka model produces a very good fit, the coefficients of the variables in the model would appear to be very unreliable guides to the influence of individual variables on the level of fatalities. This is a common problem in models containing independent variables which are highly correlated with each other. Adding or removing variables from the regression can alter the values of the other coefficents substantially while altering the percentage of variance explained by very little.

Assuming that there is a (small) downward step in fatalities after 1973, should it be attributed to the national 55mph speed limit? There could be other explanations. In 1974 the death rate per vehicle mile decreased in the United States by 15.4 per cent. Across the border in Ontario it also decreased by 15.4 per cent. But Ontario did not experience an energy crisis. There were no physical shortages of petrol and no reductions in speed limits. This interesting fact was discussed at the 1978 Congressional hearings when Ontario witnesses presented evidence. One witness (Pierce 1978, p.188) speculated that publicity about the American energy crisis might have "rolled across the border and affected things somewhat." This seemed to Mr. Goldwater for the Congressional committee an inadequate explanation.

"Mr. Goldwater. 'You haven't explained why that happened.'

Mr. Lonero [principal Ontario Government safety witness (1978)]. 'I wish we knew, sir. 1974 was a very good year for traffic fatalities all around the world. Virtually every motorised country experienced the same drop. There is a mythology in the field that bad times economically go along with relatively few fatalities, and it was a bad year economically'." (p.189)

Ontario did not get round to reducing its speed limits until January 1976 when the limits were lowered on expressways from 70 to 60 mph and on most other provincial highways from 60 to 50 mph. At the same time Ontario introduced a seat belt law. A study by the Ontario Ministry of Transportation and Communications (1980) concluded that the reduction in fatality rates for vehicle occupants associated with these two safety measures combined was "not statistically significant". (Pierce, 1980 p.12)

In Britain no belt law was passed and the energy crisis speed limits on motorways were in force for only a few months. In both Britain and the United States fatalities decreased by 18 per cent between 1972 and 1975. Both countries experienced fatality increases beginning in 1976. But in Britain they were much more modest and temporary. In Britain by 1980, after all the energy crisis speed limits had been repealed, the number of deaths was 6 per cent below the 1975 level. In the United States where the speed limit was retained the 1980 level was 15 per cent above the 1975 level.

Between 1980 and 1982 road accident fatalities in the United States decreased by 14 per cent. Hedlund et al (1984) find this decrease difficult to explain.

"Unlike 1974, when the oil crisis and the national 55 mph speed limit changed everyone's driving behaviour, there are no apparent reasons for the current decline. Travel increased in each of the past two years, by 1.5% in 1981 and 1.4% in 1982 – modest increases, but increases nevertheless. There were no gas shortages. Travel speeds have not changed markedly, and if anything have increased. Passenger cars are getting smaller, as more Americans seek fuel efficiency. These factors all suggest that fatalities should increase rather than decrease." (p.248)

Despite the fact that the Partyka model accounts for the decrease very well (it over-estimates in 1982 by 1.6 per cent), Hedlund et al still manage to attribute some of the decrease to safety measures. About one twentieth of the decrease they think might be attributable to an increase of about one per cent in seat belt wearing rates – to about 12 per cent; however, the evidence reviewed in Chapter 5 suggests that much larger increases in wearing rates to much higher levels have not produced detectable effects in other countries. About one sixth of the decrease they think might be attributable to campaigns against drinking and driving. This estimate is based on evidence which suggests that between 1980 and 1982 there was a decrease of between .3 per cent and 2.6 per cent in the numbers of dead drivers with measurable amounts of alcohol in their blood. However, evidence from Britain, reviewed below, suggests that the number of dead drivers with excessive blood alcohol levels is a very unreliable guide to numbers of fatalities.

It is not impossible that seat belts and drunk driving campaigns have had the effects attributed to them by Hedlund et al, but their method of identifying and estimating these effects is not convincing, consisting as it does of post hoc rationalisation. They have identified variables which **might** have had an effect in the desired direction, but ignored evidence which suggests that these variables have a very poor record as predictors. They have also ignored the possible effects of the other variables, such as car size and speed, which they had postulated should have had effects in the opposite direction.

A caveat   Hedlund (1984) notes that when data became available to project the Partyka model into 1983 the model produced the worst fit

in 24 years. The model predicted an increase in deaths in 1983;
instead they continued to decline. There is a longstanding
suspicion to be found in the road accident literature that accident
frequencies are influenced by the state of the economy. Using
unemployment variables the Partyka model has achieved a very good fit
with a small number of variables. But the coefficients of the model
can vary considerably depending on what other variables are included
or excluded, and their interpretation is not obvious. The perfect
model has yet to be discovered.

Great Britain

The Smeed Model Figure 7.2 describes the country's fatal road
accident history since 1926. So far no statistical model exists to
account for the ups and downs of the graph over the whole of this
period. The Smeed Law can describe the gross trend in deaths per
vehicle, but there is considerable variation about this trend. It is
unlikely that a satisfactory model for the whole of this period will

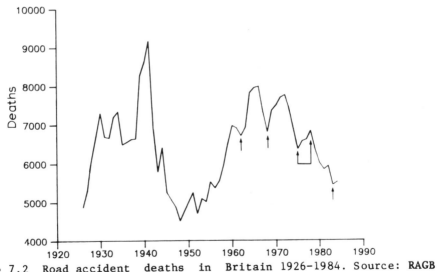

Figure 7.2 Road accident deaths in Britain 1926-1984. Source: **RAGB**
1983, Table 1. Arrows are referred to in the text.

ever be developed because parallel time series for likely independent
variables are not available.
Figure 7.3 shows that there have been large changes over time in
the proportion of total road deaths attributable to different modes of
travel since 1949. (1949 is as far back as a reasonably consistent

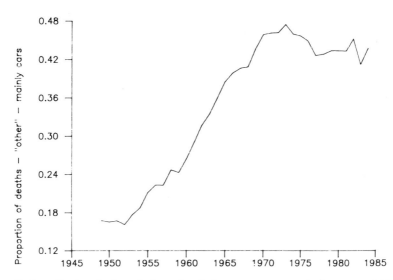

Figure 7.3a "Other" fatalties (mainly car occupants) as a proportion of total road accident deaths. Source: RAGB 1983, Table 1.

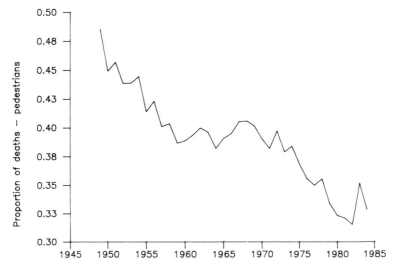

Figure 7.3b Pedestrian deaths as a proportion of total road accident deaths.

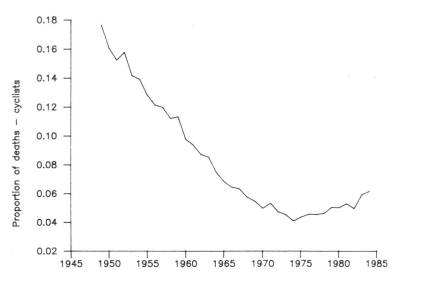

Figure 7.3c Cyclist deaths as a proportion of total road accident deaths.

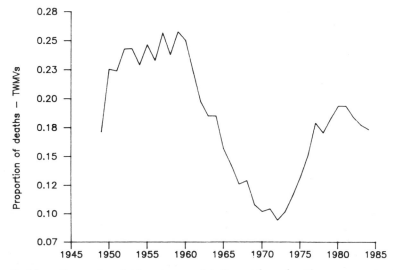

Figure 7.3d   Two wheeled motor vehicle rider deaths as a proportion of total road accident deaths.

series of traffic volume measurements are available.)

Despite the variability over time in the proportions attributable to different classes of road user, the total number of deaths relative to the volume of traffic has behaved in an impressively stable manner: the slope of the straight line in Figure 7.4 shows that for the past 35 years the death rate per vehicle kilometre has decreased, on average, by 4.7 per cent per year. Figure 7.4 represents a variation on the relationship modelled by Smeed. The volume of traffic is a more precise measure of exposure to road accident risk than simple vehicle numbers. Unfortunately a consistent series of traffic volume measurements is not available for years before 1949.

Figure 7.5 illustrates the way in which traffic growth rates have varied over the years. During years in which traffic increased by more than 4.7 per cent road deaths tended to increase, and during years in which traffic increased by less than 4.7 per cent they tended to decrease. Figure 7.6 provides an indication of how accurately deaths can be estimated by the modified Smeed model. The model describes the underlying trend fairly well and calls attention to interesting departures from this trend.

The Partyka Model   Before discussing this trend, and departures from it, it will be compared with the results achieved by applying a modified version of the Partyka model to British data (see Appendix at the end of the Chapter). The fit of the model (Figure 7.7a) is not as good as that achieved by the original Partyka model applied to United States data. With the exception of 1968, which has been modelled explicitly, the trend identified is generally similar to that shown for the same period in Figure 7.6.

For the period 1960-1984 data are available to model road deaths for different modes of travel separately. The results are shown in Figures 7.7b - 7.7d. The coefficients of the independent variables in the model vary considerably depending on the class of road user to which the model is applied. When it is applied to Two Wheeled Motor Vehicles all the signs of the coefficients are reversed, with the exception of that of the '1968 only' variable (see Appendix).

Government Intervention   At various points in time governments in Britain have implemented measures whose intended effects should have been visible in the form of large downward steps in these graphs. The four most widely publicised measures affecting road safety in Britain since the Second World War where introduced in 1962, 1967, 1974-77 and 1983. The 1962 Traffic Act imposed new speed limits, increased the maximum fines for speeding and careless driving by 150 per cent, and introduced the "totting-up" procedure whereby drivers could be disqualified for three offences. The Road Safety Act of 1967 made it an offence to drive with over 80 mg. of alcohol per 100 ml. of blood. Between December 1973 and April 1977 various speed limits were

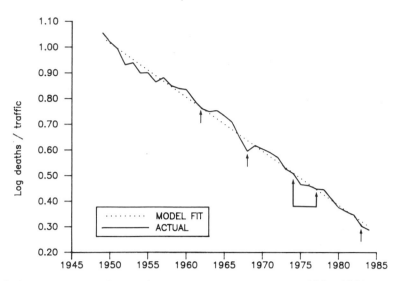

Fgure 7.4 Road accident deaths in Britain per 100 million vehicle
kilometres.   Sources: **RAGB** 1983, Table 1, **Road Accidents** 1970,
DoE, HMSO 1972, **TSGB**, relevant years.

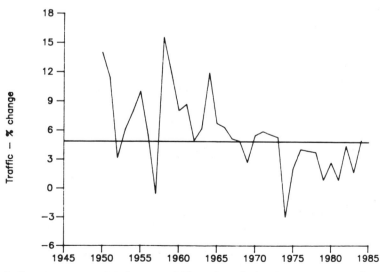

Figure 7.5   Motor vehicle traffic in Britain: percent change over
previous year.   Source: **Road Accidents** 1970, DoE,   HMSO 1972,
TSGB, relevant years.   The horizontal line represents 4.7 per cent,
the average long term rate at which deaths per vehicle mile have
been decreasing.

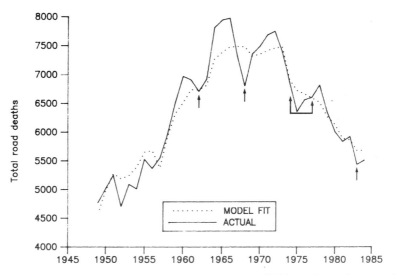

Figure 7.6 Road deaths in Britain since 1949, and estimates from a modified Smeed Model. The model fit for any given year has been calculated by multiplying the annual number of deaths per vehicle mile – estimated by the straight line in Figure 7.4 – by the volume of traffic in that year.

imposed in response to the "energy crisis" and then repealed; they were introduced as a fuel conservation measure, but were warmly welcomed by safety experts as a safety measure. At the end of January 1983 the wearing of seat belts in the front seats of cars and vans became obligatory. When these measures are viewed against the trends identified by the Partyka model and the modified Smeed model it is difficult to make a case for any of them having had any lasting effect.

1962: the Traffic Act   The penalties provided by law for motoring offences are intended to act as incentives to safer driving – disincentives to law-breaking being equated with disincentives to unsafe behaviour. The objective of the new speed limits, larger maximum fines, and the totting-up procedure was to increase the severity of the punishment for the most persistent offenders. However, changing the law did not necessarily lead to a change in practice; although the maximum fines for speeding and careless driving had been increased by 150 per cent, the average fine did not increase at all (Plowden 1971, p. 455). Following the implementation of the measures contained in the 1962 Traffic Act the number of road

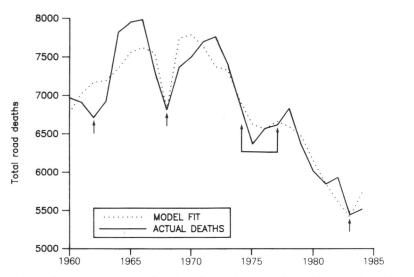

Figure 7.7a Total road deaths in Britain 1960–1984, and estimates from modified Partyka Model.

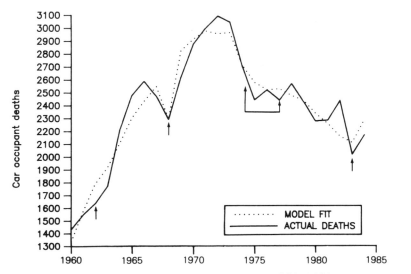

Figure 7.7b   Car occupant deaths in Britain 1960–1984, and estimates from modified Partyka Model.

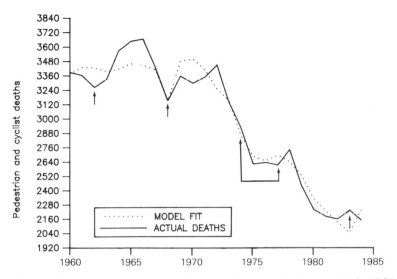

Figure 7.7c Pedestrian and cyclist deaths in Britain 1960-1984, and estimates from modified Partyka Model.

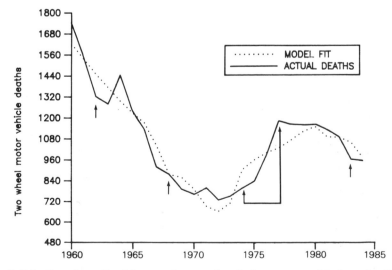

Figure 7.7d Deaths of riders of two wheeled motor vehicles in Britain 1960-1984, and estimates from modified Partyka Model.

accident deaths, which had fallen over the previous two years, climbed
more steeply than the trends identified by the models until reaching
a post-war peak in 1966. Perhaps the increase would have been even
greater without the 1962 Act. Perhaps not.

1967: the breathalyser   The introduction of blood alcohol limits
in October 1967 coincides with an abrupt departure from the trend of
the model illustrated in Figure 7.6. In the graphs in Figure 7.7 1968
stands out as a very large decrease; in Figure 7.7 this decrease has
been modelled explicitly. Between 1966 and 1968 there was a 15 per
cent decrease in total road deaths. It appears likely that the
breathalyser deserves credit for a substantial part of this
decrease. The number of over-the-limit dead drivers dropped from 25
per cent to 15 per cent. The number of deaths between 2200 and 0400
hours (the period in which most drink-drive offences are committed)
dropped by 31 per cent. However the effect was temporary. Since the
introduction of the 80mg. blood alcohol limit in 1967 the number of
road accident deaths has decreased substantially, but drunken
driving has **increased**. By 1969 the percentage of drivers killed in
accidents while over the legal limit, which dropped sharply after the
introduction of the breathalyser, was back above its pre-law level
(DoE 1976). Between 1966 (before the Road Safety Act) and 1975 the
number killed on the roads decreased by 31 per cent, but the
proportion of drivers killed with excess alcohol increased by 36 per
cent (DoE, 1976, para. 3.10). Since 1966 both the volume of
motoring and the amount of alcohol consumed have increased. There are
now far more drivers with more alcohol in them on the road than
before 1966.
  Table 7.2 shows the way in which the percentage of over-the-limit
dead drivers has varied since 1973. Between 1973 and 1975 the

Table 7.2. Drivers killed in Great Britain: percentage over
the legal blood alcohol limit.

	Two wheel motor vehicle	Car and other motor vehicle
1973		33
1974		36
1975		38
1976		38
1977		32
1978	29	33
1979	31	32
1980	29	32
1981	28	31
1982	29	36
1983	21	31

Sources: **RAGB** 1978 Table X, **RAGB** 1983 Table XXI.

percentage increased and road accident fatalities decreased, and between 1976 and 1978 the percentage decreased markedly while road accident fatalities increased. Perhaps the increases in fatalities would have been greater, and the decreases smaller without the 1967 Road Safety Act. Perhaps not.

1973-1977: speed limits   In December 1973, a blanket speed limit of 50mph was applied to all roads in Britain not already subject to a lower limit. At the same time petrol prices were increased by 20 per cent, followed by another increase of 20 per cent in February 1974, and a further increase in April; between December 1973 and April 1974 petrol prices increased by about 57 per cent. The motorway speed limit was restored to 70mph at the end of March, and in May the 70mph limit was restored to other all-purpose roads previously subject to that limit. In November 1974 the limit on some all-purpose roads was reduced to 50mph and on others to 60mph. Finally, in April 1977 Parliament agreed that the 50 and 60mph limits on all-purpose roads should be raised again to 60 and 70mph – in the face of protest and dire predictions by safety experts.
   In 1974 and 1975 the total number of road deaths decreased. In 1976, 1977 and 1978 they increased. Figures 7.3 and 7.7 show that the contribution of the different modes of travel to the changes in the total numbers of deaths in these years varies considerably. Between 1975 and 1978 there was an increase of 465 in the total number of road deaths per year, but most of this increase (325) was accounted for by motorcyclists. In 1977, after the last of the energy crisis speed limits was repealed, the total number killed – excluding motorcyclists – decreased. After 1978 deaths for all modes decreased markedly. Perhaps the decreases would have been greater if none of the lower speed limits had been repealed. Again, perhaps not.

1983: seat belts   Seat belt wearing rates in Britain were about 30 per cent for a number of years prior to 1982. For most of 1982 they were close to 40 per cent. In January 1983 they began to rise in anticipation of the seat belt law, and in February 1983 they rose sharply to about 95 per cent – where they have remained. Judged by the modified Smeed model there were fewer deaths than expected in 1983 and 1984: 244 less in 1983, and 171 less in 1984. Judged by the Partyka model there were 30 more deaths than expected in 1983, and 219 fewer in 1984. As can be seen from Figures 7.4, 7.6 and 7.7 these departures are small relative to the size of the annual variations in numbers of deaths, and relative to departures from the model in previous years.
   There are, however, some interesting differences in the behaviour of the graphs for different classes of road user. Figure 7.3a shows that in 1982 car occupant fatalities increased relative to all other fatalities, decreased in 1983, and increased again in 1984. Figure 7.3b shows that pedestrian fatalities, as a proportion of total

fatalities, decreased in 1982, increased in 1983 and decreased in
1984. Cyclist fatalities as a proportion of total fatalities decreased
in 1982 and increased in both 1983 and 1984. Table 7.3 compares the
road death statistics for these years with the expectations of the
models.

Table 7.3 Differences between recorded deaths and model
predictions; figures in () are standardised residuals –
values greater than 2.0 are considered "significant"
departures from the trends of the models.

Deaths	1982	1983	1984	R-squared
Total (Fig. 7.7)	+314	+30	−219	87.9
	(1.23)	(0.13)	(−1.29)	
Car occupant	+282	−93	−120	92.6
	(2.40)	(−0.84)	(−1.54)	
Pedestrians & cyclists	+25	+190	−88	94.9
	(0.22)	(1.75)	(−1.14)	
Two wheeled motor veh.	+1	−97	−19	89.9
	(0.01)	(−1.23)	(−0.34)	
All excluding twmv	+314	+127	−200	92.5
	(1.45)	(0.63)	(−1.39)	

With the exception of car occupant fatalities in 1982, none of the
departures from the predictions of the models is very significant. The
overall pattern is consistent with the possibility that there has been
a small, or zero, change in total road accident deaths, but a shift in
the burden of risk from car occupants (covered by the seat belt law)
to pedestrians and cyclists. (The "two wheeled motor vehicle" category
is difficult to interpret because at the same time that the seat belt
law came into effect, the law was changed to prohibit learner
motorcyclists from using machines with engine capacities greater than
125cc.)

In 1983 pedestrian and cyclist fatalities increased while the
model predicted a decrease (Figure 7.7b). The suspicion that this
might be associated with the seat belt law is strengthened by the fact
that the increase in pedestrian and cyclist fatalities in 1983 is
attributable entirely to cars and vans; the number killed by heavy
goods vehicles and public service vehicles decreased in that year –
see Table 7.4.

Interpreting the seat belt evidence   One aspect of the data which
creates problems of interpretation is the increase in car occupant
fatalities, against the trends of the models, in 1982. If this
increase is considered to herald a new trend, not represented by the

Table 7.4   Pedestrians   and   cyclists killed   in   two-party
             accidents.

	Hit by car or van			Hit by HGV or PSV		
	Pedestrian	Cyclist	All	Pedestrian	Cyclist	All
1982	1176	153	1329	263	78	341
1983	1297	184	1481	257	64	321
1984	1236	169	1405	251	85	336
% change						
1982-83	+8.7	+20.3	+11.4	-2.3	-17.9	-5.9
1984-82	+5.1	+10.5	+5.7	-4.6	+9.0	-1.5

Source: Road Accidents and Casualties Great Britain - Fourth
Quarter 1984, Department of Transport, Table 10.

models, which could have been expected to continue, then the decrease
in car occupant fatalities in 1983 could be considered a large
departure from the new trend - i.e. possibly a benefit attributable
to seat belts. If, however, 1982 is considered to be an unexplained
departure from a well established trend, then the 1983 figures might
simply represent the reassertion of that trend - i.e. no seat belt
effect. Figure 7.8 illustrates the way in which the modeller's
conception of the process being modelled can affect the conclusions
drawn. If one fits a linear trend to the data over a two year period,
and assumes that this trend will continue indefinitely into the
future, one is likely to come to conclusions concerning the efficacy
of seat belt legislation which are very different from those suggested
by the above graphs.

In 1982, the percentage of drivers killed who were over the legal
blood alcohol limit increased from 31 per cent to 36 per cent and
decreased again in 1983 to 31 per cent. Table 7.2 shows that this
represents a large change relative to the recent history of these
statistics. Might this account for some of the unexplained increase in
car occupant fatalities in 1982 and the decrease in 1983? Certainly
it is a large change compared to the change to which Hedlund et al
ascribe credit for fatality reductions in the United States
(see above). Unfortunately, in Britain, no clear relationship has been
established between this measure of the amount of drunken driving and
variations in road accident deaths.
The success of the Smeed and Partyka models in capturing much of
the variability in road deaths, over periods of 36 and 25
years respectively, suggests that the decrease in road deaths in
1983 might well have occurred without any government intervention.
The fact that the Partyka model works reasonably well in both the
United Sates and Britain lends it added credibility. The success of
the Partyka model in accounting for the variation in road deaths for
different categories of road users, as well as for the aggregate,

hints at complex interactions between categories of road user. Changes in economic and employment circumstances can produce changes in attitudes toward risk, changes in exposure to risk, and changes in mode of travel. For example, getting a well paid job could engender new confidence in an unemployed teenager and enable him to trade his

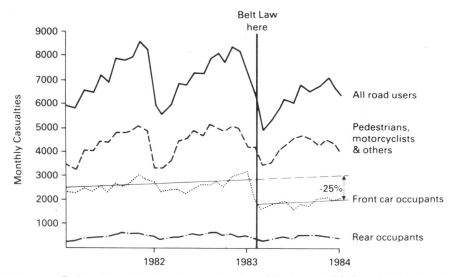

Figure 7.8 A method of analysis (Mackay 1984) which leads to conclusions favouring seat belt legislation. Comparison with Figure 7.2 suggests that the level of resolution at which one views the data can be very important. What appears to be an upward trend in Figure 7.8 (based on monthly data over a two year period), appears in Figure 7.2 as a minor pause in an established downward trend.

bicycle for a motorcycle. Another might trade a motorcycle for a car. Loss of a job by a motorist might lead to loss of confidence, loss of car, and a reduction in the amount of travel, and a consequent reduction in exposure to risk on the road. Loss of a job in a category of employment in which average incomes and car ownership levels are high could be expected to have different consequences from those following the loss of a low paid job. There are, however, possibly insurmountable obstacles in the path of efforts seeking to capture such effects in a statistical model. Accident data are not routinely collected in a way which permits the identification of the employment circumstances of the individuals involved. Also there are no reliable time series data for the "black economy", which is widely believed to have grown rapidly in recent years. The non-labour force contains unknown numbers of people employed

unofficially, as well as people who are unemployed unofficially.
The zig-zag endings on graphs 7.3a and 7.3b are consistent with the possibility that the seat belt law in Britain decreased car occupant fatalities and increased pedestrian and cyclist fatalities, and that the effect was temporary — that both sets of road users adjusted to their changed circumstances in ways that reestablished their previous levels of risk.

Speed

There is a sense in which all injuries resulting from motor vehicle collisions can be attributed to excessive speed. Speeds which are too high for the road or traffic circumstances can result in loss of control, or an inability to stop or take evasive action in time. And where collisions do occur injury results only where the forces resulting from the speed at impact exceed the protective shock-absorbing capabilities of the vehicle. Of the offences listed in Table 7.1 involving driving, speed limit violations account for the greatest number of convictions

Ever since Britain's Red Flag Act of 1865, which restricted traction engines to 4mph on turnpikes and 2mph in towns, excess speed has been a primary target for those concerned with promoting road safety. But achieving safe driving speeds by means of legislation has proved very difficult. A "safe" speed is not a constant. It varies widely according to class of road, type of vehicle, road surface, visibility, traffic conditions, and skill and state of mind of the driver. An appropriate speed limit for one configuration of circumstances can be too low or too high for others. A fixed speed limit is an extremely blunt tool for promoting road safety.

Compounding the bluntness of the instrument is the lack of consistency with which it is applied. Table 7.2 presents some results from a Department of Transport speed survey.

Table 7.2 Speeds of Cars in Miles per Hour on Different
Classes of Road in Unconstrained Conditions

	Mean speed	85th percentile	Speed limit	per cent above limit
Single carriageway	44	52	60	5
Dual carriageway	58	68	70	12*
Motorway	68	79	70	40

* includes motorcyclists, but sample dominated by cars.
Source: RAGB 1983 Table XIV.

7. Behavioural solutions: USA and Great Britain

The figures for dual carriageways and motorways relate to traffic in the near carriageway (i.e. slowest carriageway) only, so it is plausible to assume that if traffic in the faster lanes had been included the majority of motorists on the motorways would have been revealed to be law breakers. The figures suggest some interesting things about the behaviour of motorists and police. It appears that on single carriageway roads motorists are much more law abiding. This suggests that the speed limit on the single carriageways surveyed was excessive relative to most drivers' perceptions of a safe speed. Further support for this view is found in comparisons with results of similar surveys of single carriageway roads in earlier years when the speed limit was 10mph lower. When the speed limit was raised there was no significant increase in mean speeds or 85th percentile speeds, only a decrease from 19 per cent to 5 per cent in the number breaking the law (RAGB 1983, Table XIII). It appears that traffic on the single carriageway roads is largely self-regulating in terms of speed.

For the dual carriageways the evidence is less clear. Comparison with the results of earlier surveys going back to 1975 shows a slow but steady increase in speeds. In 1977 the speed limit on these roads was raised from 60 to 70mph, but the increase in speeds is not clearly related to this change. Over the period 1975 to 1983 mean speeds increased from 52 to 58 mph. Reasons for this increase could include the improved performance of cars, a diminishing concern with energy shortages, or a diminishing enthusiasm on the part of the police for charging speeders. (While speeds were increasing the number of findings of guilt for speeding offences was decreasing (TSGB 1973-1983 Table 2.52).)

On the motorways it appears that the speed limit is set below the level that most drivers think is safe. This view is shared by the police. In evidence to the House of Commons Transport Committee the Association of Chief Police Officers stated

"Speed limits in this country are in a mess. ...The proliferation of unecessary and unenforceable speed limits is not only an unacceptable burden on police resources, they also bring perfectly proper speed limits into disrepute. ... There is a case for raising the speed limit on motorways to 80mph." (ACPO, 1984)

There is in Britain an explicit attempt to seek democratic guidance in setting speed limits by consulting the behaviour of drivers. In March 1984 the speed limit for buses, coaches and lorries on dual carriageways was raised from 50 mph to 60 mph on the grounds that the previous limit was not being observed. The Secretary of State for Transport was reported to have justified this measure as follows.

"Speed limits needed to be realistic, if not the majority of drivers tended to break them and this made enforcement impractical. It brought the law into disrepute." (**The Times** March 9, 1984)

Britain's Department of Transport refers to the 85th percentile "guideline" in setting speed limits. If more than 15 per cent of traffic exceeds an established limit this is considered evidence for raising it on the grounds that it is "unrealistic" (Hamer 1985).

If speed limits are intended to address a safety problem, then the limits set for different classes of road in Britain would appear to be arbitrary; per vehicle mile, motorways are much safer than other roads with lower speed limits. Yet it is the subject of **motorway** speed limits that provokes the most public controversy. At the time of writing (early 1985) it is the subject of heated debate in British newspapers. It is argued by opponents of an increase that if the speed limit were raised to 80mph one would still find the same percentage of law breakers, and average speeds would increase. But the experience of raising the limit on single carriageway roads suggests that this would be the case only to the extent that current speeds are inhibited by the existing speed limit rather than by the motorists' perceptions of risk.

International comparisons provide little support for the view that lowering, or raising, the motorway speed limit would have a significant effect on death and injury rates. Germany, at the time of writing, has no speed limit on most of its autobahns. Germany has a much higher death rate than Britain per vehicle kilometre (in 1982 3.5 deaths per 100 million vehicle kilometres in Germany and 1.9 in Britain). Germany cities, with their **Verkehrberuhigung** - literally traffic calming - zones, have a reputation for managing their urban traffic affairs rather better than most countries. It is argued plausibly by Klau (1985) that "for the last decade at least [German traffic managers] have set a model for the rest of the world to follow." One would expect, therefore, that German autobahns would account for a disproportionately large share of German road accident fatalities. But they account for a disproportionately small share. Although the death rate per vehicle kilometre on autobahns is higher than that on motorways, in 1982 the autobahn death rate per vehicle mile in Germany was 26 per cent of the national average rate for all roads; in Britain the motorway death rate per vehicle kilometre was 37 per cent of the national average rate (**Unfall-Verhutungsbericht Strassenverkehr**, 1983 p.43 and **RAGB** 1982 Table 25). Thus, relative to their national accident rates, German autobahns appear to be safer than British motorways.

Bermuda is sometimes cited as an example of the extent to which limits could be lowered if the political will existed (e.g. Kahn 1976). It has a maximum speed limit of 20mph. It has a very small population (about 55,000) and its road accident statistics are therefore likely to exhibit considerable annual variation. But averaging the figures over the past ten years yields a death rate per motor vehicle of 3.4 per 10,000, a level which comfortably exceeds that of Britain with a similar number of vehicles per head. Very few car occupants are killed. 81 per cent of fatalities were riding two wheeled motor vehicles (**Bermuda Digest of Statistics** 1984).

Since the watershed year of 1973 there have been numerous studies making claims for the safety benefits of the speed limits imposed in the aftermath of the energy crisis. Almost all of these studies suffer the same limitation as the seat belt studies discussed in Chapter 5. They are unconvincing because they lack effective controls. In the mid-1970s some countries passed belt laws, some countries imposed speed limits, some countries did both, and some countries did neither. During this period Britain had no belt law, and it imposed and then repealed lower speed limits; and its safety record over this decade compares favourably with that of most other countries. Similarly Ontario enjoyed the "energy crisis drop" without either a speed limit or a belt law, and by the time it passed both the "effect" was not statistically significant.

A study by Scott and Barton (1976) demonstrated, using monthly accident data, a convincing, but short lived, decrease in road accidents on roads in Britain which were subject to the energy crisis speed limits. They found no similar change on roads where the established 30/40mph speed limits remained unchanged. But it remains unclear whether the decrease was caused by the speed limit, or concern to save fuel, or whether the willingness to observe the speed limits was the result of an anxiety about energy shortages. Whatever the cause, since that time, the speed limits have been repealed, concern about fuel shortages has diminished, speeds have increased, and fatalities have decreased still further.

Very little seems to be known about the safety effect of the enforcement of speed limits. Hauer and Ahlin (1982) summed up the state of knowledge as follows.

"In spite of several decades of practice and research, definitive knowledge about the safety effect of speed law enforcement does not seem to exist."

Most research in this area, including the Hauer and Ahlin study, concentrates on trying to identify effects within very restricted

Table 7.3   Effect of speed limit on the
             Baden-Wurttemburg Autobahn

	Sections with speed limits	Sections with no speed limit	
		Nearby	Total
Fatalities	-38%	+30%	-20%
Injuries	-18%	+20%	+ 2%

Source: Road Research Laboratory 1963, Table 6.11

geographical areas. Such studies, like the blackspot studies discussed in Chapter 4, risk missing "migration" effects. Table 7.3 reports the results of a study of the effects of a speed limit imposed on sections of autobahn in Germany.

The report concluded, "if it is assumed that, in the absence of the speed limit the different types of accidents would have changed by the same amounts as in the nearby parts of the motorway, the apparent effect of the speed limit has been to reduce fatalities by 52 per cent (based on rather small numbers) and the number of persons injured by 32 per cent." But if this assumption is not made, Table 7.3 might be considered prima facie evidence of accidents migrating from the sections of the autobahn with speed limits to nearby sections without.

Drink

Drunken driving is another obvious target for safety campaigners. There were 98,000 convictions for impaired driving in Britain in 1983, making this, in the eyes of the law, the next most important driving offence after speeding (the careless and neglect categories of offence listed in Table 7.1 embrace a multitude of different offences). The potential safety benefits to be gained by controlling this offence are sometimes claimed to exceed even those attributed to speed limits and seat belt and helmet laws: "If we could really succeed in controlling the drinking and driving problem we would probably reduce our deaths by 25,000 a year." (B.A. Boas, NHTSA quoted by Pettifer and Turner 1984, p.226)

There is little optimism amongst students of the problem that such results are achievable. In 1983 the journal **Accident Analysis and Prevention** devoted an entire issue to the problem of impaired driving. The guest editor's introduction (Vingilis 1983) provides a good indication of the record of achievement in this area up to that time. The tone of the editor's comments is as informative as their content.

"Once again, drinking and driving has come to the fore as a public concern. The beginning of every decade over the past 30 years has seen a surge of interest in, and concern over, drinking and driving. This concern has led to millions being spent throughout the world on countermeasures, with little measurable success in reducing the problem. As one of the harbingers of drinking-driving research recently wrote to me concerning one of my review articles, 'I have learned a lot from reading it, but feel disappointed that so little has been achieved since I last worked in the field.' But this seems to be a general feeling and may simply mean that I am getting old."

Vingilis went on, in his introductory comments, to speculate about the reasons for this lack of success. He singled out two: "we seem to have few definitive answers because methodological flaws in many of our studies preclude them", and "we researchers have been afraid to explore new ground and venture into the complexities of social and psychological theories."

However, the despairing tone which characterises much of the literature on drinking and driving appears to stem not so much from the failure to find answers, but from the answers which are found. Ross (1982) in a wide ranging survey of the effect of legislation intended to deter drinking and driving concluded that the most that had been achieved anywhere was a temporary effect. Typically, legislation has been introduced to the accompaniment of intensive publicity aimed at persuading potential offenders that the risk of apprehension had been greatly increased. Again typically, drivers soon learned that the increased risk of apprehension was negligible and reverted to their previous habits.

Most European countries, Canada, Australia, New Zealand and many American states have **"per se laws"** which deem it an offence to drive with blood alcohol concentrations above a specified level (Jonah and Wilson 1983). Such laws are like speed limits in that the behaviour (or in this case physical state) deemed criminal is not dangerous **per se**. The justification for outlawing driving above given speeds or with blood alcohol concentrations above given levels, is that these behaviours and states are associated with increased probabilities of accidents. Also like speed limits, **per se** drink driving laws are known to be extremly blunt instruments. The range of accident probabilities displayed in Figure 1.1 suggests that an individual motorist's blood alcohol level is a very poor predictor of his accident involvement. Such laws are also unusual in that, except in cases of gross violation, motorists do not know with certainty whether at any given time they are breaking the law or not.

For drink-driving offences the breathalyser might be considered to play a role equivalent to the speedometer for speeding offences. But even if made widely available it would be a much less satisfactory instrument unless it were used like a speedometer for continuous monitoring. Because alcohol absorption rates vary so widely between individuals, and depend also on eating patterns and physical activity, even if a motorist were to check his alcohol level before setting-off on a trip it would not guarantee that he would remain within the law for the duration of his trip.

Laws which make a blood alcohol concentration above a given level a crime **per se** are also unusual in that they depend for their "success" on ignorance. The uncertainty which is associated with the offence of over-the-limit driving is often held to be of vital importance. The Blennerhassett Report noted that people often sought guidance about how much they could drink without breaking the law. The Report thought that such curiosity should be discouraged.

"Such requests ... suggest a widespread and dangerous assumption that it is safe to drink up to that level. Yet by

the time he reaches it a driver's ability is virtually certain
to impaired by drink. It ought to be far more widely understood
that impairment is progressive and begins to develop at a level
much lower than the legal limit." (DoE 1976, p.19)

The British consumer magazine **Which** was criticised for
publishing the information (October 1984) that the maximum number of
glasses of wine that a person could drink while remaining below the
legal limit is five, and that "the average man" could legally drive
two hours after consuming a bottle of wine. This information was
accompanied by the advice that "if you are likely to drive the safest
rule is not to drink at all." But this is regarded as Utopian advice
by Britain's Department of Transport. Its 1984 Christmas season
campaign against drinking and driving, bowing to reality, was based
not on advice not to drink at all, but on the slogan "Stay Low". This
campaign was accompanied by no quantitative guidance to help motorists
decide how low was low enough.

Examination of "alcohol-related" accidents suggests that drinking
drivers involved in fatal accidents are different in significant ways
from drivers convicted of driving while intoxicated. Zylman (1975)
found that they were more likely to be young, agressive and to engage
in high speed or dangerous driving. He contrasted these drivers with
the typical driving-while-intoxicated offenders who were "more likely
to have been fumbling along slowly attempting to negotiate their trip
without incident." (quoted in Jonah and Wilson 1983)

Drunk driving is widely denounced as wicked and immoral and
deserving of harsh punishment, especially when it results in death or
injury. It is a crime that arouses strong passions and crusading
zeal. Opinion polls (e.g. **Which** October 1984) frequently report a
majority in favour of harsher penalties. But opinion polls are
notorious for discovering that people are in favour of righteousness
and against sin. In practice it has proved to be an elusive offence
which is impossible to define with precision, which, in varying
degrees, is indulged in by millions of people, and which is regarded
by large numbers of non-teetotalers with profound ambivalence.

It is frequently argued that examples of temporary success
achieved by some drink-drive "blitzes" prove that the problem could be
solved by a combination of more draconian penalties and more vigorous
enforcement. Scandinavia is often held up as an example of what can
be achieved by draconian drink/drive legislation vigorously enforced.
But Ross (1976) has shown that the available data furnish no support
for the legislative deterrence thesis. His interrupted-time-series
analysis revealed no effect of the legislation on the relevant
accident statistics.

Ross's analysis suggests that severe drink-drive legislation is
only likely to "work" where it ratifies well established public
opinion. Ross notes the existence of a politically powerful
temperance tradition in Scandinavia. Many people considered drinking

and driving a serious offence before it was formally designated as such by legislators. The absence of a detectable effect of Scandinavian drink-drive laws on accident statistics suggests that the laws were symptomatic of a wide-spread concern about the problem, and that most people likely to obey such laws were already obeying them before they were passed.

Incentives

The New Hampshire Insurance Company currently sells in Britain a policy called "Chauffeur Plan" which offers up to £100 per week to motorists who are disqualified for motoring offences, including drunk driving. An advertisement for the policy states that "under the pressures of living in a modern society it is not always the 'bad' driver who gets caught for breaking the speed limit or any of the many highway regulations." This insurance is not only condoned by existing law, it is subsidized; the advertisement calls attention to the fact that companies and the self employed can claim their subscriptions against tax.

Such insurance is an incentive to law breaking, especially to drunken driving. To the extent that the purpose of laws regulating motoring is the promotion of safety, it is also an incentive to increased risk taking. It is acknowledged in the insurance business that insurance can, and usually does, alter behaviour. It is frequently pointed out, for example, that the consumption of medical services is powerfully encouraged by medical insurance, and that people insured against fire or theft take fewer precautions against fire or theft.

This phenomenon is known as "moral hazard", the implication being that people ought not to behave differently just because they are covered by insurance. In more neutral language moral hazard "is the degree to which the bringing into existence of a contingent contract itself leads to a change in the probabilities on which the contract was concluded" (Dowie 1980, p.23). The degree of moral hazard can vary widely, from someone buying insurance and then deliberately burning down his house, to a slight reduction in vigilance. It has been noted by economists that the behavioural changes stimulated by insurance, excepting extreme forms such as arson, are a sign not so much of immorality as of rational economic behaviour (Pauly 1968). To the extent that risk taking behaviour is governed by both the probable frequency and magnitude of possible adverse consequences, then something that reduces the magnitude is likely to increase the frequency, and vice versa.

This reasoning underpins all safety incentive programmes. Fines, or even imprisonment, are intended to substitute for, or add to, the adverse consequences of behaviour which it is sought to discourage. Conversely rewards for desired behaviour also seek to alter the perception of the costs and benefits associated with particular actions. With a few exceptions, such as no-claims discounts on insurance premiums, most official attempts to promote road safety rely on punishments rather than rewards.

There is no clear agreement about the appropriate levels of enforcement and severity of punishments required to achieve desired changes in motoring behaviour. In the United States in the 1980s a very strong lobby emerged demanding much more severe punishments for drunken driving. However, Jonah and Wilson (1983) argue that more severe punishments for drunken driving will have little effect so long as the probabilities of being caught remain below a level that most drivers consider negligible.

At various times numerous incentives to safe driving have been proposed to supplement existing highway safety legislation. Wilde (1976) suggests that such measures might be classified under four headings: reductions in the rewards of risk - such as paying truck and taxi drivers by the hour instead of by the trip or kilometre; reductions in the penalties for caution - such as flexible working hours to reduce the penalty for being late to work; increases in the cost of risks - such as fines for not wearing seat belts; and increases in the rewards for caution - such as greater reductions in the cost of insurance for accident free drivers.

. Unfortunately, all the examples chosen to illustrate this classification of safety incentives have serious snags. Attempts to regulate the method of payment for truck and taxi drivers would be virtually impossible to apply to self-employed drivers and would place regulated transport concerns at a serious competitive disadvantage. Mandatory flexible hours again could not apply to the self employed, would wreak havoc with commercial activities which depend on punctual collaboration, and would have no effect on the driving of someone who wanted to get to work early in order to get home early. The limitations of the seat belt proposal have been elaborated in Chapter 5. Interference with existing rate setting practices of insurance companies in order to have the riskier drivers subsidise the safer drivers would require the state to dictate all motor insurance rates. Sound commercial practice dictates that insurance companies should seek to ensure that each risk category should pay its way. If premiums for safer drivers were set at a level which required subsidy by the more dangerous drivers, then safe drivers would become a category of risk that the insurance companies would have no incentive to insure.

While the disincentives to safety embodied in insurance policies such as "Chauffeur Plan" are readily apparent, it is rarely noted that the same objections apply equally to all other forms of motor accident insurance. Without insurance an accident in which a driver is responsible for killing or injuring someone else would spell financial ruin. With insurance the financial consequences of irresponsible motoring are reduced enormously. In most countries motorists are required by law to purchase an extremely powerful incentive to irresponsible driving.

Training

While training is a perennially popular safety measure with legislators and safety organisations, there appears to be a fairly strong consensus in the safety literature that it has achieved very little. There are two main reasons: it tends to increase the population at risk, and it develops skills which encourage the taking of additional risks.

Training and testing are usually prerequisites for venturing independently unto the public highway. For the use of motor vehicles these prerequisites are usually formal and official; in most countries motorists must pass driving tests before they allowed to drive unaccompanied by a qualified driver. The preparation of children for confronting the hazards of the road is usually done by means of a combination of parental coaching, school training, and formal, though voluntary, safety courses. There is therefore a direct connection between training and exposure to risk. Until people are qualified they are not allowed to take certain risks. In Connecticut when driver education was eliminated from the curriculum of a number of school districts for reasons of economy, the number of road accidents involving teenage drivers decreased relative to the number in school districts which retained driver education (IIHS, 1985).

While it is sometimes recognised that qualification leads to greater exposure to risk, training is still defended on the grounds that the exposure would take place anyway or because the risky activity for which people are trained is in some way desirable. The purpose of training is therefore to reduce the level of risk per unit of exposure. However, there is evidence to suggest that motorcyclists with training are involved in more accidents than those without (Raymond and Tatum, 1977, Kraus, Riggins and Franti, 1975). And Williams and O'Neil (1974) found that drivers with specialist training for off-highway racing had worse on-highway accident records than ordinary drivers; they were more skilfull drivers, doubtless, but not safer. Robertson (1983) reports the results of a number of studies of the efficacy of road user education programmes and finds a dearth of evidence of beneficial achievement. He concludes that "research on drivers generally produces no support for the educational approach" (p.92).

Behavioural Solutions: Conclusion

Road accidents present a serious and most intractable problem. The annual death toll varies over time and from country to country, but this variability has no clear connection with measures implemented in the name of safety. The Partyka model does not preclude the possibility that all the safety measures implemented in the United States since 1960 might have had a steadily increasing effect. Possibly without these measures all the increases in fatalities would have been greater and all the decreases smaller. But it is difficult to see how such a claim could be verified.

The editor of **Accident Analysis and Prevention** (Haight 1984) has observed a tendency to a selective use of evidence in the interpretation of accident rates: "very often it turns out that when one of these rates has a slight downturn, everyone is eager to claim it, but when it goes back up again, no one wants to have anything to do with it." The Partyka model whose results are discussed above presents a particularly difficult challenge to those who would claim the downturns for particular road safety measures. Partyka insists that the model simply illustrates a "coinciding of changes among variables" and does not imply that safety programmes are unrelated to fatality decreases. However, for safety programmes to be related to the fatality decreases represented in Figure 7.1 a large measure of coincidence must be invoked. With the possible exception of the contentious credit awarded to the "1974 and after" variable, the closeness of fit of the model would appear to leave little room for government intervention to account for any of the year-to-year variation in fatalities.

APPENDIX

Application of the Partyka Model to Britain

Figure 7.7 displays the results achieved by applying a modified version of the Partyka Model to disaggregated road accident fatality data for Britain. t-ratios for regression coefficients are given in parentheses.

Figure 7.7a

Total fatalities = - 20630 (-2.46)
                   + 1.7428 X employees in manufacturing / 1000 (2.74)
                   + 0.3003 X employees in work, other / 1000 (1.44)
                   + 0.3041 X non-labour force / 1000 (3.54)
                   + 0.9563 X unemployed / 1000 (1.66)
                   - 752 if 1968 (-2.40)
                   - 413 if 1974 or later (-2.09)

Figure 7.7b

Car occupant
fatalities   = - 26738   (-6.92)
                   + 0.900 X employees in manufacturing / 1000 (3.07)
                   + 0.417 X employees in work, other / 1000 (4.34)
                   + 0.524 X non-labour force / 1000 (13.23)
                   + 0.617 X unemployed / 1000 (2.32)
                   - 371 if 1968 (2.57)
                   - 258 if 1974 or later (2.84)

Figure 7.7c

Pedestrian and cyclist
fatalities   = - 2838 (-0.75)
                   + 0.696 X employees in manufacturing / 1000 (2.41)
                   - 0.074 X employess in work, other / 1000 (-0.78)
                   + 0.060 X non-labour force / 1000 (1.55)
                   + 0.328 X unemployed / 1000 (1.26)
                   - 256 if 1968 (-1.80)
                   - 293 if 1974 or later (-3.27)

Figure 7.7d

TWMV fatalities = + 12738
                  - 0.150 X employees in manufacturing / 1000 (-.72)
                  - 0.088 X employees in work, other / 1000 (-1.29)
                  - 0.319 X non-labour force / 1000 (-11.33)
                  - 0.150 X unemployed / 1000 (-0.79)
                  - 64 if 1968 (-0.62)
                  + 187 if 1974 or later (+2.90)

Data sources: fatalities - **RAGB** relevant years; employment - **Economic Trends** No. 10, p.99, HMSO 1985, and **Employment Gazette**, April 1985, Vol. 93, No. 4, Historical Supplement No.1, Table 1.2, HMSO. Some 1984 data provided prior to publication by the Central Statistical Office.

8 Hypotheses and Lotteries

Summary of the Statistical Evidence

There have been gross decreases over time in all motorised countries in road death rates per vehicle and per vehicle mile. There are also gross differences in these rates between countries; the rates which prevail today in countries with few cars are similar to the rates which prevailed in the currently motorised countries in their early stages of motorisation. These gross differences conform well to the Smeed Law (Chapter 2).

All countries also experience variations from year to year in numbers of road deaths relative to population. In the initial stages of motorisation the per capita death rate increases rapidly and then levels off (see Figure 2.3.48). In both Britain and the United States road death rates per capita in the early 1980s were very close to those of the mid-1920s. There has been no clear trend in per capita death rates since the 1920s, and the variation about the average rates is very much smaller than the changes that have been experienced in per vehicle rates. In Britain the motor vehicle death rate per 100,000 population rose from virtually nothing at the turn of the century to 11.1 per 100,000 population in 1926, up to 16.2 in 1934, down to 9.3 in 1948, up to 15.1 in 1966 and down again in 1982 to 10.8. By contrast the death rate per vehicle in Britain is now less than one thirtieth of the rate in 1909.

There is no convincing evidence in national road accident fatality statistics relating safety legislation or programmes to any of the decreases that have occurred in either the per vehicle or per capita death rates (Chapters 3-7). There is convincing evidence that variations in numbers of fatalities are associated with economic changes (Figures 7.1 and 7.7).

Hypotheses

There are a number of related hypotheses which might account for the apparent lack of responsiveness of road death statistics to the efforts of the safety regulators. They all assume that road users respond to safety measures in a way that compensates, at least partially, for the intended safety benefit. The idea that road user behaviour might negate the effects of safety measures has been around in the safety literature for some time. Smeed in his 1949 paper notes

"There is a body of opinion that holds that the provision of better roads, for example, or the increase in sight lines merely enables the motorist to drive faster, and results in the same number of accidents as previously. I think there will always be a tendency of this sort, but I see no reason why this regressive tendency should always result in exactly the same number of accidents as would have occurred in the absence of active measures for accident reduction. Some measures are likely to cause more accidents and others less, and we should always choose the measures that cause less."

Taylor, in a 1964 study employing measures of galvanic skin response, reported evidence which suggested that drivers respond to variations in driving conditions in a way which tends to keep tension and anxiety at a relatively stable level. This he interpreted as indicating that subjective risk was maintained at a near constant level through a great variety of driving conditions. In a 1966 study entitled "Feedback in Accident Control" Cownie and Calderwood argued that "accidents are the product of a basically simple closed-loop process". They also anticipated the accident migration phenomenon discovered in subsequent empirical work (see Chapter 4).

"[There is a suspicion that] the role of material causes is not so much a generator of accidents as a centre of attraction of accidents from elsewhere in the system. In other words, material causes may determine the distribution of accidents without affecting greatly their total number. What has been called the 'black spot' approach to accident control may be no more than a method of spreading accidents more uniformly in the system." (my emphasis)

Such ideas emerged as the focus of controversy in the mid-1970s with the publication of studies by psychologists Naatanen and Summala (1974 and 1976), Peltzman (1975), an economist, and Wilde (1976, 1982), a psychologist. They all rested on models of driving behaviour which assume a direct link between a driver's perception of risk and his behaviour. More recently Fuller (1984), also a psychologist, has devised yet another model; it characterises driving as a "threat avoidance" activity. They all make the point, most emphatically, that economists and psychologists expect risk compensation to occur. The accumulated wisdom of both disciplines leads them to the conclusion that people react to changes in their surroundings that promise benefits (rewards) or threaten costs (punishments). This conclusion is supported by common sense and observation of everyday life. It would be extraordinary if behaviour did not alter in response to changes in perceived threats.

The Present Debate

The debate over these models is, so far, inconclusive. At the time of writing the work of Wilde is at the centre of the controversy. Wilde argues (1982a) that "the accident rate is ultimately dependent on one factor only, the target level of risk in the population concerned which acts as the reference variable in a homeostatic process relating accident rate to human motivation." In essence Wilde's model, illustrated by Figure 8.1 is extremely simple. It suggests that people have "risk thermostats". The settings of these thermostats can vary over time for individuals, and can also vary between individuals; typically the thermostats of young male motorcyclists will have very high settings, while those of middle aged women will be very low. The model also suggests that any "non-motivational" safety measure, (i.e. one which does not alter the setting of the thermostat), which is accurately perceived by a motorist, will result in behavioural adjustments which reestablish the level of risk with which the motorist was originally content.

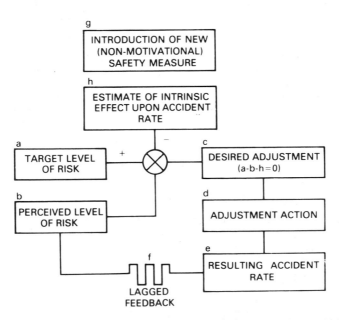

Figure 8.1. Wilde's Risk Homeostasis Model. Source: Wilde 1982.

Wilde's work has attracted criticism from a number of different directions. A good sample of these criticisms can be found in the commentaries which follow his paper in the journal **Risk Analysis** (Vol.2, No.4, 1982). His thesis is most unpopular with engineers and the devisers and enforcers of safety regulations; it directly challenges the claims made for the safety benefits of most of their work. It has also been criticised by others who accept the principle of **risk compensation**, but who consider that **risk homeostasis** postulates a precision of response which is not supported by available data. Evans (1984b) exemplifies this sort of criticism. He has encapsulated his position in a very simple equation which he calls the "human behaviour feedback model".

Actual safety change = (1+f)x(engineering safety change)

where **engineering safety change** is a measure of the safety change which would result from an engineering change (say better brakes, or improved crash protection) in the absence of any behavioural response, and f is a parameter which measures the amount of behavioural reponse or "feedback" in the system.

If there is no feedback, f will equal zero, and the engineering safety change will achieve its full expected (by the engineer) safety change. If compensation is complete, $\underline{f}$ will equal −1, and there will be no safety benefit; this represents risk homeostasis. Evans applies his model to a review of the safety literature and concludes that risk homeostasis represents a very special case. In practice he argues f can assume a range of values from less than −1, (over-compensation or false sense of security) to positive values (change in the direction "expected" but greater than expected). He accepts that

"The risk homeostasis approach ... could, in principle, be universlly correct in the long term. That is, the users could have a desired level of risk taking, and once all the information was finally received and absorbed, the previous risk taking level could be reestablished. ... [but] because of the ever changing nature of a multiplicity of factors in the traffic system, such a theory is not readily susceptible to experimental disproof."

Evans concludes
"What is here stressed is that every estimate of the future effectiveness of a safety change must contain some assumption regarding interactive effects. Such evaluations in the past have tended to include implicitly, without any discussion, the vitally important assumption that (in the present formalism) f = 0. It is recommended that in all future estimations of effects due to safety changes in traffic systems, the

question of human behavior feedback be explicitly discussed, and the assumed value of f be explicitly and clearly stated together with the reasons for choosing it."

The focus of contention in debates about risk compensation has now shifted from the very existence of compensatory effects to their magnitude. This is a highly significant development because, as Evans notes, until very recently such effects were routinely assumed by safety planners to be non-existent.

In a 1985 paper Evans attempts to refute the risk homeostasis hypothesis. He concludes that "as an explanation of traffic safety phenomena, the risk homeostasis theory suffers from the two major deficiences that there is no evidence supporting it and much refuting it" (Evans 1984). The evidence upon which Evans bases this conclusion is summarised in his 1984 and 1985 papers. In brief, after surveying a wide range of traffic safety statistics and studies published in the safety literature, he finds the response to engineering change highly variable, and hence inconsistent with an hypothesis which predicts a precise compensatory response.

It will be argued below that Evans' refutation is inconclusive. But first the role that the hypothesis has played in the recent debates about seat belts and other forms of vehicle occupant protection will be considered. Arguments about the validity of the theory have become entangled in arguments about the efficacy of specific safety measures. The next section will attempt some disentangling.

The Seat Belt Example

In Britain before a seat belt law was passed it was repeatedly claimed by the Department of Transport that a seat belt law would save 1000 lives per year. Although this claim is now no longer being made, it provides a useful number to illustrate the magnitude of the expected "engineering safety effect" of seat belts. At the time the claim was made there were an estimated 250,000 million kilometres being travelled per year by unbelted car occupants (Adams 1982). Thus the engineering expectation was that a seat belt law would reduce the chances of a car occupant being killed by one in 250 million per kilometre travelled. A reduction in risk of such a magnitude is not directly perceptible. It can only be deduced from the statistical outcome of large volumes of motoring.

The only real test of a safety measure is whether or not it reduces the number of people killed or injured. Thus, with respect to the Wilde homeostasis model (Figure 8.1), if an effective safety measure is introduced in box g the result should be detectable in box e, the resultant accident rate. The evidence reviewed in Chapter 5 suggests that there is no beneficial change visible in the fatality statistics of countries which have passed seat belt laws which can be attributed to those laws. This conclusion has been hotly disputed.

Mackay is one of the most prominent disputants. His 1982 and 1984 papers contain most of the arguments that have been put forward in defence of seat belt legislation. He accepts (1982b) that risk compensation sometimes occurs.

In a fundamental sense, risk compensation is likely to operate in the situations where a clear feedback exists between the presentation of risk and the driver. This occurs with most primary safety characteristics such as braking, handling and night-time visibility, factors which influence accident avoidance." But,

"in the secondary area [i.e the area of crash protection], if anything, the risk compensation theory appears to be reversed."

By way of accounting for the apparent lack of effect of seat belt legislation in the evidence presented in Chapter 5, Mackay (1981a) and other have argued that the "seat belt effect" was buried under other "uncontrolled variables". To date these variables have not been named. Nor has it been explained how their presumed effects have coincided so precisely the passage of seat belt laws in so many different countries.

Unable to find a beneficial seat belt effect in the resultant accident statistics of the countries which have passed laws, Mackay has sought to refute the risk compensation hypothesis by finding a non-effect in an area where measurement problems are much more severe - box d in Figure 8.1, "adjustment action". He argues that if drivers are compensating for the added security of belts, there should be measurable differences in their driving behaviour. The evidence that he offers relates seat belt use to travelling speed. He concludes that, "contrary to the Peltzman hypothesis" an increase in risk-taking does not occur with seat belt use:

"the difference in the mean speeds, 48.01 mph for belted drivers and 47.07 for unbelted drivers was 0.94 mph. The seat belt usage rate was 36.4%. Clearly the difference in mean speeds of less than 1 mph is of little importance."

"These results suggest that seat belt use, if it does provide a sense of security, does not translate into faster driving. This is contrary to a suggestion by Adams that belt use increases the risk to other road users."

Whether one considers the fact that belted drivers were found, on average, to travel about one mile per hour faster to be of "importance" depends on one's expectations. The difference in driving behaviour needed to offset a reduction in risk of 1 in 250 million per kilometre is likely to be extremely small.

In any event this evidence does not properly address the theory which it purports to refute. Speed on its own is a very incomplete measure of risk. There are numerous other "adjustment actions" to which drivers might resort to compensate for the added security of a seat belt: driving with less care and attention, while drunk, on bad tyres, with bad brakes ... etc. The same objection can be made to the work of O'Neil, Lund, Zador and Ashton (1984) which also seeks to disprove the risk compensation hypothesis using comparisons of the driving behaviours of belted and unbelted drivers rather than comparisons of accident records. They also fail to demonstrate that their measurement methods were sufficiently sensitive to pick up the extremely small behavioural changes postulated by the risk compensation theory. The only real test of whether safety measures work is whether or not they have a beneficial effect on the relevant accident statistics. None of the driving behaviour, by either belted or unbelted drivers, observed in the studies of Mackay and O'Neil et al was reported to have resulted in a single accident, either before or after seat belt legislation.

Another problem with Mackay's evidence is that voluntary belt use, or compliance with a belt law, is associated with other driver characteristics which are in turn associated with risk. The most common excuse used for the failure of seat belt legislation to achieve its expected effect is that non-wearers belong to a high risk group (Hurst 1979, Jonah and Lawson 1983, and Hearne 1981). Thus one would expect motorists who resist attempts to persuade them to wear belts (or who defy a seat belt law) to drive more dangerously than those who are receptive to safety advice (or are law law-abiding). To test the risk compensation hypothesis by direct observation of behaviour one would need to observe the behaviour of the same drivers with and without belts. Further one would require methods of measurement capable of detecting minute differences in driving behaviour, and a way of relating detected differences in behaviour to accident probabilities.

Mackay also misconstrues the hypothesis in an important way. He asserts

"The notion is that forcing people to wear seat belts will result in drivers becoming more involved in collisions, because being forced to wear a seat belt encourages greater risk-taking behaviour. Notice the distinction between voluntary and compulsory belt use. The hypothesis only applies to those who unwillingly conform to a belt law."

The hypothesis makes no such distinction. As can be seen in box g of Figure 8.1 the hypothesis relates to "non-motivational" safety measures. This does not mean "compulsory" measures, but measures which leave the target level of risk (box a) unaltered.

8. Hypotheses and lotteries

Some Questions

McKenna (1982 and 1984) raises further objections to Wilde's risk homeostasis theory in the form of four questions: (1) Do people have a straightforward representation of risk which directs their behaviour? (For example, does an alteration in risk of one in many millions affect driver behaviour?) (2) Do people always detect the presence of safety measures? (For example might penetration resistant windscreens be psychologically invisible?) (3) Do people always completely compensate for a change in risk? (For example, do drivers completely compensate for adverse weather conditions?) (4) Is it the case that people cannot be discouraged or prevented from compensating? (For example, do people compensate for the introduction of a pedestrian precinct?) He argues that if the answer to any one of these questions is "no" then the theory is at best limited and at worst completely misleading.

Robertson also questions the ability of people to perceive and act upon extremely small changes in risk associated with safety measures such as seat belt legislation. He asks "how many of us know the precise reduction of risk of injury that safety standards have provided? (Robertson 1983, p. 142)

These questions and others can be organised around the boxes a to h in Wilde's Risk Homeostasis Model in Figure 8.1.

(a) How does one measure a "target level of risk"? Is it the case that some people are prepared to take more risks than others? Such differences are largely inferred from differences in accident rates and behaviour. But Naatanen and Summala doubt that there is such a thing as a target level of risk, and attribute accidents to the difference between subjective risk of an accident, which drivers attempt to hold at zero, and objective risk; accidents, according to the Naatanen and Summala perspective, are the result of perceptual error. There appears to be no way of resolving this issue. Even physical measures of presumed emotional states, such as galvanic skin response, are subject to alternative interpretations.

b) How does one measure "perceived level of risk"? Again, there are no unambiguous physical measures. The values attached to this variable must be inferred from measurable behaviour or accident statistics. In Wilde's model the perceived level of risk is determined by prevailing accident rates transmitted via a lagged feedback mechanism. As McKenna and Robertson suggest, the magnitudes of the numbers which combine to produce these rates present a challenge to known human abilities to make sense of very large and very small numbers.

c) How does one measure the "desired adjustment"? The desired adjustment represents the assumed net effect of three variables, none of which can be measured directly: target level, perceived risk, and estimated intrinsic safety effect.

d) The "adjustment action" represents an inferred response to a stimulus assumed to represent the net effect of three unmeasurable variables. Driving skills vary widely. How might one distinguish accidents caused by skilful, but risky, driving, from those caused by driving which is cautious but incompetent?

e) The "resulting accident rate" is the only objective variable in the model, but, except for numbers of deaths, is usually recorded with a lack of precision which renders it virtually useless.

f) What are "lagged feedbacks" and how might they be measured? There are often circumstances in which delays occur between events, and knowledge of these events reaching concerned individuals. But if it is assumed that the perception of a risk is influenced by the level of concern about risk, then it becomes very difficult to know how to allocate the causes of delay between objective and subjective factors.

g) What is a "non-motivational safety measure"? It is a measure that some group of people must have been motivated to implement in order to increase safety. Effective regulation requires a degree of active support or compliance on the part of the regulated. Hence it is difficult to distinguish motivational from non-motivational safety measures, and therefore difficult to know, when attitudes toward risk change, whether safety measures are a cause or an effect of the change.

h) How is the "intrinsic effect" of a non-motivational safety measure estimated? This act of estimation is subject to the same uncertainties that are encountered in the perception of the original level of risk (see (b) above).

Further questions might be asked about relationships between the boxes in the Wilde model. What is the nature of the relationship between "target levels of risk" and "perceptions of risk"? It does not appear to be possible to distinguish with confidence between people who knowingly expose themselves to high levels of risk, and people who take large risks through ignorance.

Ought the diagram to have an arrow joining "accident rates" to "safety measures"? Such an arrow might be said to represent societal feedback, as distinct from individual feedback.

Does the model embrace all possible forms of risk compensation? Might people compensate for road safety measures by taking risks in other areas not recorded in road accident statistics?

The Difficulty

When it comes to answering such questions the difficulty with Wilde's Homeostasis Theory, and the alternative models of road user behaviour, is that they all represent formalised speculations about mental states and processes which are unmeasurable.

8. Hypotheses and lotteries

Evans concludes his 1985 paper with a plea for theory.
"The whole traffic research field has been characterised by a most unfortunate lack of theories, true or false. It is only through formulating and testing theories that our understanding of the subject can hope to advance. Without theories we are merely accumulating an ever increasing collection of information. Theories are central to fitting information into understandable patterns, and judging whether new information supports or does not support the pattern.

The risk homeostasis theory played an important role in helping to point out that engineering changes are only one of a number of vital ingredients in traffic safety systems. In doing this it played the same positive role that other now discarded scientific theories have played in contributing to our understanding. For example, the Ptolemaic theory that invoked epicycles to explain planetary motion; the Phlogiston theory that posited the movement of a substance (phlogiston) to explain the transfer of heat from hot to cold bodies. Although these theories contributed to understanding, and in many ways were necessary steps to fuller understanding, the evidence shows that there are no epicycles and that there is no phlogiston. This paper has shown that, similarly, there is no risk homeostasis."

But Evans has not shown that there is no homeostasis. The homeostasis theory can accommodate every single piece of evidence that Evans adduces to refute it. As the dissection of the model above has shown, the model incorporates so many unmeasurable variables and unverifiable assumptions about human behaviour that it is not refutable. For example, whenever accident rates increase or decrease it is always possible to claim that the change was caused by a change in the target levels of risk, or lags in feedback, or perceptual error, rather than by engineering safety changes. Or if these defences should fail it can be claimed that risk compensation must have occurred in other areas which lie beyond the scope of the statistical evidence so far collected.

Evans' Human Behavior Feedback Model is not an explanatory behavioural theory. It is a purely descriptive model which makes no attempt to account for the behaviour it describes. It provides a useful way of summarizing a large body of evidence which suggests that engineering safety measures rarely achieve the safety benefits expected of them. But the model offers no explanation of the feedback process; "feedback" in the model is little more than a label for the difference between expected safety effect and actual safety effect.

Evans' model is "scientific" in the sense that it can be used to formulate refutable predictions. It is possible to feed the model with values for f and estimates of engineering safety effects, and to observe whether or not the equation predicts with specifiable accuracy the results of implementing a safety measure. But the values of f reported in Evans' papers (1984 and 1985) are so uncertain or contentious, and vary so widely that this is unlikely to promote an increased understanding of the behavioural causes of accidents.

Not Refutable, but Plausible?

The protean character of behavioural theories provokes scorn from "hard" scientists. If a theory cannot be formulated in a refutable form, they argue, it can be made to prove anything. What use, they ask, are theories that can be made to prove anything?

If Evans' plea for theories to account for accident data is to be answered, then, unfortunately, in our present state of ignorance about human behaviour and the workings of the human mind, inferior standards of "proof" must be accepted. Behavioural sciences are still at a pre-phlogiston stage of development, and appear likely to remain there for some time. Most accidents are attributed to "the human factor"; however, the internal workings of this factor are but dimly understood. In the literature on the related subject of gambling there are a number of contending schools of thought. The psychoanalytical school offers a fascinating collection of explanations (Halliday and Fuller 1977), including Freud's view that gambling represents a "repetition of the compulsion to masturbate" (quoted in Dowie, 1980). Behaviourists favour the view that gambling is a habit which is "learned" as a result of having "stimuli" from the environment "reinforced". Functionalists note the ubiquity of gambling as a cultural phenomenon and seek explanations in terms of its social and economic function. Dowie (1980) presents an excellent survey of the subject and concludes that all these approaches provide useful, but partial insights.

The models of driving behaviour of Wilde and the others are speculations about what might be going on inside a black box. The algorithms by which they represent their speculations are conceptual devices. The boxes in the graphic representation of Wilde's model represent black boxes within a black box. They represent phenomena which cannot be specified in a way that permits rigorous quantitative testing of the sort practiced in the hard sciences. As yet, they can be subjected only to the test of plausibility.

How plausible is Wilde's homeostasis theory? I find it highly plausible, as far as it goes. It suggests (box a, "target level of risk") that people have a need to experience a certain level of risk. This accords with the widely held view that a world totally devoid of risk would be unendurably boring. It also allows for the fact that people appear to vary in terms of their propensity to take risks. Certainly this accords with my experience of the human race; some people appear to be careful and timid, others bold and reckless.

It allows (box b) for behaviour to be governed not by objective facts, but by perceptions of these facts. It suggests (boxes c and d) that behaviour in the presence of risk (which is most behaviour) attempts to keep desired level of risk and perceived level of risk in balance; why should purposeful behaviour do otherwise? It suggests (f) that perceptions of risk are related to numbers of accidents. And it suggests (boxes g and h) that **measures to make people safer are likely to be ineffectual if people do not wish to be safer.**

It is noteworthy that advocates of safety solutions who are critical of the hypothesis do not offer any alternative theories of road user behaviour to put in its stead. So far as I am aware, none of the critics of risk homeostasis would argue that behaviour is never modified in response to changes in perceived risk; they all, I presume, slow down when they come to a sharp bend in the road. But they seem to suggest that such responses are whimsical and highly unreliable, and in the case of measures such as seat belt legislation do not occur at all.

Does the Theory Provide a Plausible Explanation?

How should one proceed with a theory which is plausible, but not susceptible to experimental disproof? I would suggest that the best that can be done is to see how plausibly it accounts for the available evidence, and how well it fares in competition with alternative explanations.

In Chapter 1 it was noted that there are persistent differences in road death rates between nations, and between groups within nations. The Risk Homeostasis Theory would attribute these differences to persistent differences in target levels of risk. In the absence of a method for measuring target levels of risk this is a less than satisfactory explanation. But evidence relating causes of death to occupational status suggests a mechanism which might account for it. Fletcher (1983) has noted large differences in death rates between different occupational groups and impressively strong correlations between the death rates of men and married women classified by their husbands' occupations. The correlation applies not only to diseases, but to suicide and other accidental and violent causes of death as well. He proffers the following hypothesis to account for this.

"The occupational environment in which a man is working directly affects his cognitive structure, the way he thinks, his experience, his beliefs about himself and how to adapt to his occupational circumstances. This experience, and his response to it, influences his wife's cognitive structure, attitudes, beliefs, and behaviour through the mechanism of marriage."

The very large decreases that have occurred over time in deaths per vehicle, or per vehicle kilometre, and the (relatively) stable number of road deaths per capita are consistent, the theory would suggest, with adaptive behaviour mediated by a (relatively) constant target level of risk. The evidence displayed in Chapter 7 in Figures 7.4 and 7.6 suggests that such behaviour might be considered a societal learning process. As exposure to road traffic (measured in vehicle kilometres) increases over time, the death rate per vehicle kilometre decreases. During periods in which the growth of exposure is rapid, the learning process cannot keep up, and deaths increase. When the growth in exposure is low (or negative) the learning process gets ahead of the threat, and deaths decrease. Such an interpretation could also account for the fact, noted in Chapter 4, that oil rich middle eastern countries which have experienced exceptionally rapid traffic growth rates have more road deaths than predicted by the Smeed Law. Such an interpretation is also consistent with the economic relationships embodied in the Partyka model. When the economy is prospering traffic increases; when economic growth slows down traffic grows more slowly, or occasionally decreases. Thus exposure to the risk of a road accident varies with the state of the economy.

It has been noted for some time in the road safety literature that there appears to be a connection between the level of the economy and the level of road accident deaths (e.g. Partyka (1984), Hedlund et al (1984), Peltzman (1975), and many others). It is possible that not only exposure to risk, but also attitudes toward risk might vary with the state of the economy. It has been noted (e.g. Toffler 1980) that a great many things - from fashions in dress to sexual mores - vary with ups and downs of the economy. One might speculate with the help of the Risk Homeostasis Theory, that in times of economic prosperity life in general seems more secure, and people spend a greater proportion of their risk budgets on voluntarily selected risks, while in bad times, when people feel more at risk economically, they attempt to maintain their target levels of risk by cutting down on risks of a more voluntary nature.

Lord Bellwin, speaking for the Department of Transport in one of the seat belt debates in 1981, and presumably briefed by the Department's statisticians and safety experts, declared that the fluctuations in the numbers of road accident deaths were difficult to explain. He said

"In this country, road traffic deaths have dropped by 900 over the past two years, which is a very considerable number by any standard. Apart from the fact that we have had a Conservative Government for the past two years I can think of no other obvious reason for this improvement." (Hansard (Lords), June 11, 1981)

The strong correlation established by the Partyka model between employment variables and road accident fatality decreases suggests the possibility that the Government deserves more credit for this improvement than it might wish to claim.

The apparent lack of effect of safety measures as diverse as speed limits, blood alcohol limits, helmets, seat belts, vehicle safety regulations and road improvements can also be comfortably accommodated by the compensating mechanism postulated by the theory.

The Scope of the Theory

The evidence reviewed above has been shown to conform quite well to the expectations of the Risk Homeostasis Theory. However, it might be objected that this is but a demonstration that the theory can "prove" anything. If one selects evidence and makes the appropriate assumptions the theory can be made to fit the evidence and vice versa.

Most of the evidence discussed above relates to road accident fatality statistics. But there is no reason inherent in the theory to suppose that compensation for changes in the risk associated with road accidents should be confined only to behaviour which can be measured in road accident fatality statistics. In answer to one of the questions posed by McKenna above, the theory does suggest that people would compensate for the introduction of a pedestrian precinct. It also suggests that if motorcycles were to be banned, young men would find other outlets for their risk taking proclivities - they might range from sky-diving to glue sniffing.

Further, there is no reason to suppose that compensating behaviour should be confined only to areas of physical risk. Collinson and Dowie (1980) distinguish three types of risk: physical, monetary and social. The three appear to be related. People sometimes take physical risks in anticipation of monetary or social rewards. Also, as noted above, risks in one area may substitute for risks in others. Playing the stock market, betting on horses, or supporting contentious theories are activities which might serve in place of risk taking on the road to maintain target levels of risk. But it is difficult to imagine an experiment which could confirm or refute the theory with respect to any particular activity; there are simply too many ways in which compensation could occur.

The theory suggests that if government intervention succeeds in reducing the level of risk in one area, or activity, or time, it will pop up somewhere else - unless the intervention has succeeded in reducing the target level of risk. Figure 8.1 suggests that this may well be the case, and that target levels of risk may be very difficult to change.

The graphs represent indices of death by accident and violence (by all causes) for 31 countries over a period of 75 years. The indices are standard mortality ratios; this means that the effect of differences between countries, or over time, resulting from differences in age and sex distributions have been removed. The

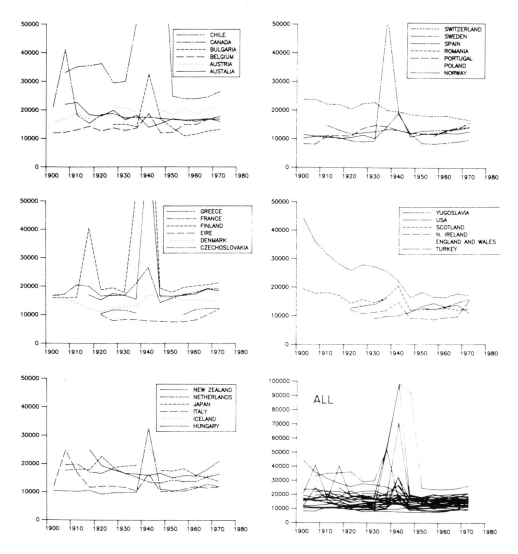

Figure 8.1 Indices of death by accident and violence (all causes, including homicide and suicide) for 31 countries. The indices are standard mortality ratios derived with a factor of 10,000. England and Wales for the period 1951-1975 served as the basis of standardisation. Source: International Mortality Statistics, M. Alderson, MacMillan, 1981, Table 177.

indices represent averages for periods of five years, e.g. the last value shown for each country represents its average standard mortality ratio for the period 1971-1975; for this reason the graphs should exhibit much more stability than graphs, such as Figure 7.2, which represent annual variations.

Interpreting data covering such a long time and so many different countries is notoriously difficult. The data cover a period in which the international conventions for classifying causes of death underwent a number of changes. The quality of the data can be assumed to vary widely over time and between countries. However, with few exceptions the data, like the road accident fatality data for Britain and the United States, exhibit no clear long term trend - there is a very slight upward drift apparent in most of the graphs after the Second World War. It appears, if the data are to be trusted, that over a period of 75 years, a period in which medical services have greatly improved, and in which all countries have conducted numerous inquests and safety inquiries, passed volumes of safety regulations, and appointed large numbers of safety regulation enforcers, that the graphs of the rates of accidental and violent death have remained remarkably flat - with the exception of marked spikes mostly associated with wars or very large natural disasters.

It should be noted that this flatness does not appear remarkable to some historians and demographers. In a survey of death by accident and violence in Britain since the thirteenth century, Hair (1971) discovered changes over time in the particular causes of accidental and violent death, but no apparent trend in the rate for all causes of death by accident and violence. Although rates in 1970 were below mid-nineteenth century rates, they were higher than estimates for most preceding centuries. He concluded

"British society throughout the centuries has struggled to control violence, and has frequently succeeded in taming one form - only to find another emerging. The axe of the drinking companion and the neighbour's open well were regulated, to be replaced by unruly horses and unbridged streams; when these were brought under control it was the turn of unfenced industrial machinery and unsignalled locomotives: today we battle with the drinking driver."

In an article entitled "Prospects for mortality decline in England and Wales", Benjamin and Overton (1981) construct a number of alternative scenarios. Their "optimistic" scenario incorporates the assumption that up to the year 2018 "the risk of accidental death remains the same, as some of the improvements in the environment are balanced by the appearance of new hazards" (p.25).

Lotteries

It has been argued that the Risk Homeostasis Theory depends upon the ability of individuals to perceive accurately, and react accurately to, minute variations in levels of risk. It is argued, for example that if the Risk Homeostasis Theory is to be invoked to account for the fact that the expected benefits of seat belt legislation have not materialised, then individuals must be reacting accurately to changes in the risk of death of the order of one in 250 million per car occupant kilometre. Not necessarily.

Driving might be considered as a morbid lottery in which the top prizes are fatal accidents. The random number generator that produces each day's winning numbers in this lottery has millions of moving parts, lethal machines erratically piloted by fallible humans. Each day these machines zoom, criss-cross, and occasionally collide — with each other, with pedestrians and cyclists, or with roadside obstacles. Individually these collisions are unpredictable, but the total number of winning tickets drawn every year behaves with remarkable consistency — usually varying by less than five per cent from one year to the next.

With every lapse of concentration or error of judgement a road user buys another lottery ticket. The chances of a winning ticket being drawn during any one kilometre of motoring are, as we have noted above, extremely small. The tickets are very easy to acquire. They can be bought by driving after a few extra drinks, by running on a worn tyre, by going a bit too fast, by driving when sleepy, or angry, or preoccupied, by showing-off, by skimping on maintenance .... etc. But the chances of any particular ticket being a winning one are negligible. Just as in a conventional lottery, the number of winning tickets drawn is probably a small but fairly constant proportion of the number of tickets bought. In Britain in 1982 on an average day 16 top prizes were won in the automotive lottery; in the United States there were 120 per day.

Some countries consistently have more fatal road accidents relative to their populations than other countries. Citizens of the United States, for example, with great regularity kill each other on the roads at an annual rate about 85 per cent higher than that achieved by Britons. But in both countries the chance of a fatal accident per risk taking decision must be one in hundreds of millions. While the percentage difference in per capita fatality rates is large, the difference in risk per decision is still measured in hundred-millionths, a difference of a magnitude not directly perceivable. Chapters 1 and 2 provide other examples of persistent large differences in road death rates between countries and between groups within countries.

Although most individual motorists could not say even approximately what risks they are taking, their collective behaviour implies judgements in the face of uncertainty that are, on average, amazingly precise. Wilde (1982, p.216) cites other examples of judgements which are individually highly erratic but which, averaged over large groups, are extremely accurate. The simplest and perhaps most convincing illustration of this phenomenon is the earliest example cited. Gordon (1924) asked 200 people to place a set of ten weights in rank order. The differences between the weights were so small that 15 per cent of the judges could not distinguish the lightest from the heaviest. The individual rankings correlated very badly with the true ranking; individual correlation coefficients ranged from −.81 to +.95. When rankings were averaged over groups the correlation improved markedly with the size of the group; when judgements were averaged over groups of 50 the four group correlation coefficients were +.92, +.92, +.94 and +.95. It appears that large groups are much better judges of probabilities than individuals.

The populations of some countries consistently spend a greater fraction of their annual incomes on conventional lotteries than the populations of other countries, and their average annual lottery winnings per capita are also correspondingly higher. If it were the case that the average American's chance of winning a million dollars in a lottery was 85 per cent higher than the chance of the average Briton, it would not necessarily signify anything about the abilities of individuals in the two countries to calculate and act upon very small probabilities, it might simply signify that Americans, on average, gambled more. Although information exists, for conventional lotteries, to permit the calculation of the odds of a particular ticket winning, most people buying tickets in a lottery participate in ignorance of these odds.

There is widespread agreement that it would be desirable to reduce the number of top prizes in the automotive lottery. But so far, no effective way has been found, and there is disagreement about what should be tried next. Some advocate reducing the number of tickets bought, either by compulsion or persuasion; others advocate physical engineering methods for reducing the proportion of tickets that are drawn. But if motorists' gambling propensities are not moderated, reducing the proportion of tickets drawn appears to result in the purchase of more tickets. And attempts to reduce the number of tickets purchased appears to have had little more success than the attempts of governments to suppress more conventional forms of gambling.

9   The Emperor's New Clothes

In the Hans Christian Andersen fable the emperor and all his courtiers and all his subjects – with one exception – participated in a grand conspiracy of self delusion. With the help of a pair of dubious tailors they persuaded themselves of the exquisite textures and intricate patterns and beautiful colours and overall magnificence ... of something that did not exist. This chapter contemplates the possibility that a similar phenomenon may be affecting judgements about the effect of measures aimed at promoting road safety.

The fable suggests that once an idea, however preposterous, becomes accepted by, and espoused by, established authorities it can become extremely difficult to dislodge. The idea becomes self-reinforcing. Authorities cite prior authorities, until the idea accumulates an authoritative pedigree. The idea acquires its own defence mechanism. Anyone incapable of seeing the Emperor's new clothes is "unfit for his situation, or unpardonably stupid." The fact that large numbers of other people believe the idea can become sufficient reason for believing. After a while evidence is no longer required.

The evidence justifying the original seat belt law in Victoria seemed very convincing. Detailed study of accidents, and experimental evidence, both supported the idea that in an accident a car occupant's chances of emerging unscathed would be dramatically improved if he were wearing a seat belt. The statistical evidence from Victoria, after its law was implemented, appeared to provide ample justification for compelling people to use seat belts. The rising trend of the 1960s in the numbers killed and injured on the roads levelled-off in the 1970s (see Figure 5.20). The life saving ability of seat belt legislation became a "fact".

This fact became the basis of seat belt campaigns all round the world, culminating in the passage of legislation in over thirty countries (Mackay 1982a). In each country, a central plank in the case for a seat belt law was the list of other countries which had already passed laws. As the list grew longer the plank appeared to grow stronger. Over time, certainly in Britain, the number of established institutions advocating legislation also grew. The British Medical Association, the Royal Society for the Prevention of

Accidents, The Royal College of Surgeons, the Royal College of Nursing, the Automobile Association, the Royal Scottish Automobile Club, and the Society of Automotive Manufacturers and Traders, are but some of the influential organisations which lent their names to the cause of legislation. In the House of Lords debate (June 11, 1981), Lord Avebury offered the list of institutional supporters as compelling evidence for legislation. "Why, after all," he asked, "would these institutions seek to mislead the public?"

But none of these organisations, and none of the countries which followed the lead of Australia, produced any compelling new evidence. They all cited the original Australian evidence, or other people citing the Australian evidence, or other people citing other people etc.. In all other countries the experience of legislation was disappointing to say the least. As Tingvall (1982) observes, "in almost every other country there probably exists a negative difference between the real effects and the expected effects of the number of killed and injured car occupants."

The principal piece of evidence presented in Britain to justify legislation was the Transport and Road Research Laboratory Report, "The Protection Afforded by Seat belts", by Grime (1979). This report examined two sorts of evidence: the effect of seat belts in crashes, and the effect of legislation in Australia. Grime stated in 1979, three years after the last of the thirteen countries covered by Figures 5.2 to 5.20 had implemented its law, "For direct evidence on deaths, however, it is necessary to rely on recent Australian data." (All the rest of the evidence surveyed in his study related to the beneficial effect of seat belts in crashes.) Why this was necessary, with the experience of a least twelve other countries available, was not made clear. Certainly none of the twelve other countries provided convincing evidence of legislation having had a beneficial effect on death rates.

By 1981 however so many countries had passed laws, and the belief in the efficacy of these laws was so deeply entrenched, that the disappointing statistical results did not present a serious challenge to this belief. The "confounding variables" theory was invoked to explain the results. What has not been explained is why the seat belt effect was thought to be so clearly visible in Australia, but so obscured by confounding variables everywhere else, and why these confounding variables appear to have been so consistently biased in their effect in countries which passed laws. Mackay states (1981b) "I simply cannot accept that there is a sudden switch in driver behaviour just because the wearing of seat belts is made compulsory." If one rules out the possibility of a behavioural change in response to the implementation of a safety measure, then an apparent lack of beneficial effect becomes evidence of the work of confounding variables.

As in the Hans Christian Andersen fable, people are grossly offended by the suggestion that something they believe in might not exist. Norman Fowler, Britain's Secretary of State for Transport at the time, was publicly accused at a British Medical Association conference of being "an accessory to murder" for opposing seat belt legislation.

"It is time for anger, it is time to tell the Minister of Transport that his failure to enforce the wearing of seat belts is tantamount to being an accessory to murder. And murder it is - mass murder." (Dr. Stanislaw Gebertt, quoted in The Times, 1.7.81)

During the Parliamentary debate which preceded the passage of the British seat belt law, various Members of Parliament suggested in various ways that I was "unfit for my situation or unpardonably stupid" for having the temerity to question the beneficial effect of seat belt legislation (Adams 1981b).

"The document [Adams 1981b] is extraordinary for a research worker ... I have had correspondence with many parts of the world from people who wish to prove to me, as I hope to prove to the House, that that piece of research was, as I have said before, bogus." (David Ennals, former Secretary of State for Health)

"... the so called new evidence of Mr. Adams ... He has produced an eccentric paper and has made the preposterous suggestion that wearing belts encourages people to drive more dangerously." (Roger Moate)

"Those who have attempted to look at the problem seriously find the evidence of Dr. Adams's paper highly spurious and bogus." (Roger Stott) (Hansard July 28, 1981)

And outside Parliament, Dr. Mackay declared that I was "doing the academic world a disservice." (1981c)

Research into the subject of road safety arouses strong emotions - for entirely honourable reasons. The duty of a researcher is to establish, so far as possible, what is true and what is false. If a researcher uncovers a truth with serious implications for the well-being of the public, his duty as a citizen obliges him to pursue these implications into the realms of public policy. The fact that safety research involves matters of life and death tends to create a sense of urgency in both researchers and public policy campaigners. These are often one and the same, and as a consequence attitudes and issues more appropriate to the latter sometimes intrude into the domain of the former.

Gatherings of road safety researchers tend to have an evangelical atmosphere. For example, in 1981, the American Association for Automotive Medicine and the Ontario Ministry of Transportation and Communications jointly sponsored a conference in Toronto on occupant restraint (AAAM 1981). The papers presented to the conference were "scientific" papers devoted to examining the effectiveness of methods of restraint and the medical significance of such methods. The purpose of the conference, was summarised in its agenda which declared it to be:

"A three-day Symposium highlighting the medical and public health aspects of occupant restraint, and the need for physician commitment to influence public policy, research and education aimed at increased usage of occupant restraint devices." (my emphasis)

In 1984 in Detroit the American Association for Automotive Medicine and the Society of Automotive Engineers jointly sponsored a symposium entitled "Advances in Seat Belt Restraint Systems" (SAE, 1984). The chairman's foreword declared the purpose of the symposium to be "bringing recognition to the gravity of the crash injury problem and the safety benefits of seat belt use."

A second foreword, contributed by Lee Iacocca of Chrysler, declared "seat belts are the most effective device ever developed for saving lives and preventing injuries." And the leading paper (Trinca) urged America to emulate Australia and make the wearing of seat belts compulsory; the paper argued that "a simple act of political courage would save countless American lives in road crashes."

Although both conferences purported to consider scientific evidence about the efficacy of legislation, their real and publicly proclaimed purpose was to win adherents to their cause. Clearly evidence which cast doubt upon the wisdom of this cause would have been unwelcome at these conferences.

For a great many in the safety field the issue has been settled and there is no need to consider further evidence. In February 1985 4000 copies of a safety booklet entitled **Road Safety Notes** were published by Derbyshire Constabulary. The following exerpt is taken from the booklet's leading comment.

"I am saddened by the rumblings of John Adams of the Geography Department of University College London, who apparently is leading the critics of the new seat belt legislation. At a recent Road Safety Conference in Detroit, John argued that the value of belting up to save lives and injury is open to question as a result of his findings. **Not knowing what his findings are,** I cannot challenge them. But I cannot fail to ask him – why since the introduction of compulsory seat belt use has there been a marked decline in fatal and serious injury ..." (my emphasis)

The atmosphere in which research on road safety questions is conducted can be morally intimidating. Anyone who cannot see the dramatic effects of road safety regulation in the United States risks being labelled by the **American Journal of Public Health** as an "ignorant nihilist" who is "symptomatic of a sick society" (Yankauer 1981). In the House of Lords debate on June 11, 1981 Lord Underhill insisted "it would be terribly dangerous if credence were to be given to any arguments against the benefit of wearing seat belts." Such pressures could well lead to a bias in the selection of evidence which is published. Such a bias would seem to be the only way of reconciling the numerous small scale studies which appear to show a safety benefit following legislation, with aggregate national statistics which do not. For example, the American Seat Belt Council has repeatedly cited (1978a, 1978b, 1980) a study of admissions to 16 hospitals in Sweden. The study compared the last three months of 1974 (before belt legislation) with the last three months of 1975 (after legislation). It showed a decrease in collision related admissions of 29 percent. The fact that in Sweden as a whole after legislation the number of deaths and injuries to car occupants **increased** slightly (see Figure 5.15) suggests that it must have been possible to find other sets of hospitals and/or months which showed an opposite result; but such results appear not to have been published.

Knowing that the publication of findings which could undermine public confidence in a safety measure is likely to invite the charge of dangerous irresponsibility - or implication in mass murder - could well cause many publishers, editors and researchers to hesitate. An example can be found in the May 1984 issue of **Traffic Engineering and Control**. The paper on accident migration by Wright and Boyle, cited in chapter 4, was followed by a paper by K.W. Huddart of the Greater London Council, the authority which Wright and Boyle acknowledge as having "provided help and advice without which the research would not have been completed." Huddart describes the paper by Wright and Boyle as "provocative" and declared that the GLC dissociated itself from its results. He also said

"We cannot agree that the evidence is sufficient to say that accident migration is a real effect, and we are certainly concerned that such a statement could unwarrantably impair road safety work. ... The danger of this type of paper is that it could reduce road safety workers' confidence in their work."

Such a statement must reduce the confidence of road safety researchers that they can publish findings which undermine confidence in established practices without impairing their chances of assistance from the principal source of road accident data for London.

British Self-Censorship

In the Hans Christian Andersen fable the Emperor sent his most trusted ministers to report on the progress of his tailors. The ministers were alarmed at their inability to see what they thought they were supposed to see, and reported back that work was progressing splendidly.

The Department of Transport insisted for many years that a universally obeyed seat belt law would save 1000 lives and 10,000 injuries a year in Britain. In 1981, a few months before the Parliamentary debate which led to the passage of a seat belt law, **New Scientist** reported (April 9 1981) that the Department was undertaking a review of the findings of my paper on the efficacy of seat belt legislation (Adams 1981b); the evidence reviewed in my paper suggested that seat belt laws had had no effect, with a hint of a perverse effect. The Department's review (DTp April 1981) was not made available to Parliament, and remained secret until shown unofficially to **New Scientist** in 1985 (reported in issue of February 7, 1985).

The Department's review included a comparison of road accident death statisticss for 8 Western European countries which had passed belt laws with those for Britain and Italy which had not – all countries which had been included in my study. It dissaggregated the data further than I had done, examining the statistics for "car users", "two-wheeler users", and "others" separately, and it subjected the data to more, and more sophisticated statistical tests than I had done; but it came to the same conclusion – the evidence was consistent with a finding of no effect, with a hint of a perverse effect. The report stated

"It is difficult to assess the effect of seat belt legislation in countries which legislated within a few years of the fuel crisis in 1974, particularly with few comparable data for countries without a seat belt law. A simple model suggests no change in death rates, and an 11% (+ or -2%) **increase in injuries** for all classes of road user, to have been the effect of the law. However, comparison with two `no-law' countries – and common sense – suggest that this increase results from the model [i.e the Department's model] being too simple, and that **there is no significant law effect**. A larger data base would be needed to test a more realistic model.

This 'o effect' conclusion appears to be at variance with the Department's estimates (for front seat occupants only). However, these related to voluntary wearing. It is perhaps conceivable that the estimated savings might be realised if voluntary wearing rose to 100%, but it is hardly possible to verify this." (DTp April 1981, p.13)

The report ventured its conclusions cautiously. It stressed the need for a larger data base before the question could be settled with confidence. The data base employed in the Department's study embraced Finland, Spain, Belgium, Netherlands, Norway, Sweden, Denmark, Germany, Italy and Great Britain. The data base upon which most seat belt laws in the world rest is that of Victoria in Australia, a state with a car population roughly equal to that of the city of Detroit.

9. The Emperor's New Clothes

It would appear that the standards of proof required of those on opposite sides of the debate are not equal.

The report also stressed that the Department's oft repeated claims for the benefits of a seat belt law were based upon extrapolations of data relating to crashes, and took no account of possible behavioural changes following a seat belt law. It insisted that "international comparisons provide the only information about the effect of compulsory seat belt wearing, both on car ocupants and on other road users." Thus at the time of the Parliamentary debate which led to the passage of Britain's seat belt law, the best informed speculation within the Department of Transport, based on the only information considered relevant, suggested that a law would have no effect, or possibly a perverse effect.

During the debates in both the Lords and Commons the old claim that a law would save 1000 lives plus 10,000 serious injuries a year was repeated frequently. In a debate in the House of Lords on June 11, 1981 Lord Nugent, mover of the amendment to the Transport Bill making seat belt wearing compulsory, commented on the findings of my paper.

"The evaluation of the significance of that paper depends upon the analysis of these global figures - the figures include all users: pedestrians, cyclists, motorcyclists and so on - to show what is related to passengers and drivers only, which is what we are talking about. I have asked the Transport and Road Research Laboratory for their comments on this interesting paper but it will take the laboratory some time to obtain detailed statistics from these countries. I hope that the Transport and Road Research Laboratory will then publish a reply. In the meantime, the laboratory adhere to their former forecast of the potential saving of life and limb from the measure." (Hansard (Lords) June 11 1981, col.324)

One month later Lord Nugent added
"I should be very surprised if, when it is time to make a complete analytical study of ... Adams' figures and his thesis, they are found to stand up to any serious argument." (Hansard (Lords) July 8 1981, col.722)

On July 7 1981 The Royal Society for the Prevention of Accidents (president- Lord Nugent) sent a letter to every Member of Parliament stating

"Dr. Adams has recently published a paper advancing the thesis that the wearing of seatbelts may actually increase road accidents by encouraging a sense of false security. His paper presents road accident trends in several foreign countries to support his view. His paper requires detailed analysis with the aid of much background information from the countries concerned before an authoritative comment can be made upon it. RoSPA and the Transport and Road Research Laboratory are undertaking these studies, meantime it is relevant to record that Dr. Adams does uneqivocally state that wearing seatbelts greatly improves the chance of avoiding injury."

This letter throws a revealing light on the campaigning methods of RoSPA. While publicly stating that much more work needed doing before they could comment authoritatively on my findings, privately they had been briefing selected Members of Parliament for three months with a document which asserted confidently that my conclusions were "absurd" and "without foundation" and that I "exhibited, at best, a layman's understanding of the situation." (The quality of the analysis in the document (dated March 1981) was such as to make it unsurprising that it was never published.) Their letter of July 7th twists my observation that in a crash ones chances of surviving unscathed are improved if one is wearing a belt, into an "unequivocal" statement that wearing seat belts improves the chances of avoiding injury.

The Secretary of State for Transport admitted during the debate in the Commons (July 28, 1981) that in the light of "recent work" things did not seem as clear as they had previously, but went on to say: "I stress that there should still be savings. No one would deny that." And Lord Bellwin began his contribution to the debate in the Lords (June 11, 1981) by saying "I should begin by emphasising the Government's firm belief that seat belts themselves save lives and substantially reduce the chances of serious injury."

Why was the Department of Transport's report not published? Why was Parliament not informed, before debating whether or not to pass a seat belt law, that the only relevant study undertaken by the Department indicated that such a law would have no effect, or possibly a perverse effect? A possible answer is suggested by the report itself. The Department was alarmed by, and disinclined to believe, evidence that contradicted its established position. The author of the report rejects the possibility, suggested by his statistics, that seat belt legislation might have a perverse effect, because such a possibility goes against "common sense". He also says, commenting on the results of his analysis of the injury statistics, "the predominance of positive effects (increased numbers of injuries) is alarming ..." In dealing with the evidence on seat belt legislation the Department of Transport and the Royal Society for the Prevention of Accidents manifest the symptoms of people, like the emperor's ministers, in whom a will to believe is in conflict with evidence.

United States Government Research

One further topical piece of research deserves attention. It is an opinion survey conducted by the U.S. Department of Transportation. In early 1984 I received a letter (dated Nov. 14 1983) from the U.S. Department of Transportation. It was addressed "Dear Concerned

Citizen". It explained that the DOT was trying to make a difficult decision - whether to require manufacturers to provide automatic crash protection in cars produced for the American market. It sought my comments. In order to ensure that my comment was fully informed, it sent me 81 pages of information on the issue.

Among the facts provided one finds the Department of Transportation's estimate that 10,200 - 14,300 lives could be saved every year if everyone wore an automatic belt. The DOT solicited answers to 91 different questions, but not one entertained the possibility of risk compensation. Nowhere in the 81 pages is the idea mentioned. The method by which the Department derived its estimate of the number of lives that would be saved excludes the possibility of risk compensation; the calculation is based upon estimates of the effect of legislation on wearing rates, and the effectiveness of belts in crashes. Nowhere does it allude to any of the evidence which shows that the expectations for the effect of seat belt legislation based on such calculations have everywhere been disappointed. At the foot of the letter itself was a small sketch of an open seat belt buckle, accompanied by the slogan
"Get it together! SAFETY BELTS SAVE LIVES".

The Department of Transportation has spent many millions of dollars on unsuccessful efforts to persuade people to use seat belts (IIHS 1977). The possibility that such attempts might have been not only unsuccessful but also misguided appears not to be one which the Department is currently investigating.

In the Hans Christian Andersen fable the origin of the belief in the Emperor's new clothes is attributed to the deception of the Emperor's tailors. In the case of road safety the origin of the belief in the efficacy of legislation has no such simple explanation. A willingness to believe in things for which there is no evidence is a common phenomenon. Rain dancers, legislators and safety experts all have an understandable readiness to claim credit for favourable events which appear to be associated with their activities.

If the road accident death toll goes up and down with the economy, as the Partyka model and much other evidence suggest, and if safety regulatory agencies are striving continuously to reduce this toll, then sometimes their efforts are bound to coincide with decreases in the death toll. In the United States the National Highway Traffic Safety Administration is the Federal Government agency charged with striving continuously to reduce the road death toll. The success of the Partyka model in accounting for almost all the fluctuations in the death toll with employment variables alone leaves very little room for the efforts of the NHTSA to account for anything. Hedlund is chief of the Mathematical Analysis Division of NHTSA and Partyka, Arnold and Cerrelli also work for the NHTSA. This perhaps accounts for the assertion in Partyka's paper (1984) that her statistical achievement does "not imply that other factors (such as safety programs and improvements) are unrelated to fatality decreases," and for the straining by Hedlund et al (1984) to give seat belts and alcohol programmes a share of the credit for the post-1980 fatality decrease. Partyka's model does not **prove** that the efforts of the road safety regulators have been ineffectual, but it implies that this may be the case.

Road safety research is a purposeful business. It is described in the introduction to **Road Safety** (RRL, 1963) as "the scientific study of the road traffic system ... with the fundamental aim of finding ways of reducing the number of road accidents or their severity." It is understandable that researchers and institutions with many years effort invested in this activity should be resistant to the idea that road accident fatalities might simply go up and down with the economy. Despite all their hesitations and qualifications, Hedlund et al remain convinced that the efforts of "the safety community" must have had something to do with the decrease in fatalities since 1980, and that if they try harder they can achieve further reductions. They conclude their attempt to explain the post-1980 traffic fatality decrease as follows:

"The safety community can take great pleasure in the 1981 and 1982, and preliminary 1983 results, but cannot expect these trends to continue without considerable effort." (1984, p.261)

The Naked Truth

Sweden provides the most graphic example of the Emperor's New Clothes Syndrome. Figure 9.1 is a poster from a Swedish safety campaign to encourage motorcyclists to wear helmets. The title of the poster is "The Naked Truth" but it is not necessary to read Swedish to comprehend the visual message of the poster - Riding fast on a powerful motorcycle is extremely safe so long as you wear a helmet - and anyone who cannot see the safety effect is either "unfit for his situation, or unpardonably stupid."

Ever since discovering this poster in 1980 I have been conducting a survey of motorcyclists' attitudes. It is not a scientific survey; my sample consists only of motorcyclists that I encounter at work or socially, mostly university students. Each rider is asked to imagine two sets of circumstances. In one the rider is wearing a helmet and visor, heavy leather jacket and trousers, and heavy duty boots; in the other he is bareheaded and wearing a T-shirt, shorts and sandals. They are then asked how these different circumstances might affect their driving behaviour. Without exception they have replied that in the less protected state they would drive more carefully. This suggests that the Swedish safety specialists responsible for the poster may have hit upon a novel method for reducing motorcycle accidents.

Figure 9.1 "The Naked Truth". A Swedish safety poster urging motorcyclists to wear helmets.

10   Risk and Freedom

"I recognise that there is hardly an issue that raises more
passions and more feelings throughout the country than the one
before us. We have been arguing about it for 10 years." (Roger
Moate MP, exaggerating only a little, in the Parliamentary
debate on seat belt legislation, **Hansard** July 28, 1981)

For ten years the arguing referred to took place between the
defenders of life, and the defenders of liberty. The idea that seat
belt legislation might not work struck most participants in the
debate as a novel one. Ivan Lawrence, opposing the bill, described
the evidence of Adams (1981b) as "astonishing and unexpected"; Roger
Moate, supporting the bill, referring to the same evidence observed,
"this is the first time opponents of compulsion have had something
that they regard as significant on which to latch." But for the most
part the debate, like all those that had gone before, focussed on
the balance which was presumed to need striking between the life
saving benefits of legislation, and the loss of freedom that such
legislation would entail. (Opposition to seat belt legislation has the
reputation of being a "right-wing" cause, but in Britain the
opposition spanned the whole political spectrum. Amongst those voting
against were Michael Foot former leader of the Labour Party, Jo
Grimond former leader of the Liberal Party, and Enoch Powell on the
right of the Conservative Party.) The two following contributions to
the debate exemplify the perspectives which distinguished the
participants on opposite sides of the issue.
"The question is whether it is right that we should legislate
on this matter. Is it desirable? Are we called upon to limit
the liberties that we are here to defend? The answer, taking the
broad view of the whole of human activity, must be that we are
not." (Percy Grieve MP, **Hansard** July 28, 1982)
"This proposal does not represent any interference with
basic freedom in the political, spiritual, psychological and
constitutional senses. Objection to it has nothing to do with a
love of liberty, but derives from the sheer exasperation of
being made to do just one more thing in this higly-regulated
State. However that one more thing takes only two seconds to do
and gives an enormous advantage in terms of safety." (Toby
Jessel MP, **Hansard** July 28, 1982)

10. Risk and freedom

The Cream Buns Argument

The essential feature of a law compelling people to wear seat belts, which distinguished it in the eyes of its opponents from most other road safety legislation, was the fact that it was a law designed to protect people from themselves. A number of opponents of the law produced lists of things, or activities, which are considered dangerous or unhealthy – smoking, drinking, mountain climbing, eating cream buns ... – and argued that if a law were passed the same principle which was invoked to justify making driving without a seat belt an unlawful act could be, and should be for reasons of consistency, invoked to prohibit all other items on their lists.

The supporters of the law replied to this argument in various ways. The most popular reply was a variation on the argument used by Toby Jessel, quoted above, to the effect that the loss of freedom at issue was trivial, and could be justified by the enormous safety benefit which would be gained. In any event Mr. Jessel insisted, if smoking, mountaineering, drinking and overeating were banned or curtailed by law then the activity itself would be inhibited, whereas the wearing of seat belts does not prevent anyone from driving where he wants.

The comparison with mountaineering is instructive. Consider the view of Michael Thompson (1980), a member of the successful British Everest expedition in 1975.

"High standard Himalayan climbing is, quite probably, the riskiest business there is: the chances of being killed are around 1 in 8 or 1 in 10 per expedition. ... The fact that it is also an expensive business makes it difficult to understand why anyone should choose to engage in it and scotches right at the outset the sort of explanation, favoured by some, that people take risks becasue they are poverty stricken. ... The aesthetics of high standard mountaineering are such that a proposed route is only felt to be worthwhile if there is considerable uncertainty as to its outcome."

One of the arguments for compelling people to use seat belts is that other interests are affected when someone is killed or injured in a road accident; the ambulance and rescue services, hospitals, taxpayers and dependants are the most commonly cited. If it is right to proscribe activities which risk imposing a burden on others, then the greater the risk, the stronger should be the case for proscription.

Thompson went on to note that the first British ascent of Everest led to a great increase in the popularity of mountain climbing, and an increase in the number of climbers killed. This led to safety codes, training schemes and Mountain Leadership Certificates. And even more people were killed. Thompson comments wryly on the growing regimentation in Outdoor Pursuits Training: "a programme inspired originally by a great achievement is now poised to bring about a situation in which such an achievement will be impossible." Insisting that a mountaineer use a safety rope, or wear approved clothing, does not prevent him climbing where he wants any more than requiring motorists to wear seat belts prevents them from driving where they want. But in both cases it changes the nature of the experience.

A **Sunday Times** article on the hazards of winter mountaineering encapsulated the apparent irrationality and ambivalence of participants in such risky ventures in its headline: "What to wear to risk your life as safely as possible" (Feb. 23 1984).

"Irrational" Risk Taking

The mountaineering example can be pursued further. The reasons why mountaineers voluntarily subject themselves to such high risks has been much, and inconclusively, discussed, not least by mountaineers themselves. Dostoevsky suggests an explanation

"What a man needs is simply and solely independent volition, whatever that independence may cost and wherever it may lead. ... I repeat for the hundreth time that there is one case, and only one, when a man can consciously and purposely desire for himself what is positively harmful and stupid, and even the very height of stupidity, and that is when he claims the right to desire even the height of stupidity and not be bound by the obligation of wanting only what is sensible. After all, this height of stupidity, this whim, may be for us, gentlemen, the greatest benefit on earth, especially in some cases. And in particular it may be the greatest of all benefits even when it does us obvious harm and contradicts our reason's soundest conclusions on the subject of what is beneficial – because it does at any rate preserve what is extremely dear and extremely important to us, that is our personality and our individuality."
(**Notes from the Underground**)

Might he be right? And if so, might his explanation apply not only to mountaineers, but to ordinary motorists as well? Mr. Jessel spoke of the "sheer exasperation of being made to do just one more thing in this highly regulated State." But why should a regulation exasperate someone when the thing that it compels him to do is good for him? Every regulation that compels behaviour that might otherwise be freely chosen reduces the scope of independent volition. Perhaps it is not only mountaineers who value independent volition highly. Perhaps if it is threatened people seek to defend it, either by flouting the regulation, or by reasserting their risk-taking "rights" in other areas.

The Risk Homeostasis Theory also suggests that a rigorously enforced law which seeks to compel people to be safer than they voluntarily choose to be can succeed only if people can be prevented from reasserting their risk-taking desires in other unregulated areas; such comprehensive regulation lies beyond the ambition of the most authoritarian of regimes. Although Wilde and Dostoevsky express it rather differently they both suggest that laws intended to protect people from themselves will not work **because** they infringe personal freedom.

In no country without a seat belt law do voluntary belt wearing rates approach 50 per cent. Yet many democratic countries have passed belt laws, and the evidence of opinion polls suggests that the laws usually have the approval of substantial majorities. A law reflecting the will of the electorate compelling people to behave in a way in which they could voluntarily choose to behave would seem to be a manifestation of collective doublethink; people who do not wear seat belts voluntarily, but who support a law compelling themselves to wear seat belts, are choosing through their elected representatives to be safer than they choose to be. It should not be surprising if their behaviour turns out to be inconsistent with their publicly proclaimed desire to promote road safety.

Reducing the Scope of Independent Volition

Most safety experts agree that the "human factor" is responsible for most accidents, but they argue heatedly over what should be done about it. The human factor has been much studied and found to be intrinsically fallible. One response to this discovery has been to conclude that this factor is incorrigible, and to advocate measures to limit the opportunities available to it to take risks.

"In terms of human vision and aural and intelligence limits, we must compensate through evolving telecommunications and microprocessing devices (the ultimate of which may very well be a brain implant) which will increasingly take over the complex driving task from the human, reduce decision-making to an absolute minimum especially at high speeds, and clarify information and traffic regulation at all points of decision. Only in these ways can a unified, systematic thrust reduce the world-wide highway death toll." (Cantilli 1981)

This proposal is to be found in the introductory chapter of a book entitled **Road Safety** (Foot, Chapman and Wade eds). While brain implants might be considered rather extreme remedies by many road safety practitioners, this passage nevertheless exemplifies the sense of urgency with which they approach their job, and the draconian nature of the solutions which many are prepared to entertain. The next quotation is taken from the concluding paper to the General Motors International Symposium on Human Behaviour and Traffic Safety in 1984.

"We are heading for an intelligent, knowledge and rule based model of the driver that will be capable of dealing with a wide variety of realistic, complex situations. In other words, we are heading for a psychologically plausible expert system or, if you like, a robot driver. At least that is what we should be heading for." (Michon 1984 in "A critical review of driver behaviour models: what do we know, what should we do?")

The ultimate safety purpose of intellectual exercises which reduce drivers to robots is to make drivers more robot like. Robots, at least well designed ones, do not have accidents. If researchers succeed in reducing the act of driving to its robotic essentials they will be better placed to regulate the behaviour of human drivers in such a way as to eliminate the causes of accidents.
Another paper at the General Motors Symposium confronted the issue of freedom directly, and concluded that on the road it should be sacrificed for safety.
"We need rules and, with the human motivational basis in mind, we have to enforce people to these rules. We know that enforcement is efficient if it is intensive enough but we also know that police enforcement is too expensive and it is feasible in major roads only. Why not hence develop efficient automized enforcement!

Twelve years ago, Naatanen (1972) proposed that a large register number should be painted at the top of each car in order to make possible to identify deviant drivers from an airplane or helicopter. With present technology, the basis for efficient enforcement could be an automized identification system, a black box which would be installed in each car at the factory. It would be a passive device, powered from the detection system, and the communication would use radio waves. The detection stations would be movable, except for the detectors in the pavement, and they would be able to check speed, driving at signals or other features in driving and, in the case of conviction, they would store the register number, date, time, and type of conviction on a magnetic tape.

Many of you certainly think that we do not want such a Big Brother. But we should remember that we already have such a Big Brother in aviation, the total accident loss of which is only a fraction of that of road traffic. And this proposal only means the same what the police officers are currently doing: they measure speeds of the cars, they identify those driving too fast in order to stop them and write a ticket. The automatic system would do only the same, and it would do it reliably. (Identification would be checked carefully.) (And, of course, such an identification system would be a dream to a traffic researcher.)

We can also argue that it is a democratic system. If we have laws for controlling traffic why should they not be enforced. It should be possible to prevent endangering other people's life by a car as is often the case with fast and deviant driving." (Summala 1984)

Technological advance has undoubtedly provided new possibilities for observing and controlling the behaviour of road users. It is now possible to provide vehicles with electronic number plates which can be read by roadside monitors. The information collected by the monitors can be processed by a central computer for any purpose designated by the controller of the computer. Hong Kong is now installing such a system to be used for electronic road pricing, but in principle there is no reason why the technology cannot be used for automating the enforcement of speed limits, for tracing stolen cars, or for keeping track of any vehicle of interest to the controller of the computer. There is in principle no reason why the enforcement of drink/drive legislation could not also be automated with the use of on-board testing equipment, with the results relayed via roadside monitors to a central computer. Beyond this lie future possibilities for automating the driving task itself by means of computer linked on-board radar. (A useful review of current and future possibilities can be found in **Computer Controlled Urban Transportation**, (Strobel ed, 1982).)

Safety Regulations and Sanctions

The idea that accident losses can be reduced by means of regulations accompanied by sanctions rests on an assumption that is central to the Risk Homeostasis Theory – that road users can be deterred from taking one kind of risk by the imposition of a substitute risk, the sanction for breaking a safety regulation. The substitute risk is usually financial, a fine, but it can also be social if breaking the law is stigmatizing; incarceration as a punishment for very serious offences might be considered to embrace all forms of risk – financial, social and physical.

It is frequently argued with respect to speed limits and drink/drive laws, that if regulation does not work it is because the substitute risk is not large enough or certain enough (e.g. Summala, quoted above, and Jonah and Wilson 1983). This explanation begs two important questions. Why are sanctions not sufficiently large or certain? How large and/or certain would they have to be to make a significant impact on the numbers of road deaths and injuries?

Summala, in the passage quoted above, hints at a possible reason, and dismisses it – **Big Brother**. It is well established that people behave differently if they think they are being watched. This phenomenon has become known as the "Hawthorne Effect", after the name of the factory in which it was first discovered. Researchers studying the results of changes in working practices designed to increase productivity, concluded that certain behavioural changes were caused not by the new practices, but by the fact that the workers were being observed. "High profile policing – the ostentatious monitoring of speeds, or searching for TV licence evaders are two examples – makes use of this phenomenon. The temporary operation of a Hawthorne effect may account for the temporary effect of short-lived safety campaigns such as drink-driving blitzes.

If there were the political will speed limits and alcohol limits could be lowered, the new technologies of observation and control could be applied pervasively, far more resources could be devoted to enforcement, and penalties could be made much harsher. Certainly there are lobbies and pressure groups campaigning vigorously for more, and more effective regulation, but there are also lobbies and pressure groups who favour less. At any given time the level of regulation in a democracy might be presumed to reflect the prevailing consensus, or balance between contending pressure groups. Where regulations attempt to compel behaviour which a substantial proportion of the population considers excessively prudent they are widely flouted with impunity. It appears in Britain, for example, that for many people breaking the speed limit and drinking and driving are not stigmatizing offences. In these areas the police, judges and juries, and the motoring public have settled for a level of compliance with the law considerably below what could be achieved, if the will existed.

Summala and many others see road accidents as a problem mainly attributable to "deviant drivers". Campbell (1973) suggests that this is not so. His study suggests that attempting to identify and ban motorists with bad accident records would not affect the greater part of the problem. The worst 1.3 per cent of the drivers in his study had had two or more accidents in the two years prior to the start of the study, but banning them would not have prevented 96.8 per cent of the accidents that occurred in the following two years. He concluded that, while it is possible to identify accident prone groups with two or three times their share of accidents, most accidents are caused by "normal but fallible drivers".

The great difficulty in reducing the number of road deaths by means of regulation is, paradoxically, that driving is so safe. It is very difficult to deny people something they might want, such as a few drinks, or driving a few miles over the speed limit, for the benefit of having their risk of being killed reduced by a probability measured in ten-millionths per mile driven. And it is difficult to get people to take seriously the idea that doing something that might increase the risk of a fatal accident by this imperceptible amount is a "crime". The frequency with which many road safety regulations are currently flouted in most motorized countries suggests that these regulations may be straining the democratic limits of driver perfectibility.

Criminal law establishes behavioural norms. It labels deviant, and imposes sanctions on, those who violate these norms. The behavioural norms enshrined in the criminal law of a truly free society will reflect majority opinion. If most accidents are caused by "normal but fallible drivers" taking risks which they judge to be acceptable, then attempts to prevent such events by the application of the criminal law are unlikely to succeed. The law is unlikely to work because it rests upon a logical contradiction: it rests upon the assumption that the great majority are deviant.

Altering Independent Volition

"It follows from the Theory of Risk Homeostasis that lasting accident reduction ... cannot be achieved by means of merely providing road users with more opportunity to be safe, but that safety **can be enhanced by measures** that **increase people's desire to be safe.**" (Wilde, 1982a)

"You will exclaim ... that after all nobody is trying to deprive me of my will; that all anybody is trying to do is to arrange that my volition will of its own accord fall in with my normal interests, the laws of nature, and arithmetic. ... you are wanting to wean man from his old habits and correct his will to make it conform to the demands of science and common sense." (Dostoevsky, **Notes from the Underground**)

All the approaches to "the road accident problem" reviewed so far, including Wilde's have been systematic. That is they treat accidents as the output of a "system", in the belief that if the system can be sufficiently well understood it can be modified to make it produce fewer accidents. The researchers cast themselves in the role of scientific servants to a benign authority which, with their advice, will intervene to effect the necessary modifications.

The Risk Homeostasis Theory and the evidence reviewed in earlier chapters suggest that attitudes toward risk are the principal, if not the only, determinant of numbers of accidents. Although accidents, after the event, can usually be attributed to specific causes, before the event they are perceived as very small risks. Although the theory is of little use for explaining individual accidents, it suggests that the total number of accidents incurred by a group of people over a period of time will be determined by the number and size of risks taken. If the number and size of risks taken reflects a willingness to take risks (what Wilde calls the "target level of risk") the number of accidents can be altered only by altering this willingness.

Parents of young children attempt this continually. When children are very young their safety is guarded by engineering methods. They are kept behind bars in cots and playpens. Their play environment is rendered as foolproof as possible by doing things such as covering electical outlets and removing dangerous objects. They rapidly outgrow such solutions. Then begins a protracted and anxious period of training and attitude inculcation during which children are led to assume a steadily growing share of responsibility for the safety of both themselves and others. This process involves the establishment of norms of acceptable behaviour and the use of punishments for violating these norms. Gradually parental authority weakens. The most dangerous time, measured by accidental death statistics, is between the ages 15 and 19, a period during which full responsibility is usually formally handed over.

Handed over to whom? While there is general agreement that parents ought to be responsible for the safety of their children (schools are said to act in loco **parentis** with respect to such matters), there is much disagreement about the extent to which the State ought to assume responsibility for the safety of its citizens. In particular, ought the State to take over the parental role of shaping attitudes toward risk? Wilde's theory raises an awkward possibility. Perhaps the annual toll of accidental death and injury is the toll that society desires.

Surely not! Are not accidents by definition events which no one wants or intends? Yes. But it seems that people are ambivalent. They do not desire accidents, but they do desire risk. Those responsible for the advertising budgets of car manufacturers have a large financial interest in assessing accurately the attitudes and motives of their potential customers. The conclusions they have drawn from their intensive market research are evident in their advertising. Excitement, exhilaration and performance are the themes that sell most cars - **adrenalin** is a word that features frequently in car advertisements at the moment. One of the most frequently recurring themes in car advertising is that of a high performance car being pushed to its limit. It is true that manufacturers sometimes also advertise the safety features of their products, but the overall message is at best ambivalent. Current Goodyear tyre advertisements provide a good example; a tyre which is claimed to make "a major contribution to road safety" is called the "Grand Prix-S". The conclusion of those who have probed the psyches of motorists deeply seems to be that motorists, like mountaineers, wish to risk their lives as safely as possible. But if a given large number of people take a given number risks of a given size, then the result will be a predictable number of accidents.

Should the State, acting in loco **parentis**, attempt to influence the risk-taking desires of adults in order to reduce the accident toll? Such intervention is not without precedent. In a recent controversial case in Britian a convicted sex offender was offered the

choice of a long prison term, or hormone treatment to supress his sex
drive. He chose the treatment (reported in **The Guardian**, December 4,
1984). Accident statistics suggest that the potential life saving
benefits of supressing risk-taking desires are very large. If, for
example, young men could somehow be equipped with the same behaviour
patterns and attitudes toward risk as young women their accidental
death rate would decrease by about two thirds.

What Should We Do?

· "Risk, it seems to me, is very closely linked to the
quintessentially human attribute of curiosity, which itself
becomes, in a rationalised form, the urge to discover and
innovate - by any standards a positive virtue. ... Risk implies
progress, definite movement, and advance from A to B. It is
associated with such concepts as growth, enterprise, dynamism,
acceleration, progress, upsurge, the process of stimulating and
energizing. All action implies risk." (Paul Johnson, 1976,
quoted in Collinson and Dowie 1980)

"The most difficult and time-consuming committee with which I
am currently involved concerns itself with safety and health at
work - trying to create a state of zero risks for employees in
their work environment." (Clive Jenkins, General Secretary,
Association of Scientific, Technical and Managerial Staffs,
Sunday Times, December 9 1984)

"Prudence is a rich ugly, old maid courted by Incapacity."
(William Blake, **Proverbs of Hell**)

Debates about safety are usually highly polarised. On one side are
to be found extreme libertarians who are prepared to brook no
interference with individual liberty - the gun lobby in the United
States is a well known example. On the other side one finds
organisations dedicated to the prevention of all accidents - the best
British example is the Royal Society for the Prevention of Accidents.
Those concerned to strike a balance between these two points of view
are usually shouted at by both sides.
In contemplating how the balance might be struck it is useful to
consider an example where the balance has been radically altered.

Japan

In Japan, as in most other countries, the road death toll
increased steadily and substantially after the Second World War. By
1970 it had reached a level (16,765 deaths) which prompted political

166

action. In that year the Fundamental Law Related to Road Safety Measures was put into effect. The law established the Central Council on Traffic Safety Measures with an influential chairman, the Prime Minister.

The Japanese approach to the road safety issue was impressively thorough - to most Western eyes draconian. The programme involved engineering measures, safety regulations and attempts to mould attitudes. Expenditure on road safety increased dramatically through the 1970s reaching a level of 1000 billion yen per year (about $6 billion) by the early 1980s. Most of this money was spent on the "improvement of the physical environment of road traffic" (Koshi 1984).

There was also vigorous activity in other areas. Japanese speed limits are very low. Of the 100,000 km of trunk roads in the country, 230 km have speed limits of 60 km/hr, 20,000 km have a limit of 50 km/hr, and the remainder have limits of 40 km/hr or less. Motorway speed limits are often 80 km/hr and nowhere exceed 100 km/hr. Passing is prohibited on virtually all two lane roads, even in rural areas. The legal blood alcohol limit is 50 mg per 100 ml of blood and is enforced by random breath tests. Road traffic laws are rigorously enforced. In 1983 one licence holder in 3.7 was subject to an "enforcement notice" for a road traffic offence (Koshi 1984). This compares with about one in 10 in Britain.

Penalties are severe. 1.8 million drivers had their licences suspended or revoked in 1983 (1 out of every 27). Government and private company employees can be fired without retirement benefits if involved in serious accidents while under the influence of drink. There are twelve special prisons exclusively for road traffic law offenders (Turner and Pettifer 1984). Throughout the 1970s more than 10,000 drivers a year were sentenced to prison for involuntary manslaughter or injury offences (Japanese Governemnt White Paper, 1980, Table 49).

The programme confronted attitudes toward risk directly. Pettifer and Turner (1984) describe the start of a day in one of the prisons for traffic offenders.

"Behind the barbed wire at Ichihara Prison, on the outskirts of Tokyo, hardened traffic offenders file out of the Dormitory of Hope. Dressed in white pyjamas and with shaven heads, they parade at dawn each day to recite a prayer of penitence in front of the Monument of Atonement, a memorial to road victims."

The Japanese Government White Paper on Transportation Safety (1980) describes the objective of the programme for offenders.

"The prisoners are provided with guidance in order to cultivate a spirit of obeying laws and a sense of responsibility and respect for human life... Group treatment or therapy of traffic offenders ...[aims] to bring about a reawakening or strengthening of the individual's basic sense of traffic safety consciousness."

But it is not only offenders who are subjected to official attitude moulding. The National Government budget for the "establishment of safe driving habits" was 41 billion yen in 1982 (about $160 million). This money was spent to ensure that "traffic safety consciousness should be stabilized in peoples' minds through organized activities in daily life." (p.110) The Government promotes safety publicity campaigns, safety fairs and conferences, school safety programmes, essay contests and other competitions, and an enormous number of national and local safety groups ranging from the Japan Traffic Safety Movement to the Traffic Safety Boy Scouts "in order to lift the nation's consciousness in the safety area."

Between 1970 and 1980 the number killed on the roads in Japan decreased by 48 per cent. By 1980 Japan had been transformed from a country with a bad road accident record into a country with one of the world's best accident records. What lessons can be drawn from this experience?

Given the comprehensive nature of the attack on road safety, and the fact that many measures were implemented simultaneously, it is extremely difficult to allocate credit for its achievements to specific components of the programme. Most of the money was spent on engineering measures, but it is not clear that these measures deserve the credit; there are numerous examples from other countries of engineering improvements being consumed as performance benefits rather than safety benefits. The statistics relating to the enforcement of road safety laws suggest that stricter regulation might deserve part of the credit. To the extent that compliance reflects general acceptance of the regulations, it appears that altered attitudes may have contributed to the reduction in the road death toll. After decreasing every year from 1970 to 1979 the road death toll turned up again in the early 1980s. Koshi (1984) observes that whatever might have been achieved in Japan in the 1970s by the applications of "conventional safety measures" such measures are now approaching their "saturation levels".

"One out of every 3.7 drivers is already caught each year and it will probably not be that helpful to catch any more drivers. ... The regulations have been decided rather arbitrarily by the local traffic police and are often inconsistent with the practices of the majority of drivers. ... The police have been trying to force drivers to obey blindly the speed limits rather than to teach them how to determine the proper speeds in actual traffic conditions."

"The only way that is left for us now to obtain further reduction of accidents is to improve drivers' behaviour."

But the experience of Japan suggests that behaviour

modification measures may also have their "saturation levels". Certainly the appropriateness for more individualistic Western societies of many of the Japanese endeavours to alter the national consciousness is questionable. In countries where it is held that it is the duty of governments to listen to what the people want, rather than to tell them what they should want, such measures are unlikely to be effective. It should also be noted that, impressive though Japan's fatality reductions of the 1970s may seem, by the early 1980s its road death rate, measured either per head of population, or against the Smeed Law, was very close to that of Britain, where a much more relaxed approach to road safety regulation prevails.

The Law of Diminishing Returns

Koshi's application of the term "saturation level" to conventional road safety measures in Japan is most appropriate. It describes a state of affairs known to economists as diminishing marginal returns. It is a commonly accepted fact of life in most areas of human endeavour. It can be found wherever the efforts of man run up against a natural limit. In economics it has acquired the status of a "Law". A popular text book illustration of the phenomenon used by economists relates to the maximum possible yield of an acre of land. There comes a point when no matter how hard a farmer works, or how much fertiliser or water he applies to his acre he cannot make it yield any more food. A similar state of affairs is currently causing concern to those in charge of health budgets. In developed countries most of the diseases which yield a high return in lives saved for money spent have been subdued. A growing proportion of medical expenditure is being spent on practices which yield progressively less in terms of lives saved or prolonged. It has been estimated that half an average person's lifetime medical expenses are now incurred during his last six months (reported in **Time** December 10, 1984). There is no limit to the amount that can be spent in pursuit of immortality, but there appears to be a very sharp limit to what can be achieved.

If risk taking is an inescapable human attribute, then the safety campaigner's pursuit of a state of zero risk will be as futile as the physician's pursuit of immortality. Haight (1985), editor of **Accident Analysis and Prevention**, makes the following observation

"Many years ago, it was not unusual to hear the opinion that we should aim at the total removal of all traffic accidents, or at least at the elimination of their consequences in terms of human suffering and property damage.

"Nowadays, I am sure that most people realize that this is a goal not likely to be achieved, but some would say that even so, it is a desirable goal. I would like to argue that it is not only unrealizable, but actually undesirable as a goal."

10. Risk and freedom

It is an undesirable goal because it recognizes no limit to costs that can be legitimately incurred in its pursuit. Consider the case of the Ford Pinto fuel tank discussed in Chapter 1. The injured victim's lawyers argued that Ford had "consciously and wilfully" disregarded the safety of people who bought the car. The jury accepted the argument and awarded the victim $128 million in damages. What had Ford done to deserve such punishment?

It was discovered that Ford had undertaken a cost benefit analysis of an alternative location for the Pinto's fuel tank which would have made it less likely to rupture when hit from behind. This safety improvement would have cost $11 per vehicle. On a vehicle fleet of 12.5 million cars and light trucks this would have cost $137 million. It then calculated that the omission of this safety improvement was likely to cost "180 burn deaths, 180 serious burn injuries, 2100 burned vehicles." At $200,000 per death, $67,000 per injury and $700 per vehicle it estimated the total safety benefit at $49.5 million. The estimated cost exceeded the benefit so the proposed safety improvement was rejected. The jury evidently considered this a callous calculation.

It was not so much a callous calculation as an absurd one. Whenever cost-benefit analysis is applied to questions of life and death it runs up against the impossibility of attaching a meaningful value to human life. The jury apparently thought that $200,000 was a derisory value to place on a human life. The conventions of cost benefit analysis require potential losses to be valued at a price that the losers would consider fair compensation. For the loss of a life this is clearly infinity. Convention requires the benefits to be valued at the price that potential beneficiaries would be prepared to pay. Immortality is not available at any price, and ability to pay is limited by income.

If the 12.5 million vehicles in the Ford calculation were to have travelled an average of 100,000 miles each, the added risk of being killed in a vehicle with the "dangerous" fuel tank per mile travelled would have been 1 in 6.9 billion. The safer alternative fuel tank location did not promise invulnerability, or even complete protection against a ruptured fuel tank; it offered an extremely small extra margin of safety. If offered a device costing $11 which promised a safety benefit of this magnitude, many people might prefer to spend it instead on a smoke detector for their homes, or a better lock for the front door, or a good meal, or a book, or ..... If the pursuit of zero risk becomes an over-riding objective there will be no money to spend on anything else.

But the costs incurred in the pursuit of zero risk are not exclusively monetary. Freedom must also be sacrificed. In a world without risk there can be no scope for the exercise of independent volition. The Law of Diminishing Returns also applies to costs incurred in the form of loss of freedom. If the level of risk to which people choose to subject themselves is greater than zero, then no amount of control short of padded cells and straitjackets is likely to achieve a regulator's objective of zero risk.

The conflict that exists between personal freedom and safety is an issue that is now being confronted directly by those concerned with the care of the elderly. In Britain the National Corporation for the Care of Old People has published a report entitled **Rights and Risk** on the problem of maintaining civil liberties in old age. The report argues that more risk is an acceptable price to pay for more freedom.

"I believe that old people are too often smothered by the way in which services are provided. They tend to get what other people think they need, not what they themselves are asking for, and all too often this can start them on a vicious spiral of loss of independence, and loss of confidence which can leave them apathetic human shells, 'warehoused' in a nursing home or geriatric ward. A two year old child has more choice than patients in some longstay wards and there are situations where a prisoner undergoing brain-washing is the nearest analogy." (Norman, 1980)

The pursuit of more safety is relentless and without any obvious stopping point short of zero risk. There is currently in the United States a pressure group called the National Coalition for Seat Belts in School Buses. It is reported to have 40 regional coordinators, and to be lobbying vigorously state capitols and school boards across the country.

It has been estimated that there are 390,000 school buses in the United States travelling 3 million miles a day transporting 21.5 million children to school. Since 1977 the NHTSA estimates that an average of 12 school bus occupants a year have been killed, making the school bus system one of the safest modes of travel available. At between $1200 and $1500 per bus it would cost about $500 million to equip the national school bus fleet with belts. There is no evidence that this would save **any** lives. The leader of the campaign for belts in school buses is quoted as saying "Parents don't want 'minor' injuries. They don't want **any** injuries". (quotation and statistics from IIHS 1985b)

In Germany a device costing about £100 called "Auto Notfunk" has been developed which will transmit an SOS signal to a network of receiving stations, which will in turn pin-point the location of the vehicle and despatch emergency services. The network of receiving stations would cost an estimated £300 million and have an annual running cost of £100 million. It has been estimated by the advocates of the system that every minute cut from the period between an accident and the arrival of the emergency services will effect a one per cent reduction in road deaths, and that the full system would reduce road accident deaths by about 20 per cent - about 2000 lives per year (Reported in **The Guardian**, March 25, 1985, and **RAC World**

March 1985). A fleet of helicopters to provide continuously hovering intensive care units would be a logical extension to such a system, if the money were available.

Another invention reported recently (**Sunday Times** April 7, 1985) is also claimed to be capable of preventing 20 per cent of road accidents. This is the percentage of accidents which it has been estimated are caused by drivers dozing at the wheel. The device is strapped to the drivers head. It detects jerks of the head and responds with an ear-splitting buzz to wake the driver up.

Therefore?

If a society's accident toll reflects that society's desire to take risks, if there is no way to reduce the toll without reducing the desire, and if it is considered unacceptable for Governments to attempt to regulate citizens' desires, is there any justification at all for governments interfering in matters of safety? I think yes.

The evidence and theories reviewed to this point suggest strongly that measures with the potential to make people safer tend to get consumed as performance benefits. This is not to argue that none of the performance benefits is worth having. I offer an example from my neighbourhood in north London.

For some time my local residents association has been campaigning for measures which will slow down traffic on a busy road in our locality. It is regarded as a dangerous road, and parents such as myself forbid their younger children to cross it unaccompanied. There have been meetings with the local authority officials responsible for road safety, and they insist that, judged by their accident statistics, it is not a dangerous road. This is consistent with the Risk Homeostasis Theory; the road looks dangerous and so people respect it. The theory suggests that if traffic were slowed down people's behaviour would change. More people might cross the road, people might take less care in crossing, and parents might no longer forbid their children to cross it unaccompanied; a potential safety benefit for pedestrians might be consumed as a performance benefit. There might well be no reduction in accidents, but there would still be a benefit for local people. The neighbourhood would become a more pleasant place in which to live. The freedom of motorists would be reduced, while the freedom of pedestrians would be increased.

It was noted in Chapter 1 that there are considerably fewer children under the age of 15 killed in road accidents now than there were in 1927. This does not mean that the roads have become safer. Traffic has increased enormously since 1927 and the roads have become much more dangerous. If children played in the streets today with the same heedlessness to traffic that characterised their behaviour 50 years ago there would be slaughter on an unimaginable scale. The reduction in the juvenile road death rate has been brought about mainly by changes in the behaviour of juvenile road users. Safety for children has been purchased at the cost of their freedom. Bunge (1971) describes the process by which children are progressively deprived of traditional freedoms as traffic volumes increase.

"Where could the Indian children travel across Fitzgerald's landscape [a neighbourhood in Detroit]? Everywhere. By the time of late farm days the fences were spreading yet children could still safely use most of the roads and wander in considerable open spaces like Holman's Woods. Today the children can move almost nowhere. They are more and more caged. Expressway fences and property fences continue to go up. These fences are often built with the excuse of protecting the children from the machines, especially the automobile, but it is the machines which are being given the space taken from the children."

Haight and Olsen (1981) note that the low priority accorded to the rights of children is betrayed by the language used to discuss the accidents in which they are involved. A category commonly used in the safety literature for the classification of pedestrian accidents is "dartouts". Haight and Olsen note that a more appropriate label might be "children".

Britain's Department of the Environment (1976) explicitly nominates freedom as a major cause of juvenile accidents.

"Every year 6000 children under 10 are killed or seriously injured crossing the road. ... The seeds of these accidents are sown in traditions of independence and freedom; sometimes also in thoughtlessness and lack of care. ... the Government have launched a campaign to bring home to parents their own responsibility for teaching their children this lesson for life."

The lesson for life which is impressed upon both children and parents is one of deference to traffic. School safety programmes drill children not on their rights, but on the importance of respecting, even fearing, traffic. This is a constant theme of **Care on the Road** the monthly publication of the The Royal Society for the Prevention of Accidents. The September 1984 issue contained a valedictory article from one of its longest serving contributors (Pummell, 1984). The theme chosen for the article was the necessity of keeping young children on reins. Pummell expressed amazement at the attitude of people who objected to reins on the grounds that it is "necessary for children to be free". This, she insisted, was "a grave misunderstanding of the idea of freedom." The campaigning energies of RoSPA, and most government safety officials, are directed not at the cause of traffic accidents - traffic - but at the need for people to adapt to the growth of this cause. As traffic increases more freedoms must be sacrificed to it, or the number of accidents will also increase.

It is not only the freedoms of children which have been sacrificed. Large volumes of motor vehicle traffic, and fast traffic, are powerful deterrents to journeys by pedestrians and cyclists of all ages. This deterrent effect has resulted in the severance of communities. Appleyard and Lintell (1972) have demonstrated the way in which pedestrian journey patterns are drastically altered and communities hemmed in as traffic volumes on residential streets increase.

The severing effect of traffic is a neglected field of study. Transport planners typically have vast collections of data describing the travel patterns of people in cars, and virtually nothing on the travel patterns of people on foot in the areas through which the cars pass. Official concern for pedestrian safety often exacerbates the severing effect of traffic. Safety problems are defined in terms of injury accident statistics; if a road does not have an exceptionally high accident rate it is not officially dangerous. It is not uncommon for safety officials to be asked to look at a road considered dangerous by local residents, only for the residents to find that by the safety expert's yardstick there is no problem; and where there is no problem, they are told, they are entitled to no assistance or relief.

Where potential conflicts exist between pedestrians and large volumes of vehicular traffic they have almost invariably been resolved by requiring the pedestrians to defer to the traffic. For the sake of safety, pedestrian railings, footbridges and tunnels are deployed to confine pedestrians to a reduced number of designated crossing points. The limited survey evidence available on such schemes shows that they reduce substantially the numbers of pedestrians crossing the road. It is now beginning to be appreciated that there are alternative ways of organising the relationship between people and vehicles. A few transport planners are experimenting with a reversal of orthodox safety measures. Instead of straightening roads, removing surface irregularities, and lengthening sight-lines, they are inserting bends, obstacles and speed humps, and shortening sight lines. Instead of separating people and vehicles they are mixing them. And instead of requiring pedestrians to defer to vehicles they are attempting to devise ways of ensuring that vehicles defer to people (Monheim 1984). The **Tokyo Manifesto** of the IATSS International Symposium on Traffic Science (1984), asserting the "rights" of pedestrians, cyclists and users of public transport, is perhaps a sign that such heresies are gaining ground.

While freedom for many has been curtailed, the automotive revolution has given those with access to cars considerably more freedom than they had before. This effect has been most dramatic for older teenagers. It has been noted in chapter 1 that less than half as many children under the age of fifteen are killed in road accidents now as in 1927. By contrast the number of 15 to 24 year olds killed has increased by 80 per cent.

This migration of accidents from the younger age group to the older has been associated with a reduction in the freedom of movement for the younger group and greater freedom for the older. As public transport services have dwindled with the increase in car use, younger children have become more dependent for their mobility on the services of parental chauffeurs. With their freedom to play on the streets curtailed, and their independent mobility by public transport reduced, the road safety of this age group now is probably under greater parental control than in earlier generations. Older teenagers, however, often acquire simultaneously both the use of a car and responsibility for their own safety. The combination of lethal machinery, sudden freedom of mobility and freedom from parental control is associated statistically with a very high death rate.

A Role for Government

The conclusion that more safety regulation is unlikely to result in more safety is not original. It is essentially the conclusion to which the Committee on Health and Safety at Work came in 1972.

"The most fundamental conclusion to which our investigations have led us is this. There are severe practical limits on the extent to which progressively better standards of health and safety at work can be brought about through negative regulation by external agencies. We need a more effectively self-regulating system."

The Committee quoted the 1969 report of the Chief Inspector of Factories.

"We have now reached a state where many of the causes of serious accidents which were once common have been brought under control, at least in most places most of the time. Methods of guarding have been greatly improved ... a very large number of accidents which can readily be prevented by physical means are now prevented ... yet reported accidents continue to rise."

The Committee when on to state

"It was argued in some submissions made to us that the sheer mass of this law, far from advancing the cause of safety and health, may well have reached the point where it becomes counter-productive. We share this view. The existence of such a mass of law has an unfortunate and all-pervading psychological effect. People are heavily conditioned to think of health and safety at work as in the first and most important instance a matter of detailed rules imposed by external agencies. ... **The**

primary responsibility for doing something about the present
levels of occupational accidents and disease lies with those who
create the risks and those who work with them. The point is
quite crucial. Our present system encourages rather too much
reliance on state regulations and too little on personal
responsibility and voluntary, self-generating effort."

The conclusions, and the reasoning, of the Committee on Health and
Safety at Work in 1972 can be applied, more or less intact, to the
evidence relating to road safety in 1985.

The conclusion that safety measures redistribute risks is also
not original. It is essentially the conclusion of Evans, a senior
General Motors research scientist. Evans (1984) makes the point with
the help of two imaginary vehicles.
"Consider two fictional hypothetical vehicles at either
extremum of a safety continuum. At one end, consider a
hypothetical 'invulnerability vehicle' in which it is almost
impossible for the driver to be hurt no matter how he drives.
At the other end of the continuum, consider a 'death trap
vehicle' -- one with, say a sharp pointed steel spike positioned
a few centimetres in front of the driver's forehead. This
example has generated lively discussion regarding in which
vehicle a driver would in fact be more likely to be hurt.
However, there is essential unanimity on the question of which
car would pose a greater threat to other road users. This
admittedly contrived example invites us to think about the very
small region of this continuum that can be considered to
characterize actual cars on the road. When we consider car
mass, which is closely related to engineering safety, we find
that drivers in larger cars, which are displaced towards the
safer end of this continuum relative to smaller cars, are
involved in more crashes and constitute a greater two-car crash
threat to other cars of all sizes."

The efficient organization of transport on a large scale requires
government intervention. Roads or tracks must be built and
maintained. Public rights of way must be established, often over the
objection of individual property owners. Vehicles must be regulated
in various ways; weight limits, noise limits, pollution emission
limits must be imposed to control the environmental damage and
nuisance caused by traffic. Where public transport services enjoy a
geographical monopoly they must be regulated to protect the interests
of individual users from abuses of monopoly power. And codes of road
user behaviour must be devised and enforced; a transport system
cannot function efficiently without rules which dictate who should
defer to whom in situations of potential conflict. While there is
considerable debate about the appropriate level of government

intervention in transport there are few who would dispute that in a highly mobile society the role of government must be a large one.

It appears, however, that regulation by governments in the name of safety has done little if anything to reduce the numbers killed and injured on the roads. But it has had important side effects. Vehicle occupant protection measures appear to have been consumed as performance benefits; one can now travel farther, or faster, or with less vigilance for the same risk of killing oneself. Motorways and expressways and pedestrian/vehicle segregation measures have facilitated the flow of traffic and thereby encouraged its growth. Safety training, beginning with the very young, has inculcated an attitude of deference to motorised traffic. "Safety" measures have redistributed risks and freedoms. Children have lost much of their earlier independence, and the mobility of pedestrians, cyclists, and users of public transport has been constrained. Whether or not these changes are desirable is a political question, not a technical safety question.

Conclusions

The argument of this book rests upon two propositions: a world of zero risk is unattainable and undesired; and behaviour is influenced by perception of risk. Risk homeostasis remains a plausible but unproven hypothesis, and the data for testing it remain frustratingly elusive. But there is an abundance of evidence for the existence of risk compensation. Only the magnitude and precision of the behavioural adjustment to safety measures remains in question. In the past the advocates of safety regulation have proposed measures which addressed the most immediate and specific causes of death and injury, and placed upon the opposition the onus, both moral and scientific, to prove that they would not work. If risk compensation is accepted as an inescapable corollary to safety measures, the onus is shifted to the advocates of regulation. They ought to identify the forms of compensating behaviour most likely to be induced by the measures they propose, and show that the resulting distribution of risks and freedoms would be preferable to the existing one.

Epilogue:
seat belts in Britain

The Scott-Willis Report

In June 1985 Britain's Transport and Road Research Laboratory released a report entitled "Road Casualties in Great Britain during The First Year with Seat-Belt Legislation" (TRRL Research Report 9, Scott and Willis 1985). The conclusions of the report with respect to the effect of seat belt legislation conflict with those reached in Chapters 5, 7 and 8 of this book. Scott and Willis conclude that the law was responsible for a saving in the first year of 500 fataltities, 6500 serious injuries, and 13,000 slight casualties. They conclude that there was no evidence of an adverse effect on "unprotected road users" - cyclists, pedestrians and motorcyclists.

The differences between my conclusions and those of Scott and Willis can be accounted for by the statistical models used, the data fed into the models, and the adjustments which Scott and Willis have made to their model to help it fit their data.

The Model

Scott and Willis use a multiplicative model having the following form.

$$C = V^V \exp (k + t.T + x.D + e)$$

Where C is the number of casualties (monthly),
  V is the traffic volume for the corresponding vehicle type and road class,
  T is time in months since December 1978,
  D is a dummy variable representing the presence of absence of seat belt legislation (ie D = 0 in the before period, and = 1 in the after period),
  e represents the residuals measuring lack of fit, and
  k is a "multiplier" estimated by the fitting program (it is allowed to take different values in each month of the year to allow for seasonal

variation), and

v is a parameter estimated by the fitting program.

The model was applied to casualty data for a number of different classes of road user - car and van occupants, pedestrians, cyclists, motorcyclists, heavy goods vehicle occupants, and public service vehicle occupants. The objective was to estimate the value of x, which Scott and Willis interpret as measuring the change in casualty frequency attributable to the introduction of the seat belt law.

It was the original intention of Scott and Willis to apply the model to monthly data for the period covering the years 1979-1983. The model fails a rather elementary test. It cannot postdict. If projected back into the period before 1979 it does not fit the data. The inability of their model to fit earlier data is the reason given by Scott and Willis for not using pre-1979 data.

"Earlier data were not included because there are known to have been marked changes in accident rates at about this time, so that figures from earlier years would have formed a doubtful basis for the analysis."

For some classes of road user the model did not fit very well even when applied to a period of only five years. Scott and Willis' solution to this problem was to reduce still further the limited number of years to which they applied their model. They observe:

"While it would have been interesting to investigate the reasons for this, and possibly fit a more complex model to describe the varying trend, it was decided that this would not be worthwhile (and, in any case, might not be successful). Instead the procedure adopted in such cases was to eliminate the earlier part of the period, and fit a model of the above form to the most recent data for which the trend appeared to be consistent, the view being taken that the most recently observed trends gave the best basis for prediction purposes."

The Data

Table E1 lists the road users classes and casualty severity classes to which Scott and Willis apply their model.

All the casualty statistics used by Scott and Willis, with the exception of the fatality statistics, have been widely rejected as being unfit for analysis. Summala (1985), for example, observes "only the figures involving fatalities are reliable among the different indicators of accident losses." An American study of the validity of police reported accident data (Shinar, Treat and McDonald 1983) found that "the least reliable data concerned vertical road character, accident severity, and road surface composition." They report that in

Table E1. The data used by Scott and Wilson

	Fatal	Seriously Injured	Slightly Injured	Fatal + Serious	All
Car					
Drivers	x	x	x	x	
Front seat passengers	x	x	x	x	
Rear seat passengers	x	x	x	x	
Drivers - built-up	x	x	x	x	
Drivers - non-built-up	x	x	x	x	
Occupants - single veh.	x	x	x	x	
Occupants - mult. veh.	x	x	x	x	
Van occupants	x	x	x	x	
Pedestrians					
Hit by cars or vans				x	x
Hit by HGVs or PSVs				x	x
Pedal Cyclists					
Hit by cars or vans					x
Hit by HGVs or LGVs					x
Motorcyclists					
Hit by cars or vans					x
Hit by other vehicles					x
Heavy goods vehicles			x	x	x
Public service vehicles			x	x	x

"Built-up" refers to areas with speed limits of 40mph or lower. "Non-built-up" refers to areas with higher speed limits. HGVs are Heavy Goods Vehicles. PSVs are Public Service Vehicles. Source: Scott and Willis (1985), Research Report 9.

over 30 per cent of the cases examined in their survey injury accidents were recorded by the police as accidents involving property damage only.

In Britain a TRRL study of 3641 casualties seen at a large accident hospital between 1974 and 1976 (Hobbs, Grattan and Hobbs 1979) found that nearly 28 per cent of the casualties seen at the hospital were not recorded by the police. The injury statistics analysed by Scott and Willis are police statistics. The degree of under-reporting varied with the type of road user. Table E2 summarises the findings of Hobbs et al.

Table E2 does not convey the full extent of the problem. An unknown number of injury accidents are not recorded by the police or hospitals. There is no legal obligation to report an injury to oneself in a road traffic accident. Thus in cases where a driver receives an injury as a result of behaviour which constitutes a motoring offence there will be a strong incentive not to report it. The number of unreported injuries almost certainly increases as the

Table E2. Under-reporting of casualties to police.

| | Percentage not reported | | | |
	Slight	Serious	Fatal	Total
Vehicle occupants	18	9	0	14
Pedestrians	40	18	0	27
Cyclists	71	59	0	66
Motorcyclists	46	27	0	36
All road users	34	21	0	28

severity of injury decreases. It is likely that police statistics for minor injury accidents suffer from the same bias that affects police statistics for petty crime - that to an unknown extent they measure the resources devoted to collecting them rather than the actual number of accidents.

There is further uncertainty attaching to the "serious injury" category. Separating slight injuries from serious requires police officers without medical qualifications to be able to distinguish sprains from fractures, minor shock from major shock, slight cuts from severe cuts, and to be able to recognise the symptoms of internal injury. In addition to the problem of applying the injury definitions Hobbs et al note that the the definition of the "serious" category is unsatisfactory; it embraces "injuries ranging in severity from detention in hospital for observation only [i.e. sometimes no injury at all] to spinal cord injury resulting in quadriplegia." Hobbs et al categorised the 3641 cases in their survey according to both the DTp's criteria, and the Abbreviated Injury Scale, the internationally recognised scale for the clinical classification of injury. According to the A.I.S. classification 405 of the non-fatal injuries were "severe," "serious," or "critical", and 3143 were "moderate," or "minor," or not injured at all. According to the DTp classification there were 1532 "serious" injuries and 2020 "slight" injuries. Thus the number of serious injuries judged by the DTp criteria was about three times the number obtained when the A.I.S. classification was used.

Table E1 shows that the road user categories for which definitional problems and recording difficulties are most serious, and under-reporting greatest, i.e. "unprotected road users," are the categories for which Scott and Willis rely upon the least reliable data. The reason they give for not using fatality data in their analysis of "unprotected road users" (pedestrians, cyclists and motorcyclists) is that the numbers are too small. To a considerable extent this is a problem of their own making. They reduce the size of their numbers by using monthly data instead of annual data. Then they reduce them still further by excluding from their analysis of "unprotected road users" all accidents occuring outside built-up areas. This is their explanation.

"Only casualties in built-up areas have been used in these analyses. The vast majority of casualties among unprotected road users occur in built-up areas, and it was thought that the inclusion of casualty and traffic data from elsewhere might only serve to obscure any effects which existed."

In 1983 20 per cent of all pedestrian fatalities, 42 per cent of cyclist fatalities and 47 per cent of all motorcyclist fatalities occurred outside built-up areas. Scott and Willis do not explain why they think the inclusion of accidents in non-built-up areas would obscure a "seat belt effect" for unprotected road users but not for vehicle occupants, whose accidents are not excluded. Certainly, as will be shown below, the effect of excluding them can substantially alter the impression given by the statistics.

It should also be noted that the reason given for not using fatality statistics for unprotected road users - that the numbers are too small - is not one which Scott and Willis apply consistently. They apply their model to fatality statisics for van drivers, van passengers, and rear seat car occupants, whose numbers are even smaller. The following are fatality statistics for 1983: 70 van drivers, 45 van passengers, 320 rear seat car occupants, 323 cyclists, 963 motorcyclists and 1914 pedestrians.

It might be argued that while the injury statistics are less accurate than the fatality statistics they should still be used because with large numbers the inaccuracies will cancel out, and large numbers make it easier to identify phenomena which are "statistically significant". Unfortunately, as will be shown below, in some cases the accurate numbers and the large numbers lead to quite different conclusions.

The Results

Figure E1 to E4 display annual casualty indices for different classes of road user for the years 1979-1983. The three severity categories - fatal, serious and all severities - have been transformed into indices, with 1979 set to 100, in order to reveal the way in which the choice of category can influence the conclusions reached.

Car Occupants. The solid line (fatalities) in Figure E1 is a magnified version of part of Figure 7.7b in Chapter 7, i.e. for the period 1979-1983. Comparison of the two figures shows how the nature of the trend estimated using the Scott/Willis model will depend on the number of years data fed into the model. If applied to data going back to 1973 the model would yield a pronounced downward trend which, projected into 1983, would produce a result much less favourable to their conclusions in favour of seat belt legislation.

Scott and Willis note that the trends identified by their model for car occupant casualties were more often upwards than downwards. As noted above, high values in 1979, which would tend to make the model yield a downward trend were systematically excluded if they were out of line with the following years. With the exception of the series for front seat passengers in built-up areas they do not specify which series they have truncated in this way, or by how much. (In the case of front seat passengers in built-up areas they apply their model to 1982 and 1983 data only.)

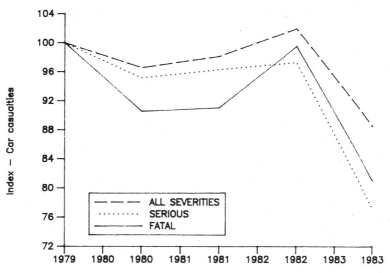

Figure E1. Indices of car occupant casualties: 1979–1983. Annual data. Source RAGB.

Another way in which they discouraged their model from yielding a downward trend was by removing the effect of the traffic variable, V. This is how they justify what they have done.

"In only two of the many series analysed did the best-fitting model ... include the traffic variable with a significant positive coefficient. In fact, in the majority of cases the best estimate of the traffic coefficient was negative (although not significantly different from zero), implying that as traffic increases casualty frequencies decline! ... However, negative relationships are not very plausible, so the traffic variable has been eliminated from the model in such cases..."

In other words, whenever their model led to the conclusion that casualties were decreasing as traffic was increasing they rejected the result as implausible and removed ·the relationship between traffic and casualties from the model to prevent it happening again. But Figures 7.4 - 7.6 provide reasons for believing that it is not at all implausible that casualty frequencies should decrease while traffic volumes increase. So long as the casualty rate per vehicle mile is falling faster than the rate at which traffic is increasing the trend in casualties can be down while the trend in traffic is up. This has been happening since 1973 and the modified Smeed model provides a plausible explanation for the phenomenon.

Pedestrians. In the case of pedestrians, where injury reporting rates are much lower than for cars, the correlation between reported non-fatal injuries and fatalities is much weaker. In 1982 the numbers reported seriously injured increased while the number killed decreased. In 1983 the number reported seriously injured decreased while the number killed increased. Using the fatality series there is no way that the model can be made to yield a rising trend because the number killed decreased every year from 1979 to 1982. The conclusions one draws from Figure E2 will depend therefore on the casualty series modelled (fatal, serious or slight) and the number of years to which the model is applied. Reasons are given above, and in Chapter 7, for preferring the fatality series applied to as many years as possible.

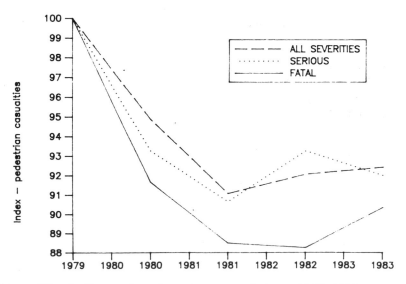

Figure E2. Indices of pedestrian casualties: 1979-1983. Annual data.
Source: **RAGB**.

Cyclists. In the case of cyclists, for the period 1979-1982, Figure E3 reveals that there is a negative correlation between serious injuries and fatalities; whenever one goes up the other goes down. The graphs for the injury series suggest that the increase in injuries in 1983 appears to be in line with the trend of the previous three years, but the graph for the fatality series suggests a sharp upward departure in 1983 from the prior trend. Table E3 shows how the exclusion of cycle accidents occurring outside built-up areas from the analysis can radically alter the impression given by the data.

Table E3   Cycle accident injury statistics 1982-83

| | Built-up | | | Non-built-up | | |
	1982	1983	% change	1982	1983	% change
Killed	187	186	-0.5	107	137	+28.0
Serious	4561	5003	+9.7	1112	1070	-3.8
All	24984	27389	+9.6	3152	3183	+1.0

Sources: RAGB 1982 Table 23 and RAGB 1983 Table 22.

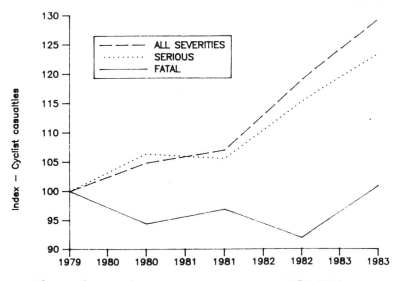

Figure E3. Indices of cyclist casualties: 1979-1983. Annual data. Source: RAGB.

It can be seen that there are very large differences between built-up and non-built-up areas in the proportion of injury accidents that are fatal. In non-built-up areas one accident in 23 is fatal. In built-up areas one accident in 147 is fatal. It has been noted in the main text that there are probably two reasons for this difference. Accidents in non-built-up areas tend to involve greater speeds, and more minor accidents in built-up-areas are likely to get reported because police and hospitals are more accessible.

Heavy Goods Vehicle Occupants. Again the injury and fatality series tell different stories (see Figure E4). Despite the fact that fatalities decreased by 12 per cent and fatal and serious injuries decreased by 2 per cent in 1983, according to the Scott/Willis model fatal and serious casualties increased by 12 per cent above the trend. As with the previous series, Scott and Willis do not say whether they have fitted their model to the whole five year period beginning in 1979, or whether they have used a truncated series, but the fact that an actual decrease in casualties is interpreted by them as an increase above the number estimated by their model for 1983, suggests that in this case they have allowed their model to register a decreasing trend. The number of fatalities is small, 59 in 1983, so the actual decrease in 1983 is not a very reliable indicator, but neither are the injury data upon which Scott and Willis rely.

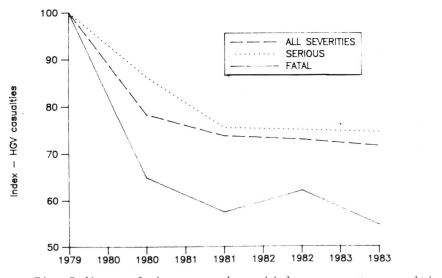

Figure E4. Indices of heavy goods vehicle occupant casualties: 1979-1983. Annual data. Source: RAGB.

Selected History

Scott and Willis cite the works of Grime, Vaughan, Vulcan, Lund and Zador in support of seat belt legislation (the shortcomings of these works have been discussed in Chapter 5), but do not deal with, or even acknowledge, the world-wide evidence presented in Chapter 5 which casts doubt on the efficacy of seat belt legislation. Most of this evidence has been in the hands of the Department of Transport for over four years. As noted in Chapter 9 it has been the subject of an internal DTp review, unpublished, which came to conclusions similar to those reported in Chapter 5.

They do not deal with any of the evidence relating to risk compensation. They note in their report that "it has been suggested" that such an effect may exist. They also say that the possibility of such an effect "cannot yet be dismissed."

Conclusion

In Chapter 7 the claims for seat belt legislation in Britain have been investigated with the assistance of two models - a modified Smeed model and a modified Partyka model. Both models have been demonstrated to have an applicability beyond the particular time period and the particular country to which they are fitted in Chapter 7. Both are accompanied by a rationale which accounts for their ability to fit the data. And both have shown an ability to follow fairly long time series through periods which include both rising and falling trends. The Scott/Willis model, by contrast, is applied to very short time series (maximum 5 years, minimum 2 years) and is supported by no reasons for believing that it is a reliable guide to either the past or the future. On the contrary, it has been accepted by its authors that it cannot postdict; and if applied to a number of 5 year periods chosen at random from the past 36 years it would clearly yield a set of wildly different predictions. The Scott/Willis treatment of unprotected road users is particularly unsatisfactory. It is based on wholly untrustworthy data and should be disregarded.

There is no agreed statistical method for determining whether or not a safety measure has achieved its intended effect. A survey of the safety literature shows that a very large number of different methods have been applied to this problem over the years. It is expected that the DTp's final report on seat belts (to be issued after this book goes to press) will make use of yet another set of statistical methods. It has been shown here, and in other chapters, that different methods can lead to different conclusions.

According to the DTp's own statistics in the 11 months after the law came into effect in 1983 the number of front seat car occupants killed decreased by 23 per cent, the number of pedestrians and cyclists killed by PSVs and HGVs in two-party accidents decreased by

7.5 per cent, and the number of pedestrians and cyclists killed by cars and light vans in two party accidents increased by 8 per cent.

It is argued in Chapter 7 that these facts are consistent with the possibility that the seat belt law decreased car occupant fatalities (below prevailing trends) and increased pedestrian and cyclist fatalities (above prevailing trends), and that both effects were temporary. But we are dealing with possibilities and probabilities, not certainties. In evaluating competing claims resting upon possibilities and probabilities it is often helpful to view them in the company of other similar "experiments". The evidence reviewed in Chapter 5 suggests that there is no convincing evidence that any other country which has passed a seat belt law has enjoyed a beneficial effect. If Britain **has** enjoyed a beneficial effect, it is the odd nation out. Those claiming a beneficial effect for Britain ought to offer an explanation for this phenomenon.

References

AAAM (American Association of Automotive Medicine) 1981: Proceedings: International Symposium on Occupant Restraint. AAAM, PO Box 222, Morton Grove, Illinois.

Abbess, C., Jarrett, D. and Wright, C.C. 1981: Accidents at blackspots: estimating the effectiveness of remedial treatment, with special reference to the 'regression-to-mean effect'. Traffic Engineering and Control, 535-542.

Accident Facts, published annually, National Safety Council, Chicago.

ACPO (Association of Chief Police Officers) 1984: minutes of evidence, the House of Commons Transport Committee Report on Road Safety, Vol. III, HMSO.

Adams, J.G.U. 1981: Transport Planning: Vision and Practice, London, Routledge and Kegan Paul.

Adams, J.G.U. 1981b: The efficacy of seat belt legislation: a comparative study of road accident fatality statistics from 18 countries. Occasional Paper, Department of Geography, University College London.

Adams, J.G.U. 1982: The efficacy of seat belt legislation. Society of Automotive Engineers, SAE paper no. 820819, Warrendale, PA. Also published in SAE Transactions 1982, 2824-2838.

Adams, J.G.U. 1983: Public safety legislation and the risk Compensation hypothesis: the example of motorcycle helmet legislation. Environment and Planning C, vol. 1, 193-203.

Adams, J.G.U. 1984: Smeed's Law, seat belts and the emperor's new clothes. paper presented to the International Symposium "Human Behavior and Traffic Safety", Warren Michigan, September 23-25. To be published in a book with the same title, edited by L. Evans and R. Schwing (Plenum Press, 1985, in press).

Appleyard, D. and Lintell, M. 1972: The environmental quality of city streets: the residents' view point. American Institute of Planners Journal, March, pp. 84-101.

ASBC (American Seat Belt Council) 1978a: Evidence to Safety Belt Usage. See DoT below.

ASBC 1978b: Seat Belt Use Abroad. Suite 460, 1730 Pennsylvania Avenue, Washington D.C.

ASBC 1980: International Seat Belt and Child Restraint Use Laws. Suite 460, 1730 Pennsylvania Avenue, Washington D.C.

Asogwa, S.E. 1980: The crash helmet legislation in Nigeria. Accident Analysis and Prevention, vol. 12, 213-216.

Australian House of Representatives Standing Committee on Road Safety, Report on Passenger Motor Vehicle Safety, May 1976, Parliamentary Paper no.156/1976.

Baker, S.P. 1980: On lobbies, liberty, and the public good. **American Journal of Public Health**. vol. 70, 273-274.

Benjamin, B. and Overton, E. 1981: Prospects for mortality decline in England and Wales. **Population Trends** 23, HMSO, 22-29.

Blalock, H.M. 1960: **Social Statistics**. McGraw Hill, New York.

Bohlin, N.I. 1967: A statistical analysis of 28,000 accident cases with emphasis on occupant restraint value. Proc. of 11th STAPP Conference, SAE, New York.

Bohlin, N.I. and Aasberg, A. 1976: A review of seat belt crash performance in modern Volvo vehicles. Proc. of Seat **Belt Seminar**, conducted by the Commonwealth Department of Transport, Melbourne.

Bohlin, N.I. 1977: Fifteen years with the three point safety belt. Proc. of 6th Conference of IAATM, Melbourne.

Borkenstein, R.F. 1972: A panoramic view of alcohol, drugs and traffic safety. **Police** 16, 6-15.

Bunge, W. 1971: **Fitzgerald: Geography of a Revolution**, Schenkman Publishing Co., Cambridge, Mass.

Campbell, B.J. 1973: Accident proneness and driver licence programs. Paper presented to the First International Conference on Driver Behavior, organized by the International Drivers' Behavior Research Association, Zurich, Switzerland.

Campbell, B.J. 1978: Evidence to Safety Belt Usage. See DoT below.

Cantilli, E.J. 1981: Highway safety: past and future. See Foot, Chapman, Wade (eds).

Chenier, T.C. and Evans, L. 1984: **Motorcyclist Fatalities and the Repeal of Mandatory Helmet Wearing Laws**. General Motors Research Publication GMR-4832, September 25.

Chodkiewicz, J.P. and Dubarry, B. 1977: Effects of mandatory seat belt wearing legislation in France. Paper presented to 6th Conference of IAATM, Melbourne.

Collinson, D. and Dowie, J. 1980: Concepts and classifications. **Risk and Rationality**, Block 1, Unit 1, of Open University Course on Risk, Open University Press.

Cownie, A.R. and Calderwood, J.H. 1966: Feedback in accident control. **Operational Research Quarterly**, vol. 17, no. 3, 253-262.

Crinion, J.D., Foldvary, L.A. and Lane, J.C. 1975: The effect on casualties of a compulsory seat belt wearing law in South Australia. **Accident Anlysis and Prevention**, 81-89.

Derbyshire Constabulary 1985: **Road Safety Notes**. Operational Support Division, Butterly Hall, Ripley, Derby.

DoE (Department of the Environment) 1976: **Drinking and Driving**, London, HMSO (known as the Blennerhassett Report).

DoE 1976b: **Transport Policy: A Consultation Document**, vol. 1, HMSO.

DoT (US Department of Transport) 1978: **Safety Belt Usage**.

Hearings before the subcommittee on investigations and review, of the committee on public works and transportation, US House of Representatives (95-39), US Government Printing Office.

DTp (Department of Transport) April 1981: Seat belt savings: implications of European statistics. Study report in New Scientist February 7, 1985. It may, or may not, be available on request from STG Division, 2 Marsham St. London SW1.

Dowie, J. 1980: Gambling and Gamblers. The World of Monetary Risk, Block 2 Unit 6 of Open University Course on Risk, Open University Press.

Duff, J.T. 1971: The effects of small road improvements on accidents. Traffic Engineering and Control, 244-245.

Ebbecke, G.M. and Shuster, J.J. 1977: Areawide impact of traffic control devices. Transportation Research Board Record 644, Transportation Research Board, Washington D.C.

Evans, L. and Wasielewski, P. 1983: Do drivers of small cars take less risk in everyday driving?. General Motors Research Publication, GMR-4425.

Evans, L. 1983: Accident involvement rate and car size. General Motors Research Publication, GMR-4453.

Evans, L. 1984: Driver behavior revealed in relations involving car mass. Conference paper, General Motors Symposium on "Human Behavior and Traffic Safety". To be published in a book with the same title, edited by L. Evans and R. Schwing (Plenum Press, 1985, in press).

Evans, L. 1984b: Human behavior feedback and traffic safety. General Motors Research Publication, GMR-4766.

Evans, L. 1985: Risk homeostasis theory and traffic accident data. General Motors Research Publication, GMR-4910.

Fletcher, B. C. 1983: Marital relationships as a cause of death: an analysis of occupational mortality and the hidden consequence of marriage - some U.K. data. Human Relations. vol. 36, 2, 123-134.

Foldvary, L.A. and Lane, J.C. 1974: The effectiveness of compulsory wearing of seat belts in casualty reduction. Accident Analysis and Prevention, 59-81.

Foot, H.C., Chapman, A.J. and Wade, F.M. 1981: Road Safety: Research and Practice, New York, Praeger.

Fuller, R. 1984: A conceptualization of driving behaviour as threat Avoidance. Ergonomics, vol.27, no.11, 1139-1155.

Gordon K. 1924: Group judgements in the field of lifted weights. Journal of Experimental Psychology, vol. VII, 398-400.

Grime, G. 1979: The Protection Afforded by Seat Belts, Transport and Road Reasearch Laboratory Report, SR449, Crowthorne, Berks.

Haight, F. and Olsen, R.A. 1981: Pedestrian safety in the United States: some recent trends. Accident Analysis and Prevention, pp. 43-55.

Haight, F.A. 1984: chairman's introduction to first session of General Motors Symposium on Human Behavior and Traffic Safety. To be published in a book with the same title, edited by L. Evans and R. Schwing (Plenum Press, 1985, in press).

Haight, F.A. 1985: The developmental stages of motorization: implications for safety. Mimeo, Pennsylvania Transportation Institute, Penn. State University, University Park PA 16802.

Hair, P.E.H. 1971: Deaths from violence in Britain: a tentative survey. Population Studies, Vol. 25, No. 1, 5-24.

Hakkert, A.S., Zaidel, D.M. and Sarelle, E. 1981: Patterns of safety belt usage following introduction of a safety belt wearing law. Accident Analysis and Prevention, 65-82.

Halliday, J. and Fuller, P. (eds) 1977: The Psychology of Gambling, Penguin.

Hamer, M. 1985: How speed kills on Britain's roads. New Scientist, 21 February, p. 10.

Hauer, E. 1980: Selection for treatment as a source of bias in before-and-after studies. Traffic Engineering and Control, 419-421.

Hauer, E. and Ahlin, F.J. 1982: Speed enforcement and speed choice. Accident Analysis and Prevention, 267-278.

Hearne, R. 1981: The intial impact of the safety-belt legislation in Ireland. An Foras Forbartha RS255.

Hedlund, J. 1984: Recent United States traffic fatality trends. Conference paper, General Motors Symposium on "Human Behavior and Traffic Safety". To be published in a book with the same title, edited by L. Evans and R. Schwing (Plenum Press, 1985, in press).

Hedlund, J., Arnold, R., Cerrelli, E., Partyka, S. Hoxie, P. and Skinner, D. 1984: An assessment of the 1982 traffic fatality decrease, Accident Analysis and Prevention, pp.247-261.

Huddart, K.W. and Dean, J.D. 1981: Engineering Programmes for Accident Reduction, in Foot, Chapman and Wade (eds).

Huddart, K.W. 1984: Accident migration - true or false. Traffic Engineering and Control, 267.

Hurst, P.M. 1979: Compulsory seat belt use: further inferences. Accident Analysis and Prevention, 27-33.

IIHS (Insurance Institute for Highway Safety) 1985: Teenage Drivers, Watergate 600, Washington D.C.

IIHS 1985b: School Buses and Seat Belts, Status Report, Vol. 20, No.5.

IRF (International Road Federation), World Road Statistics, Table IV, published annually.

Jacobs, G.D. and Sayer, I.A. 1983: Road accidents in developing countries. Transport and Road Research Laboratory, England, SR807.

Jacobs, G.D. and Sayer, I.A. 1984: work in progress at the Transport and Road Research Laboratory.

Jadan, K.S. and Salter, R.J. 1982: Traffic accidents in Kuwait. Traffic Engineering and Control, 221-223.

Japanese Government 1980: White Paper on Transportation Safety, Prime Minister's Office, International Association of Traffic and Safety Sciences.

Joksch, H. 1980: Comment. Societal Risk Assessment, Albers, W.A. and Schwing R.C. (eds), New York, Plenum Press.

Jonah, B.A. and Wilson, J.J. 1983: Improving the effectiveness of drinking-driving enforcement through increased efficiency. Accident Analysis and Prevention, 463-481.

Jonah, B.A. and Lawson, J.J. 1983: The Effectiveness of the Canadian mandatory seat belt laws. Road Safety Directorate Transport Canada, TMRU 8303, in press.

Joubert, P. 1985: Written comment on Adams' paper presented to the international symposium "Human Behavior and Traffic Safety", Warren Michigan, September 23-25, 1984. To be published in book of same title, edited by L. Evans and R. Schwing (Plenum Press, 1985, in press).

Kahn, H. 1976: The Next 200 Years, William Morrow.

Klau, C.H. 1985: Trying to calm the urban motor car. Town and Country Planning Vol. 54, No.2. 51-53.

Koshi, M. 1984: Road safety measures in Japan. Paper presented to the international symposium "Human Behavior and Traffic Safety" in Warren Michigan September 23-25. To be published in a book of the same title, R. Schwing and L. Evans eds. (Plenum Press 1985).

Kraus, R., Riggins, R. and Franti, C. 1975: Some epidemiologic features of motorcycle collision injuries: introduction, methods and factors associated with incidence. American Journal of Epidemiology, pp. 74-97.

Levin, P. and Bruce, A. 1968: The location of primary schools. Journal of Town Planning Institute Vol. 54, no. 2, 55-66.

Lonero, L.P. 1978: Evidence to Safety Belt Usage. See DoT above.

Lowrance, W.W. 1980: The nature of risk. Societal Risk Assessment: How Safe Is Safe Enough?, (Schwing, R.C. and Albers, W.A. eds.) General Motors Symposia Series, New York, Plenum Press.

Lund, H.W. 1981: Komentarer til "The efficacy of seat belt legislation". The Danish Council of Road Safety Research.

Lund, H.W. 1982: personal communication.

Mackay, M. 1981a: letter to The Times, June 11.

Mackay, M. 1981b: quoted in "Belt Report Slammed", Motor, March 7.

Mackay, M. 1981c: quoted by M. Hamer, New Scientist, February

19.

Mackay, M. 1982a: **Reducing Car Crash Injuries: Folklore, Science and Promise.** Foley Memorial Lecture, published by the Pedestrians Association, 1 Wandsworth Road, London SW8.

Mackay, M. 1982b: Seat belts under a voluntary regime. Proc. IRCOBI, Koln, Germany, published by ONSER, Lyon, France.

Mackay, M. 1984: Seat belt use under voluntary and mandatory conditions and its effect on casualties. Paper presented to the international symposium "Human Behavior and Traffic Safety", Warren Michigan, September 23-25, 1984; to be published in book of same title, edited by L.Evans and R. Schwing (Plenum Press, 1985).

McKenna, F.P. 1982: The human factor in driving accidents: an over view of approaches and problems. **Ergonomics**, vol. 25, 10, 867-877.

McKenna, F.P. 1984: Do safety measures work?- comments on risk homeostasis theory. MCR Applied Psychology Unit, 15 Chaucer Road, Cambridge.

Mayhew, P. 1979: Road accident prevention: the lessons for crime control. **Home Office Research Unit Bulletin**, no.7, 25-27.

Michon, J.A. 1984: A critical review of driver behavior models: what do we know, what should we do? Paper presented to the international symposium "Human Behavior and Traffic Safety", Warren Michigan, September 23-25, 1984; to be published in a book of the same title, edited by L. Evans and R. Schwing (Plenum Press, 1985).

Monheim, H. 1984: Cars, bicycles and pedestrians using common road space. Paper to the International Association for Traffic and Safety Sciences' Symposium on Traffic Science, Tokyo.

Naatanen, R. and Summala, H. 1974: A model for the role of motivational factors in drivers' decision-making. Accident **Analysis and Prevention**, vol. 6, 243-261.

Naatanen, R. and Summala, H. 1976: **Road-User Behaviour and Traffic Accidents**, North-Holland and Elsevier, Amsterdam, New York.

NHTSA (National Highway Traffic Safety Administration) 1979 **The Effect of Helmet Usage on Head Injuries and the Effect of Helmet Usage Laws on Helmet Wearing Rates - A Preliminary Report**, US Department of Transportation, Washington DC.

NHTSA 1980: **A Report to Congress on The Effect of Motorcycle Helmet Law Repeal - A Case for Helmet Use.** US Department of Transportation, Washington DC.

Norman, A. 1980: **Rights and Risks: A Discusion Document on Civil Liberty in Old Age.** National Corporation for the Care of Old People (now the Centre for Policy on Aging) London.

NTS 1983 (**National Travel Survey**), Department of Transport, HMSO.

NRTRI (National Road Traffic Research Institute of Sweden) 1978: **Effekter av vidtagnatrafiksakerhets-atgarder under perioden 1968-1976**, Nr 156, p.6.

O'Neil, B., Lund, A.K., Zador, P. and Ashton, S. 1984: Mandatory belt use and driver risk taking: an empirical evaluation of the risk-compensation hypothesis. Paper presented to international symposium "Human Behavior and Traffic Safety", Warren Michigan, September 23-25. To be published in book of same title, edited by L. Evans and R. Schwing (Plenum Press, 1985).

Orr, L.D. 1984: The effectiveness of automobile safety regulation: evidence from the FARS data: American Journal of Public Health, 1384-1389.

Orr, L.D. 1985: Answer to Robertson. American Journal of Public Health, in press.

OPCS (Office of Population Censuses and Surveys) 1983 DH1 No. 14, Table 24.

Partyka, S.C. 1984: Simple models of fatality trends using employment and population data. Accident Analysis and Prevention, 211-222.

Pauly, M.V. 1968, The economics of moral hazard. American Economic Review, 531-536.

Peltzman, S. 1975a: The effects of automobile safety regulation. Journal of Political Economy, vol. 83, no. 4, 677-725.

Peltzman, S. 1975b: Regulation of Automobile Safety. Evaluative Studies 26, American Enterprise Institute for Public Policy Research, Washington D.C..

Pettifer, J. and Turner, N. 1984: Automania, Collins.

Pierce, J.A. 1978: Evidence to Safety Belt Usage, see DoT above.

Pierce, J.A. 1980: Safety benefits of the seat belt legislation and speed limit reduction in Ontario. Research and Development Division, Ontario Ministry of Transportation and Communications. Presented to 1979 conference of American Association for Automotive Medicine, Louisville Kentucky.

Pummel, D. 1984: Mind that child. Care on the Road, September, RoSPA.

RAGB (Road Accidents Great Britain): published annually, London, HMSO.

Raymond, S. and Tatum, S. 1977: An evaluation of the RAC/ACU motorcycle training scheme - final report, University of Salford, England.

Riley, D. 1984: Drivers' beliefs about alcohol and the law. Research Bulletin, Home Office Research and Planning Unit, HMSO.

Road Research Laboratory 1963: Road Safety. Table 6.11, HMSO.

Robertson, L.S. 1977: A critical analysis of Peltzman's "The Effects of Automobile Safety Regulation". Journal of Economic Issues, 1977, vol. XI, no. 3, 587-600.

Robertson, L.S. 1983: Injuries. Lexington Mass., Lexington Books.

Robertson, L.S. 1984: Automobile safety regulation: rebuttal and new data. American Journal of Public Health, 1390-1394.

Ross, H.L. 1976: The Scandinavian myth: the effectiveness of drinking-and-driving legislation in Sweden and Norway. Evaluation Studies - Review Annual, vol. 1, Sage.

Ross, H.L. 1982: Deterring the Drinking Driver: Legal Policy and Social Control. Lexington Books, Lexington Mass.

Ross, H.L. and McLeary, R. 1983: Methods for studying the impact of drink driving laws. Accident Analysis and Prevention, 415-428.

Royal Society for the Prevention of Accidents (RoSPA) 1981: Seat Belt Sense, Birmingham.

RoSPA 1981b: The Efficacy of Seat Belt Legislation: the RoSPA Criticisms, Birmingham, March, unpublished.

Rumar, K., Berggrund, U., Jernberg, P. and Ytterbom, U. 1976: Driver reaction to a technical safety measure - studded tires. Human Factors, 443-454.

Sabey, B.E. and Taylor, H. 1980: The known risks we run: the highway. Societal Risk Assessment. Albers, W.A. and Schwing R.C. (eds), New York, Plenum Press.

SAE (Society of Automotive Engineers) 1984: Advances in Seat Belt Restraint Systems: Design, Performance and Usage, SAE P-141.

Sayer, I.A. and Hitchcock R. 1984: An analysis of police and medical road accident data: Sri Lanka 1977-81, Transport and Road Research Laboratory, in press.

Scott, P.P. and Barton, A.J. 1976: The effects on road accident rates of the fuel shortage of November 1973 and consequent legislation. TRRL, SR236, Crowthorne Berks.

Smeed, R.J. 1949: Some statistical aspects of road safety research. Journal of the Royal Statistical Society, Series A, Part I, 1-34.

Smeed, R.J. 1968: Variations in the pattern of accident rates in different countries and their' causes. Traffic Engineering and Control, 364-371.

Smeed, R.J. and Jeffcoate G.O. 1970: Effects of changes in motorisation in various countries on the number of road fatalities, Traffic Engineering and Control, 150-151.

Smeed R.J. 1972: The usefulness of formulae in traffic engineering and road safety. Accident Analysis and Prevention, 303-312.

Smith, J.Q. 1981: Search effort and the detection of faults, British Journal of Mathematical and Statistical Psychology, pp. 181-193.

Statistics Sweden, Road Traffic Accidents with Personal Injury, published annually.

Strobel, H. 1982: Computer Controlled Urban Transportation: A Survey of Concepts, Methods and International Experiences. International Series on Applied Systems Analysis, John Wiley.

Summala, H. 1984: Modelling driver behavior: a pessimistic prediction? Paper presented to the international symposium "Human Behavior and Traffic Safety", Warren Michigan, September 23-25. To be published in a book of the same title edited by R. Schwing and L. Evans (Plenum Press 1985).

References

Supramaniam, V., Van Belle, G. and Sung, J.F. 1984: Fatal motorcycle Accidents and helmet laws in Penninsular Malaysia. **Accident Analysis and Prevention**, vol. 16, 157-162.

Taylor, D.H. 1964: Drivers' galvanic skin response and the risk of accident. **Ergonomics**, 7, 439-451.

Tingvall, C. 1982: Is Adams right? - some aspects of a theory concerning effects of seat belt legislation. **Journal of Traffic Medicine**, 41-47.

Thompson, M. 1980; Aesthetics of risk: culture or context. **Societal Risk Assessment**, R.C. Schwing and W.A. Albers eds, Plenum Press, New York.

Thrumble, D. 1983: **The Effect of Helmet Legislation on Motorcyclist Fatalities in the United States 1975-1978.** MSc Thesis, Statistics Department, University College London.

Toffler, A. 1981: **The Third Wave.** Pan.

Tolonen, J. 1984: **Profile of Injuries in Traffic Accidents: And Effects of Seat Belt Use, Speed and Mass Ratio of Vehicles**, Research Institute of Public Health, University of Kuopio, Finland.

TSGB (**Transport Statistics Great Britain**), annual, HMSO.

Trinca, G.W. 1984: Thirteen years of seat belt usage - how great the benefits. **Advances in Belt Restraint Systems: Design, Performance and Usage**, SAE P-141, 15-28.

Tukey, J.W. 1977: **Exploratory Data Analysis.** Addison-Wesley, Reading MA.

Vaughan, R.G. 1977: Seat belts - some aspects of compulsory wearing in New South Wales, Australia. **Proc. Inst. of Mechanical Engineers**, Vol. 191, 3/77.

Vingilis, E.R. 1983: Guest Editor's Introduction. **Accident Analysis and Prevention**, 405-406.

Vulcan, A.P. 1977: Victorian experience with the compulsory wearing of seat belts. Proc. of 6th International Conference of IAATM, Melbourne, January 31 - February 4.

Watson, G.S., Zador, P.L. and Wilks, A. 1980: The repeal of helmet use laws and increased motorcyclist mortality in the United States 1975-1978. **American Journal of Public Health**, vol. 70, 579-585.

Watson, G.S., Zador, P.L. and Wilks, A. 1981: Helmet use, helmet use laws, and motorcyclist fatalities. **American Journal of Public Health**, vol. 71, 297-300.

Wilde, G.J.S. 1976: The risk compensation theory of accident causation and its practical consequences for accident prevention. Paper presented at annual meeting of the Osterreichische Gesellschaft fur Unfallchirurgie, Salzburg.

Wilde, G.J.S. 1982: The theory of risk homeostasis: implications for safety and health. **Risk Analysis**, 209-225(a) and 249-258(b).

Williams, A.F. and O'Neil, B. 1974: On-the-road driving records of licensed race drivers, **Accident Analysis and Prevention**, pp. 263-270.

WHS (World Health Statistics Report) 1974: **The Ten Leading Causes of Death for Selected Countries in North America, Europe and Oceania**, 1969-1971, Vol. 27, No.8.

Wright, C.C. and Boyle, A.J. 1984: Accident 'migration' after remedial treatment at accident blackspots. **Traffic Engineering and Control**, 260-266.

Yankauer, A. 1981: Deregulation and the right to life (editorial). **American Journal of Public Health**, 797-798.

Zylman, R. 1975: Mass arrests for impaired driving may not prevent traffic deaths. Proceedings of 6th Conference Alcohol, Drugs and Traffic Safety, Toronto Sept. 1974.

Index